YEATS: The Poetics of the Self

YEATS

David Lynch

The Poetics of the Self

The University of Chicago Press
Chicago and London

The University of Chicago Press, Chicago 60637
The University of Chicago Press, Ltd., London

Printed in the United States of America
88 87 86 85 84 83 82 81   1 2 3 4 5

Library of Congress Cataloging in Publication Data

Lynch, David, 1943–
  Yeats, the poetics of the self.

  Bibliography: p.
  1. Yeats, William Butler, 1865–1939.   2. Authors,
Irish—20th century—Biography.   3. Creation (Literary,
artistic, etc.)   4. Narcissism.   I. Title.
PR5906.L9   821'.8 [B]   78–13242
ISBN 0-226-49816-6 (cloth)
    0-226-49812-3 (paper)

CONTENTS

PREFACE

This book is about what Yeats called "the choice": how he chose, or was chosen for, the creative life. It is based on his works, on the biographical evidence we have, and on the hypotheses of psychoanalytic theory. But it is not a technical book. I have imagined readers who may only know enough about Yeats or about psychology to be interested in finding out more about both, and I have organized the book in a way that I hope will encourage even my best-informed readers to approach my subject as if it were new to them too. I want them to verify—and amend—my conclusions by participating in the investigation that led me to them, and I have tried to recreate something of the sense of mystery—or at any rate the feeling of curiosity—that made the investigation interesting and exciting.

My readers should also be prepared for a certain amount of repetition. The whole story I have to tell is "over-complicated"—a term Yeats once used to describe the dramatic effect of a play he had written about fathers and sons called *On Baile's Strand*. He meant approximately what a psychoanalyst would mean by "overdetermined": the hero Cuchulain's murder of his only son had more meanings than a single scenario could express. Yeats's solution was to write a cycle of plays; my solution to a similar problem has been to write a cycle of interpretations. Each of the

vii

four major divisions of this book is a partial version of a single over-complicated story. In each, and most noticeably in the last three, a different text or group of texts is used to interpret the same events from a different point of view. Taken together, they are a "complex" that is the life a man lived, the fictions he created, and the personality we imagine: the story of a poet, mistress, and Muse; of sons and mothers; of fathers and sons; and, finally, of fathers and mothers.

What I am describing may itself sound overcomplicated. I think, however, that it is the clearest and simplest way to describe a phenomenon whose meanings are not consecutive but simultaneous. I think, too, that in the end it comes closest to conveying something of the quality of continuous repetition and elaboration that was and is the experience of Yeats—was and is, in fact, the experience of any of us. I have tried to present his life and work in a way that interprets the act of interpretation: here, as in Kurosawa's *Rashomon,* human reality is not one story but the sum of many.

The fifth and concluding part of the book is concerned with theoretical issues. The section called "Yeats and Psychology" is a short review of previous biographical and psychological work; "Art and Madness" deals with questions raised by the application of clinical theory to art. Both matters are important. The story of the poet I will tell is quite different from both the story he told about himself in *Reveries over Childhood and Youth* and the stories others have told about him elsewhere. It is also different from the account of art and artists that psychoanalytic studies of them usually give. It is above all a story of the vicissitudes of self-love, and since it is also the story of a poet, it suggests that aesthetic psychology is the psychology not of the oedipus complex but of narcissism or, as Dr. Heinz Kohut might put it, "the psychology of the self." Narcissism is not the whole story, but I shall try to show that it is the part of anyone's story that accounts for the special quality that distinguishes some of our experiences as "aesthetic." Yeats would have called it art's "visionary" quality; someone else might say that it's the way art makes you feel, so that when you feel it, you know it's art.

The relevance of the psychology of narcissism to the interpretation of Yeats will be discussed again in chapter 5; those who are interested will also find it documented in detail in the notes. The theoretical issues raised by Kohut's work, however, will not be taken up directly. This book may contribute something toward resolving them; but I will not argue, and I have tried not to assume, the merits either of his theories or of psychoanalytic theory in general here. Every fresh set of observations is an opportunity to reargue premises and to test rather than merely to confirm conclusions. If this book supports what Kohut says in *The Analysis of the Self* and elsewhere—and I think it does—it does so by making more and better sense out of Yeats. What we may come to know intellectually about the nature of the human psyche must be verified at last by what we always knew in other ways, sensually, emotionally, in "imagination, ear and eye." There is a Yeats we know that way, and I want to begin and end with him.

Richard Onorato could have written this book but decided to help me do it instead. I doubt if it ever would have been written without him. I have also had helpful readings from Professors Frederick Crews, Karen Klein, Kevin Lynch, and Aileen Ward and from Rebecca Bluestone and Joan Rockwell. Others who helped, sometimes without knowing it, were Barbara Gelpi, Nina Felshin, Richard Freadman, and Dr. Egbert Mueller. I would also like to thank Dr. Rolf Arvidson for inviting me to join his group on psychoanalysis and literature for a discussion of "Among School Children" and Dr. Paul Myerson, of the Tufts–New England Medical Center, for asking me to give the talk on "The Tower" that became the first draft of chapter 1.

Quotations from Yeats's *Collected Poems, The Variorum Edition of the Poems of W. B. Yeats, The Variorum Edition of the Plays of W. B. Yeats,* and the *Collected Plays* of Yeats are used by permission of Macmillan Publishing Co., Inc., New York; Michael and Anne Yeats; and Macmillan Co. Ltd. of London and Basingstoke and are protected by copyright.

One

MISTRESS OR MUSE

The Self-invented Man

By the time William Butler Yeats died in 1939, his reputation as a poet was secure. He was, T. S. Eliot said, "the greatest poet of our time—certainly in this language, and so far as I am able to judge, in any language."[1] If there was anything troubling or ambiguous about his greatness, those who had known him or known of him when he was alive put it down to eccentricity. Like Oscar Wilde, Yeats was a personality. His figure caught the eye, his voice the ear. Even if one cared little about his mystical philosophy or his conservative, even fascistic politics, the impression he left was problematic.

His appearance and manner were certainly striking. He dressed with great care all his life, and his manners were elaborate and courtly; we are told that even in his youth he had an air of "great dignity and authority."[2] Yet there were many who found the effect overdone. The meticulous dress was too deliberately aesthetic; the manner and gestures too theatrical; the devotion to the mystical, the aristocratic, and the sublime too affected.

1

Since his death, some of the controversy that the man once inspired has been transferred to the poet. This is undoubtedly due in part to the way in which some of his poems now seem to be merely a record of his eccentricities. Reading Yeats often leads to a complicated and unrewarding elucidation of his "mythologies," including, in his early work, the esoterica of the Wisdom tradition and later the complex psychohistorical geometries of his own "philosophy," A Vision.[3] As often as not the reader returns from such expeditions feeling more confused and irritable than enlightened. But the art, like the man, is not merely eccentric. Yeats's mythologies would be neither particularly interesting nor particularly irritating if he had not also been a great poet. As Louis Mac-Neice puts it, if he was "one of the most peculiar poets in our history ... in so far as he achieved greatness it proves, not the power of inspiration or any other such woolly miracle—all it proves is the miracle of artistic integrity."[4]

The miraculous quality in Yeats's artifice, which Eliot also praised as the "integrity of his passion for his art and his craft," has sufficed and will probably continue to suffice for most of his readers.[5] As MacNeice and Eliot imply, Yeats was great in spite of himself, a talent so formidable that his art could redeem even his most cranky and dubious peculiarities. Yeats the artist often seems, as once in the famous concluding apostrophe of "Sailing to Byzantium" he had prayed he might be, "out of nature":

> Once out of nature I shall never take
> My bodily form from any natural thing,
> But such a form as Grecian goldsmiths make
> Of hammered gold and gold enamelling
> To keep a drowsy Emperor awake;
> Or set upon a golden bough to sing
> To lords and ladies of Byzantium
> Of what is past, or passing, or to come.[6]

But his characteristic insistence that the integrity of the artist was no natural thing is also what accounts for what can be most annoying about him. Occasionally or often, depending on the reader's sensibility, his golden bird becomes a metaphor for artifice that is merely artificial. For some the Yeatsian creative miracle tends to creak a bit, to suggest the hidden wire or spring, and thus to seem of a piece with the more obviously unacceptable manifestations of his paraphernalia. It is sometimes a case, to paraphrase Keats, of the fancy cheating too well. To be impressed by the passion and integrity of a poem like "The Second Coming," for instance, is also to be imposed upon, and it is not an imposition to which everyone submits with equal pleasure:

> Turning and turning in the widening gyre
> The falcon cannot hear the falconer;
> Things fall apart; the centre cannot hold;
> Mere anarchy is loosed upon the world,
> The blood-dimmed tide is loosed, and everywhere
> The ceremony of innocence is drowned;
> The best lack all conviction, while the worst
> Are full of passionate intensity.
>
> Surely some revelation is at hand;
> Surely the Second Coming is at hand.
> The Second Coming! Hardly are those words out
> When a vast image out of *Spiritus Mundi*
> Troubles my sight: somewhere in the sands of the desert
> A shape with lion body and the head of a man,
> A gaze blank and pitiless as the sun,
> Is moving its slow thighs, while all about it
> Reel shadows of the indignant desert birds.
> The darkness drops again; but now I know
> That twenty centuries of stony sleep
> Were vexed to nightmare by a rocking cradle,
> And what rough beast, its hour come round at last,
> Slouches towards Bethlehem to be born?

The "surely ... surely" presumes and insists equally on everyone's certainty; the "now I know" reminds us how willingly we have come to accept Yeats's skill in the public staging of private and highly idiosyncratic convictions.

In assessing one's response to Yeats's poetry, then, one is faced with a paradox similar to that which faced his friends and co-workers in assessing him as a man. On one hand there is the manifest beauty of the created thing; on the other, the more or less troubling feeling that it is, after all, only artifice. It could be argued, of course, that the same might be said of any work of art. But to do so would be to leave unexpressed the distinctive quality that almost everyone discovers in Yeats's work sooner or later. The speaker of the Yeatsian lyric seems to insist more deliberately than most on his histrionic identity or, as Yeats would put it, on his "mask." Perhaps the best way to describe what distinguishes this from what we usually admire in poetry is to say that it suggests not self-expression but self-invention. *"The friends,"* as Yeats himself put it in a quatrain introducing the second volume of his 1908 *Collected Works,*

> that have it I do wrong
> When ever I remake a song,
> Should know what issue is at stake:
> It is myself that I remake.[7]

Again, one could argue that any artist might say as much; yet again, there is something in the observation that is peculiarly appropriate to one's impression of Yeats in particular. Indeed it is something of a critical commonplace to identify the making and remaking of the self as the central issue addressed by both his creativity and his mystical "philosophies."[8] As such, it was a matter that went considerably beyond the problem of self-expression. What burdened Yeats most was the difficulty of synthesizing a self to be expressed. That that self would be in conflict he took for granted; it was the fundamental sense of integrity implicit in even the most conflicting forms of self-expression that seemed to him to be truly no "natural thing." In "Sailing to Byzantium" the sense of self that most of us take most for granted—the continuity of consciousness in past, present, and future—is a consummation reserved for the created object. This way of distinguishing what came naturally from what came by art was, as he explained at the end of his life in "A General Introduction to My Work," Yeats's "first principle":

> A poet writes always of his personal life, in his finest work out of its tragedy, whatever it be, remorse, lost love, or mere loneliness; he never speaks directly as to someone at the breakfast table, there is always a phantasmagoria. Dante and Milton had mythologies, Shakespeare the characters of English history or of traditional romance; even when the poet seems most himself, when he is Raleigh and gives the potentates the lie, or Shelley "a nerve o'er which do creep the else unfelt oppressions of this earth," or Byron when "the soul wears out the breast" as "the sword outwears the sheath," he is never the bundle of accident and incoherence that sits down to breakfast; he has been reborn as an idea, something intended, complete. A novelist might describe his accidence, his incoherence, he must not; he is more type than man, more passion than type. He is Lear, Romeo, Oedipus, Tiresias; he has stepped out of a play, and even the woman he loves is Rosalind, Cleopatra, never The Dark Lady. He is part of his own phantasmagoria and we adore him because nature has grown intelligible, and by doing so a part of our creative power. "When the mind is lost in the light of the Self," says

the Prashna Upanishad, "it dreams no more; still in the body it is lost in happiness." "A wise man seeks in Self," says the Chandogya Upanishad, "those that are alive and those that are dead and gets what the world cannot give." The world knows nothing because it has made nothing, we know everything because we have made everything.[9]

Under the circumstances, it is not surprising that Yeats's record of his own personal life often seems unintended and is certainly incomplete. He began his *Autobiography* with *Reveries over Childhood and Youth* in 1916. The title sets the tone for the prose: it is a very beautiful, and appropriately poetic, series of impressions. But it is also an account, as Yeats's old friend George Russell (the mystic A.E., hardly the most practical of men) observed testily, of "pure externalities . . . . The boy in the book might have become a grocer as well as a poet."[10]

The later installments do no better. *The Trembling of the Veil* (1922) and *Dramatis Personae, 1896–1902* (1935), which take us through the poet's thirty-seventh year, are, as he had predicted as early as 1914, mostly about "other people."[11] The remaining sections, *Estrangement* (1926), *The Death of Synge* (1928), and *The Bounty of Sweden* (1925), are selections from journals kept between 1908 and 1914 and in December 1923. Despite its often considerable circumstantial interest (though even in this respect it is as often deliberately misleading) and its importance as a record of the development of Yeats's thought, the *Autobiography* as a whole has much the same "accidental" quality Yeats attributed to the events of natural life.[12] The man who sat down to breakfast with Lady Gregory and dined with Wilde, Lionel Johnson, Arthur Symons, and J. M. Synge is not the intelligible, phantasmagorical Poet; the story of the boy who did not become a grocer remains untold.

Some of the enigmatically "external" quality of Yeats's memoirs may be attributed to his unwillingness to say certain things in public. There is now evidence that he deliberately misrepresented his family life in *Reveries,* and the recently published drafts of *The Trembling of the Veil, Dramatis Personae, Estrangement,* and *The Death of Synge* indicate that he was reluctant to publish details of his own or his friends' lives that he thought were painful or in bad taste.[13] But knowing more of the facts— his sexual anxieties, or his fear of inheriting the madness that afflicted some members of his mother's family, for instance—does not necessarily put one in possession of a coherent version of the story Russell wished Yeats had been able to tell. That telling, for Yeats as for Wordsworth in the *Prelude,* was reserved for the voice of the phantasmagorical Poet himself. Like Wordsworth, though never so explicitly and always more elliptically, Yeats wrote his best autobiography when he wrote poetry. This is particularly true of the long meditative poems in his version of ottava rima that began to appear toward the end of his life. One of the best known of these, and the last, is "The Circus Animals' Desertion":[14]

I   I sought a theme and sought for it in vain,
             I sought it daily for six weeks or so.
             Maybe at last, being but a broken man,
             I must be satisfied with my heart, although
             Winter and summer till old age began
             My circus animals were all on show,
             Those stilted boys, that burnished chariot,
             Lion and woman and the Lord knows what.

II   What can I but enumerate old themes?
             First that sea-rider Oisin led by the nose
             Through three enchanted islands, allegorical dreams,
             Vain gaiety, vain battle, vain repose,
             Themes of the embittered heart, or so it seems,
             That might adorn old songs or courtly shows;
             But what cared I that set him on to ride,
             I, starved for the bosom of his faery bride?

             And then a counter-truth filled out its play,
             The Countess Cathleen was the name I gave it;
             She, pity-crazed, had given her soul away,
             But masterful Heaven had intervened to save it.
             I thought my dear must her own soul destroy,
             So did fanaticism and hate enslave it,
             And this brought forth a dream and soon enough
             This dream itself had all my thought and love.

             And when the Fool and Blind Man stole the bread
             Cuchulain fought the ungovernable sea;
             Heart-mysteries there, and yet when all is said
             It was the dream itself enchanted me:
             Character isolated by a deed
             To engross the present and dominate memory.
             Players and painted stage took all my love,
             And not those things that they were emblems of.
             [1–32]

It is in poems like this, and not in the *Autobiography,* that one begins to hear the poet telling his own story. "The Circus Animals' Desertion" is about being Yeats and writing poetry, and the man it describes is recognizable from both the impressions of others and his own "first principle" as one for whom personal history is the history of artifice: "When all is said / It was the dream itself enchanted me." The details of his dream are likely to be obscure to most readers nowadays; few of us have seen his plays about Countess Cathleen or Cuchulain or read the epic *Wanderings of Oisin*. Nevertheless, the dreamer of "The Circus Animals' Desertion" is someone we can recognize too. The poet Yeats remembers being is above all a lover ("Players and painted stage took all my love"), and his enchantment begins with the story of a "faery bride."

The faery bride is, of course, a familiar part of the "phantasmagoria" of English romanticism, particularly in Keats and Shelley.[15] For Yeats, the "last romantic," she is a Belle Dame who was both imaginary and real, the Maud Gonne of the love lyrics that, of all his works, have had the most immediate and lasting appeal. There is "The Song of the Wandering Aengus":

> Though I am old with wandering
> Through hollow lands and hilly lands,
> I will find out where she has gone,
> And kiss her lips and take her hands;
> And walk among long dappled grass,
> And pluck till time and times are done
> The silver apples of the moon,
> The golden apples of the sun.
> [17–24]

Or there is "Words":

> ... Every year I have cried, "At length
> My darling understands it all,
> Because I have come into my strength,
> And words obey my call";
>
> That had she done so who can say
> What would have shaken from the sieve?
> I might have thrown poor words away
> And been content to live.
> [9–16]

Without Maud, the poet who "might have been content to live" implies, there would have been no poetry. Yet is would be more accurate to say that without the poetry there would have been no Maud Gonne.[16]

Yeats's lifelong obsession with a woman who was capable of returning his passion in only the most ephemeral and ambiguous ways suggests issues at stake that transcend sexual desire or personal affection. As the "my dear" who inspired *The Countess Cathleen* and innumerable lyrics besides, she was not Yeats's mistress but his Muse; his need for her was equivalent to his mysterious need to "remake" himself. The story of the creative life he tells in "The Circus Animals' Desertion" begins rather than ends with mythology; where mythology begins, he reminds us in conclusion, is another question:

> Those masterful images because complete
> Grew in pure mind, but out of what began?
> A mound of refuse or the sweepings of a street,
> Old kettles, old bottles, and a broken can,
> Old iron, old bones, old rags, that raving slut
> Who keeps the till. Now that my ladder's gone,
> I must lie down where all the ladders start,
> In the foul rag-and-bone shop of the heart.
> [33–40]

What follows is an attempt to say where it all started for Yeats. I will begin, as he does in "The Circus Animals' Desertion," with an enumeration of "old themes"; I will conclude, as he does, that creativity begins with an effort to master and complete the fragments of impoverished affection, "the foul rag-and-bone shop of the heart." In later chapters the stories of Oisin and Cuchulain will become occasions for telling and retelling what we know (or have been allowed to know) about Yeats's story; here, however, I will start the story where he usually started it and where most of us usually start with him: with the dream-enchanted lyric poet and the Muse or, as he puts it in "The Tower," the "woman lost":

> Does the imagination dwell the most
> Upon a woman won or woman lost?
> If on the lost, admit you turned aside
> From a great labyrinth out of pride,
> Cowardice, some silly over-subtle thought
> Or anything called conscience once;
> And that if memory recur, the sun's
> Under eclipse and the day blotted out.
> [113–20]

"The Tower"

The tower that became the central emblem of one of Yeats's most formidable and complex versions of the poet's story was Thoor Ballylee, the Norman keep (bailey) near Coole he acquired from the Congested Districts Board for thirty-five pounds in 1917. He had been interested in the place since about 1900, and in 1915 it had begun to appear as a regular feature of his poetry.[17] In December of that year he completed "Ego Dominus Tuus," the esoteric dialogue in verse that opens when the antagonist Hic discovers the Yeatsian protagonist Ille

> On the grey sand beside the shallow stream
> Under your old wind-beaten tower, where still
> A lamp burns on beside the open book
> That Michael Robartes left, you walk in the moon,
> And, though you have passed the best of life, still trace,
> Enthralled by the unconquerable delusion,
> Magical shapes.
> [1–7]

In fact the man who suspected that he had passed the best of life at fifty had ahead of him what, by any common measure of public or private success, were to be his best years. Shortly after buying the tower, Yeats proposed to and was accepted by Georgie Hyde-Lees. In 1918 he began to restore the tower as their summer residence.[18]

> I, the poet William Yeats,
> With old mill boards and sea-green slates,
> And smithy work from the Gort forge,
> Restored this tower for my wife George;
> And may these characters remain
> When all is ruin once again.
> ["To Be Carved on a Stone at Thoor Ballylee"]

The years 1919–21, which brought the terror of the Black and Tans to Ireland, brought Yeats two children and two major books of poetry: Anne Butler (born February 28) and *The Wild Swans at Coole* in 1919; Michael Butler (born August 22) and *Michael Robartes and the Dancer* in 1921. In 1922, after the Treaty of December had created the Free State, he became a nominated member of the Irish Senate, received a

Doctor of Letters degree from Dublin University, and began work on the new Macmillan *Collected Edition* of his works. In 1923 he was awarded the Nobel Prize for literature; in 1925 he completed the project that had occupied him privately since his marriage, publishing the first version of *A Vision*, "An Explanation of Life Founded on the Writings of Giraldus and Certain Doctrines Attributed to Kusta Ben Luka." The proofs were delivered in late June;[19] in September the fifth volume of the *Collected Edition, Early Poems and Stories,* appeared; and toward the end of that month, in the midst of all that was past and passing, the man who had become in fact as well as in fantasy "the poet William Yeats," the man who was now, with the dignity of fatherhood and sixty winters upon him, with his public honors, private achievement, and refurbished Norman tower, literally the emblem of himself, began a new poem:

> I   What shall I do with this absurdity—
>   O heart, O troubled heart—this caricature,
>   Decrepit age that has been tied to me
>   As to a dog's tail?
>   Never had I more
>   Excited, passionate, fantastical
>   Imagination, nor an ear and eye
>   That more expected the impossible—
>   No, not in boyhood when with rod and fly,
>   Or the humbler worm, I climbed Ben Bulben's back
>   And had the livelong summer day to spend.
>   It seems that I must bid the Muse go pack,
>   Choose Plato and Plotinus for a friend
>   Until imagination, ear and eye,
>   Can be content with argument and deal
>   In abstract things; or be derided by
>   A sort of battered kettle at the heel.
>   [1–16]

The subject of "The Tower" is old age, and Yeats was an aging man when he wrote it. Yet the fact that we have already found the feeling of having passed the best of life recorded in a poem written ten years earlier should alert us to the presence of a characteristically "phantasmagorical" speaker. Old age is the only one of Yeats's subjects that rivals Maud Gonne in productivity and endurance; his first published work on the theme, a dramatic poem called "The Seeker," appeared in the *Dublin University Review* in 1885, the year he was twenty. It is also one of his most common ways of imagining the poet; from *The Wanderings of*

Oisin (1889) on, the speakers of his poems have a decided tendency to be, or to seem, "old with wandering." The fact that Yeats really had grown old in the pursuit of the Muse by the time he wrote "The Tower" is an example of the way fact and fantasy conspired at certain moments in his life to produce a poet who seemed "most himself" when he was also most profoundly mythological.

"The Tower" begins with what sounds like the complaint of an aging lover. His heart is young, but his body is old and (perhaps) impotent, a "caricature" in line 2 and a "battered kettle at the heel" in line 16. But the impression is misleading. "This caricature" is not his decrepit body but his "decrepit age," and as the passage proceeds it becomes clear that the "age" he means is not a time of life but a state of mind. The poet is more excited and passionate than ever before in lines 4–5. But the word we stumble over without really attending to it at the beginning of line 6 is "imagination," not desire; in line 11 it is not his mistress but his Muse whom he fears he must bid go pack. It becomes clear, too, that his is above all a creative state of mind: feeling "old" is how it feels to feel like writing the poem. The feeling is not, as I have indicated, an uncommon one in Yeats's work; we have found it in "Ego Dominus Tuus" and, for that matter, in "The Circus Animals' Desertion":

> Maybe at last, being but a broken man,
> I must be satisfied with my heart, although
> Winter and summer till old age began
> My circus animals were all on show. . . .

Curiously enough, the feeling of decrepitude that initiates creativity in "The Tower" is caused not by insufficient but, as Harold Bloom puts it, by excessive imagination.[20] The Wordsworthian cadence of "rod and fly and humbler worm" alludes to Yeats's worst fears about the imaginative impotence of aging poets. But the echo is presumably ironic; Yeats's visionary gleam is anything but fled. Reordered and relieved of its elaboration, the passage reads, "It seems that since my imagination has grown more excited, passionate, and fantastical than ever before, I must give up poetry for philosophy." Apparently there is something about what he imagines, or perhaps about imagining itself, that leaves him feeling weakened, apprehensive ("What shall I do . . . ?"), and "old." The poet must banish his Muse not because he is impotent but because he has become too passionate. The mind's excitement has begun to threaten its integrity, and its only resource seems to be the rigid intellectual control of "abstract things." Here, as elsewhere in Yeats's work, the effort to remake the self in verse begins with a depressed, hypochondriacal, and sometimes hysterical conviction that "things fall apart":

> Turning and turning in the widening gyre
> The falcon cannot hear the falconer;
> Things fall apart; the centre cannot hold;
> Mere anarchy is loosed upon the world. . . .

The remaking of the self in "The Tower" is lengthy, complicated, and not, in the end, the Yeats that most of us like best. It begins, in part II, with a protracted and digressive interrogation of "images and memories" in the ottava rima stanza Yeats preferred for such meditations and ends in part III with a senatorial last will and testament, seventy-odd lines of majestic trimeter that open with

> It is time that I wrote my will;
> I choose upstanding men
> That climb the streams until
> The fountain leap, and at dawn
> Drop their cast at the side
> Of dripping stone; I declare
> They shall inherit my pride,
> The pride of people that were
> Bound neither to Cause nor to State,
> Neither to slaves that were spat on,
> Nor to the tyrants that spat . . .
> [121–31]

and conclude,

> Now I shall make my soul,
> Compelling it to study
> In a learned school
> Till the wreck of body,
> Slow decay of blood,
> Testy delirium
> Or dull decrepitude,
> Or what worse evil come—
> The death of friends, or death
> Of every brilliant eye
> That made a catch in the breath—
> Seem but the clouds in the sky
> When the horizon fades,
> Or a bird's sleepy cry
> Among the deepening shades.
> [181–95]

This conclusion, of course, is little different in substance from the conclusion of part I. What makes this the end rather than the beginning of the poem is mostly a matter of tone. The resolute "Now I shall" that responds to the first line's anxious "What shall I do?" announces not the intellectual but the emotional resolution of the poem. The poet is no longer depressed and tentative ("It seems that I must bid the Muse go pack") about "studying in a learned school" or apprehensive about excessive imagination. Indeed his self-invented integrity ("Now I shall make my soul") is so nakedly solipsistic that its triumph seems merely rhetorical; at such moments of strange ecstasy in Yeats one may long for the humanizing ironies of poems like "The Circus Animals' Desertion":

> ... Now that my ladder's gone,
> I must lie down where all the ladders start,
> In the foul rag-and-bone shop of the heart.

Yet if what is finally made of the self in "The Tower" seems less acceptable than what is made of it in the later poem, the course of its making is in some respects quite similar. The triumphant "soul" of part III is, like the tenant of the rag-and-bone shop, the product of an elaborate reminiscence that is both a series of stories and a single story about the "heart-mystery" of the fictive life. Part II begins,

> I pace upon the battlements and stare
> On the foundations of a house, or where
> Tree, like a sooty finger, starts from the earth;
> And send imagination forth
> Under the day's declining beam, and call
> Images and memories
> From ruin or from ancient trees,
> For I would ask a question of them all.
> [17–24]

The tone is magisterial and the technique of the Nobel laureate's verse so faultless that one tends to take its considerable formal limitations completely for granted. But as the poem proceeds it becomes clear that the process of recollection is to be neither so impersonal nor so well-controlled as the poet seems to expect when he first sends imagination forth. Thus while part II does consist of a series of "images and memories" of real and imaginary persons associated with the geography of Ballylee, it is difficult to escape the impression that the poet is really remembering something about himself. It seems unlikely to be accidental, for instance, that the first two things that occur to him are descriptions of the destructive effects of excessive imagination. Beginning with the story of Mrs. French, who lived "beyond that ridge" and had a servant whose mind was so impressed by her unspoken fantasy that he once

> Ran and with the garden shears
> Clipped an insolent farmer's ears
> And brought them in a little covered dish,
> [30–32]

the poet goes on to tell about the peasant girl whose beauty was so convincingly rendered in a song that "certain men, being maddened by those rhymes," set out to see her for themselves one moonlit night:

> Music had driven their wits astray—
> And one was drowned in the great bog of Cloone.
>
> Strange, but the man who made the song was blind;
> Yet, now I have considered it, I find
> That nothing strange; the tragedy began
> With Homer that was a blind man,
> And Helen has all living hearts betrayed.
> O may the moon and sunlight seem
> One inextricable beam,
> For if I triumph I must make men mad.
> [47–56]

In coming to the story of blind Raftery and Mary Hynes, the poet has come, as if by accident, upon a story that he recognizes as peculiarly his own: the story of the Muse, of Homer and Helen, of the seduction and betrayal of "all living hearts" by the dream, of the imaginative influx before which consciousness falls apart and whose triumph is madness. And indeed the next image that suggests itself is a case in point, not only because it recalls a madman Yeats himself created but also because in remembering him the poet brings himself to a pitch of frenzy that forces him to break off and begin again:

> And I myself created Hanrahan
> And drove him drunk or sober through the dawn
> From somewhere in the neighbouring cottages.
> Caught by an old man's juggleries
> He stumbled, tumbled, fumbled to and fro
> And had but broken knees for hire
> And horrible splendour of desire;
> I thought it all out twenty years ago.
>
> Good fellows shuffled cards in an old bawn;
> And when that ancient ruffian's turn was on

He so bewitched the cards under his thumb
That all but the one card became
A pack of hounds and not a pack of cards,
And that he changed into a hare.
Hanrahan rose in frenzy there
And followed up those baying creatures towards—

O towards I have forgotten what—enough!
I must recall a man that neither love
Nor music nor an enemy's clipped ear
Could, he was so harried, cheer. . . .
[57–76]

The stanzas that follow are the part of the poem that most readers find hardest to remember. What the poet "must recall" is the history of the tower itself: "an ancient bankrupt" and "rough men-at-arms." It is, in the emotional orchestration of recollection, anticlimatic, a return to plan that ignores what imagination has really discovered. The marshaling of images and memories is complete, but the question that the poet is finally able to ask has become irrelevant. Instead, what registers most strongly in the stanzas that conclude part II is his impatience to return to what he has "forgotten":

Did all old men and women, rich and poor,
Who trod upon these rocks or passed this door,
Whether in public or in secret rage
As I do now against old age?
But I have found an answer in those eyes
That are impatient to be gone;
Go therefore; but leave Hanrahan,
For I need all his mighty memories.

Old lecher with a love on every wind,
Bring up out of that deep considering mind
All that you have discovered in the grave,
For it is certain that you have
Reckoned up every unforeknown, unseeing
Plunge, lured by a softening eye,
Or by a touch or a sigh,
Into the labyrinth of another's being;

Does the imagination dwell the most
Upon a woman won or woman lost?
If on the lost, admit you turned aside
From a great labyrinth out of pride,

> Cowardice, some silly over-subtle thought
> Or anything called conscience once;
> And that if memory recur, the sun's
> Under eclipse and the day blotted out.
> [97–120]

These last lines and the opening lines of part I are what everyone remembers from "The Tower." They express a sense of liberation, an escape from tentativeness and uncertainty, a discovery of a way of saying what was really meant all along. The speech is now, as most readers notice with approval, moving, passionate, and memorable. Moreover, there is good reason to feel, as most critics do, that this is the moment at which the "remade" poet emerges and the depressed tone of part I is transformed into the triumphant exaltation of part III. It is frequently observed, for instance, that the attractive feeling of affective release that the reader experiences here expresses the poet's cathartic self-identification with his "lecherous" creation, Hanrahan. The result is a kind of purification through acknowledgment, if not through insight: the poet is now able to transcend his anxieties or at least, as one critic puts it, to dissociate himself from the past and turn to what is left.[21] What is left, as we have already observed, is the poet's solipsistic "pride" and "faith":

> And I declare my faith:
> I mock Plotinus' thought
> And cry in Plato's teeth,
> Death and life were not
> Till man made up the whole,
> Made lock, stock and barrel
> Out of his bitter soul,
> Aye, sun and moon and star, all,
> And further add to that
> That, being dead, we rise,
> Dream and so create
> Translunar Paradise.
> I have prepared my peace
> With learned Italian things
> And the proud stones of Greece,
> Poet's imaginings
> And memories of love,
> Memories of the words of women,
> All those things whereof
> Man makes a superhuman
> Mirror-resembling dream.
> [145–65]

In effect, the man who insists so strongly on his self-invented integrity in part III has found himself, and it is evident that the alteration of his mood has a great deal to do with his having first found Hanrahan among his images and memories. What he has found in either case is less evident. Apparently Hanrahan has the answer to the question that expresses the essence of the hypochondriacal anxiety Yeats calls old age: what excites the imagination to the pitch that threatens to drive men mad? The answer is contained, we are told, in a memory that has something to do with sexual love, and particularly with the relationship between imagination and a "woman lost." But the memory itself, which would eclipse the sun and blot out the day, does not recur. Instead, it remains something implicit in the poet's recognition of himself in Hanrahan and elaborately concealed in the fiction of Hanrahan's memories, which are ambiguously both his own and those of his creator, Yeats.

The puzzle is not necessarily one that either Yeats or the poem is asking us to solve. The version of Hanrahan's story "The Tower" tells seems interesting and significant partly because it is so incomplete; we are in the presence, as we often are in Yeats's work, of the numinous and unknowable. Besides, *The Stories of Red Hanrahan* that now appear in *Mythologies* are a part of his work that few have read and fewer remember clearly. Yet the conspiracy between what is unremembered in the poem and unmemorable about Yeats's prose fiction is deceptive, for Hanrahan's "mighty memories" give us access to the explicit account of the origins of creativity that is available nowhere else. A discussion of a "mythology" that seems less interesting on its own merits is an indispensable preliminary to a discussion of versions of the poet's story that seem more interesting but are more enigmatic. The story of the "woman lost" is the first episode in the longer and more complex story of Yeats's life and work this volume has to tell.

Red Hanrahan

The full recovery of the "mighty memories" the poet appeals to at the end of part II of "The Tower" is a considerably less straightforward task than his way of referring to them implies:

I thought it all out twenty years ago:

Good fellows shuffled cards in an old bawn;
And when that ancient ruffian's turn was on

> He so bewitched the cards under his thumb
> That all but the one card became
> A pack of hounds and not a pack of cards,
> And that he changed into a hare.
> Hanrahan rose in frenzy there
> And followed up those baying creatures towards—
>
> O towards I have forgotten what—enough!

Despite its frank and spontaneous air, the passage (like many other things about Yeats) is both disingenuous and misleading. It hardly seems to stretch interpretation too far, for instance, to observe that what the poet has "forgotten" is also what he does not want to remember ("enough!"), and Wade's *Bibliography* tells us that Yeats had only recently finished preparing the *Stories of Red Hanrahan* for the fifth volume of the Macmillan *Collected Edition*.[22] The *Bibliography* also reveals that the "thinking out" of the particular story he summarizes in "The Tower" involved not one version but three, each significantly revised. Strictly speaking, Hanrahan's own "memories" and Yeats's memories of him span at their fullest extent not twenty but nearly thirty-five years, beginning with a story called "The Devil's Book" that appeared in the *National Observer* on November 26, 1892, proceeding through another called "The Book of the Great Dhoul and Hanrahan the Red" in *The Secret Rose* (1897), and finally arriving at "Red Hanrahan" in the 1905 *Stories of Red Hanrahan,* the story that, with minor changes, now appears in *Mythologies.*

At first it is not easy to see what the history of the remaking of Hanrahan's story has to do with what we are not told about its final version in "The Tower." What is being left out of the poem, as even someone who has not read "Red Hanrahan" can see, is what his magical frenzy leads him toward in the night; one has the impression, which is perfectly appropriate in the context, that the poet can remember driving Hanrahan mad but cannot remember why. Yet it cannot be accidental—and is in fact the part of his "forgetting" most likely to have been deliberate—that what Yeats is so abruptly unable to recall is that Hanrahan was driven mad so that he could become a poet. His hire for his journey, besides "broken knees" and "horrible splendour of desire," is the Muse, the "woman lost" upon whom the imagination dwells and with whom is associated the memory that would blot out the sun.

In "Red Hanrahan" the story begins, as the speaker of "The Tower" says, with a game of cards that a mysterious "ancient ruffian" turns into a midnight chase after a pack of phantom hounds. What they lead Hanrahan to is a door in a hillside that leads to fairyland. There he is greeted by an old man, who leads him to a "very big shining house." Inside he finds a woman, "the most beautiful the world ever saw," sitting asleep on a high seat, and before her are four old women, each holding a different object: a cauldron, a stone, a spear, and a sword. "Hanrahan stood looking at them for a long time ... but ready as he was with his tongue and afraid of no person, he was in dread now to speak to so beautiful a woman, and in so grand a place. And then he thought to ask what were the four things the four grey old women were holding like great treasures, but he could not think of the right words to bring out."

One by one, the old women rise up and say a word: "Pleasure"; "Power"; "Courage"; and "Knowledge." Each waits for Hanrahan to question her, but he can say nothing. They all carry their treasures out the door, saying as they go, "He has no wish for us"; "He is weak"; "He is afraid"; "His wits are gone from him"; and then they say together, "Echtge, daughter of the Silver Hand, must stay in her sleep. It is a pity, it is a great pity." Hanrahan too falls asleep, and when he wakes he is on the hillside near Slieve Echtge, but he is "not sure how he came there; for all that had happened in the barn had gone from him, and all of his journey but the soreness of his feet and the stiffness in his bones."[23]

For a year afterward, Hanrahan wanders the world without remembering who he is or where he has been, until he is no longer a "tall, strong, red-haired young man" but "very thin and worn, and his hair very long and wild." "Where have I been since then? Where was I for the whole year?" he cries as he comes to himself at last, and an old man replies, "It is hard to say where you might have been ... or what part of the world you may have travelled; and it is like enough you have the dust of many roads on your feet; for there are many who go wandering and forgetting like that, ... when once they have been given the touch." Even more important, however, is the fact that "the touch" has made him into someone who, in the stories that follow, is very much like the Yeats who remembers him in "The Tower": a famous "poet of the Gael" (in "The Twisting of the Rope"), a visionary (in "Red Hanrahan's Vision"), and the composer of a curse on old age (in "Red Hanrahan's Curse").

In spite of its puzzling symbolic machinery, the basic outline and character of the events that transform an ordinary young man into a passionate and decrepit poet are clear. "Red Hanrahan" is an episode in the history of the mind. Hanrahan is changed not by external but by internal misfortune; Yeats, like the peasant storytellers he is imitating, is giving an account of the psychogenesis of an abnormal personality, the half-mad or "touched."[24] The symptoms of this condition are already familiar from "The Tower": amnesia, physical debilitation, and an appearance that suggests "wild" emotional disorder. It is consequently not surprising to find that in the succeeding stories the new "poet of the Gael's" poems are in fact Yeats's poems: "The Happy Townland," "Red Hanrahan's Song about Ireland" and "Red Hanrahan's Curse on Old Age," to name only those now attributed to him in *Mythologies*.[25] What the story is about, in other words, is how one becomes the sort of person who writes the sort of poems that a person like Yeats would write—precisely the thing that, as George Russell observed, is missing from the *Autobiography*.

The crucial figure in the transformation of the "strong young man" into the debilitated poet is the sleeping fairy woman, Echtge, the "woman lost." At the outset, she is neither lost nor won but passive, awaiting arousal; she is, according to the old women, waiting to become the "woman won." The peculiarity of Hanrahan's encounter with her—which at first seems to imitate a familiar pattern in Western mythology and folktale—is that it requires of him a kind of behavior quite different from that of, for instance, an Achilles or an Odysseus. To awaken Echtge Hanrahan needs something more than physical prowess or intellectual subtlety. In effect his problem is to realize that there is a problem, to ask the question or, to put it in a way that suggests more of what I take to be the real irony of the situation, to become conscious of the problem. In the presence of the idealized sexual object ("the most beautiful the world ever saw") Hanrahan, the "strong young man," "ready as he was with his tongue and afraid of no person," is suddenly struck dumb and deprived of his manhood; he sees and recognizes the importance of its symbolic "treasures," Pleasure, Power, Courage, and Knowledge, but cannot muster enough of any of them in himself to ask the question that would awaken Echtge's dormant sexuality. In order to arouse her he must first become aroused himself, and the fact that he feels only a vague, numbing anxiety suggests that here, as in "The Tower," is a man who responds to the excited and passionate aspects of his sensibility as if they were over-stimulating and excessive. The house is too "grand," the woman too beautiful to be won; the correspondence between manhood and its symbols cannot be acknowledged, and Echtge, as the old women put it, must "remain in her sleep."

But however the anxiety-provoking quality in Echtge is described—and it is obviously a matter of some importance, to which I shall return in the next chapter—it is clear from the stories that follow "Red Hanrahan" in *Mythologies* that his failure to awaken her is the decisive moment in the genesis of the creative personality. As a "poet of the Gael" Hanrahan is now an exile from the company of men, doomed to the creative elaboration of a conflict between desire and anxiety, lechery and vision, excitement and depression. The second story, "The Twisting of the Rope," is about his attempt to seduce a farmer's daughter. Her mother tricks him into leaving the house and locks the door. Hanrahan walks down to the sea, where he sits down on a stone and begins to sing "slowly to himself, the way he did always to hearten himself when every other thing failed him." As he sings, he seems to see mist and shadows gathering around him, and among them "the queen-woman he had seen in her sleep at Slieve Echtge; not in her sleep now, but mocking and calling out to them that were behind her, 'He was weak, he was weak, he had no courage.'" Then it seems to him that a great water worm comes out of the sea and twists itself around him.

> And then he got free of it, and went on, shaking and unsteady, along the edge of the strand, and the grey shapes were flying here and there about him. And this is what they were saying: "It is a pity for him that refuses the call of the daughters of the Sidhe, for he will find no comfort in the love of the women of the earth to the end of life and time, and the cold of the grave is in his heart forever. It is death he has chosen; let him die, let him die, let him die."[26]

Echtge has become Hanrahan's Muse: the woman he might have won transformed into the terrifying and punitive image of the "woman lost" the poet sees as he sings.[27]

Knowing more about what was thought out twenty years ago, then, does make it easier to understand the significance of what is "unremembered" about Hanrahan in "The Tower." Unfortunately, it also raises some questions about the accuracy of what *is* remembered. There is, for instance, the famous interrogation in stanza 13:

> Does the imagination dwell the most
> Upon a woman won or woman lost?
> If on the lost, admit you turned aside
> From a great labyrinth out of pride,
> Cowardice, some silly over-subtle thought
> Or anything called conscience once;
> And that if memory recur, the sun's
> Under eclipse and the day blotted out.

The content of the accusation is evidently a crucial part of the self-recognition that transforms the depression of part I into the elation of part III. But it is by no means obvious from "Red Hanrahan" what the poet of "The Tower" finds in it to fire his indignation. Hanrahan, after all, is passive throughout, caught by the juggleries of both the old man in the barn and the artist who triumphs by making men mad. He is moved rather than motivated, taken he knows not where, or how, or for what reason, presented with circumstances whose nature and consequences he does not understand, and doomed by events he cannot remember. The 1905 version of his story is, as Yeats would have put it, a "symbolic" story, and he would have meant something like what he had found to praise that year in John Synge's *Shadow of the Glen,* whose heroine, "like everybody when caught up in great events...does many things without being quite certain why she does them. She hardly understands at moments why her action has a certain form...she is intoxicated by a dream which is hardly understood by herself, but possesses her like something half remembered on a sudden wakening."[28]

The sudden wakening from the dream and the uncertain consciousness of having acted under its enchantment is also the subject of "The Circus Animals' Desertion," and the biography of the possessed poet is the story of Hanrahan. Yet it is precisely the puzzlingly "external" and artificial quality that both the poet Yeats and the poet Hanrahan have in common that makes the depth of feeling betrayed in their confrontation in "The Tower" seem so gratuitous. The most tantalizing failure of memory in the poem occurs not when something is "forgotten" (what Hanrahan follows the hounds toward) but when something is remembered in a way that "half remembers" something else ("Admit you turned aside"). The already elaborately misleading process of self-recollection in part II, in other words, now suggests that there is yet another version of the poet's story, a version containing the "great events" at issue not only in the symbolism of "Red Hanrahan" but also in the enigmatic "memory" of "The Tower,"

> And that if memory recur, the sun's
> Under eclipse and the day blotted out.

And indeed, as we have already observed, Hanrahan's "mighty memories" do extend considerably beyond the limit of twenty years suggested by "The Tower," first to "The Book of the Great Dhoul and Hanrahan the Red" (1897) and then to "The Devil's Book" (1892). At this point, however, one's willingness to unravel the intricacies of the unremembered any farther is opposed, once again, by the unmemorable, and to a certain extent by the inaccessible. There is as yet no variorum of Yeats's prose fiction,[29] and the trouble taken to unearth the early versions of "Red Hanrahan" is not rewarded by the discovery of a forgotten masterpiece. If "Red Hanrahan" has less claim on our attention than "The Tower," its predecessors have hardly any at all. *The Secret Rose* is a relic of Yeats's "Celtic" 1890s; "The Devil's Book" is a piece of juvenilia. What makes them worth discussing here is not their aesthetic merit but their relevance to what is so puzzlingly "symbolic" about Yeats in general, about the "images and memories" of "The Tower" in particular, and specifically about the story of Red Hanrahan that "he himself created."

One's first impression of "The Book of the Great Dhoul and Hanrahan the Red" in *The Secret Rose* is that in this case the vicissitudes of creativity have been so extreme that they are indecipherable. "The Book of the Great Dhoul" seems to be a different story about a different person. Hanrahan is no longer strong, earnest, and young but a pale, dissipated man of indeterminate age. "The book of the great dhoul" (devil) is an occult work he buys called "The Grimoire of Pope Honorious," which contains a "receipt for making spirits appear." Hanrahan uses the formula to invoke the first name he thinks of, Cleena of the Wave, queen of the southern fairies. At first her form is vague and shadowy and her voice an inaudible murmur; but each time he invokes her she is more visible and audible, and he "listens to many miraculous things." Finally, after a week, he falls into an exhausted sleep, and wakes to find "a beautiful woman in a pale saffron dress looking at her own footmark in the ashes."

> ... At the sight, the memory of all the trouble women had brought upon him passed over his mind, and he cried out, "Woman, what do you want here?"
>
> She turned toward him a face so full of the tender substance of mortality, and smiled upon him with lips so full of red mortal blood that he did not recognize the immortal of his dreams; and she said to him in a caressing voice: "You have always loved me better than your own soul, and you have sought for me everywhere and in everything, though without knowing what you sought, and now I have come to you and taken on mortality that I may share your sorrow." He saw that she was indeed Cleena of the Wave, but so changed that all the trouble he had ever had from women, and all his anger against them were between him and her; and standing up hurriedly he cried: "Woman, begone out of this. I have had enough of women. I am weary of women. I am weary of life."
>
> She came over to him, and laying her hand upon his shoulder, said in a half-whisper: "I will surround you with peace, and I will make your days calm, and I will grow old by your side. Do you not

see I have always loved you? . . . I love you, for you are fierce and
passionate, and good and bad. . . . It was I who put a thought of
the Devil's Book into your head. . . ." Her importunity had made
him angry, and he flung her from him, crying: "It was not you I
loved, but the woman of the Shee." . . . But now she too was angry,
and he heard her voice, musical even in anger, and her words staid
long in his ears: "Owen Hanrahan the Red, you have looked so
often upon the dust that when the Rose has blossomed there you
think it but a pinch of coloured dust; but now I lay upon you a
curse, and you shall see the Rose everywhere, in the noggin, in
woman's eye, in drifting phantoms, and seek to come to it in vain;
it shall waken a fire in your heart, and in your feet, and in your
hands. A sorrow of all sorrows is upon you, Owen Hanrahan the
Red."[30]

It is this Hanrahan, then, that Yeats implicitly refers to in the last
stanzas of part II of "The Tower." He, not the mysteriously baffled
young man of "Red Hanrahan," is the old lecher who turns aside. Yeats's
way of confusing "half-memories" of both in 1925 also suggests that this
is the "dream" that explains the symbolic drama he had thought out
twenty years before. Both the mockery of the punitive Muse in "The
Twisting of the Rope" and the accusation of the poet in "The Tower" are
justified by their common "memory" of the overmastering rage that the
"woman won" had once inspired. Both are, like Cleena's curse, formali-
zations of the psychological consequences of Hanrahan's angry rejection
of the woman he loves "better than his own soul," the most important of
which is creativity itself: the fire and the sorrow, or excitement and
depression, that are part of the way it feels to feel like writing a poem.
Hanrahan's Rose is now the subject of Yeats's poetry, where it expresses
in particular the power of the "woman lost" to excite fantasies in which
things seem about to fall apart. There is, for example, "The Secret Rose,"
which was originally attributed to Hanrahan[31] and later became the
epigraph of *The Secret Rose:*

> . . . I, too, await
> The hour of thy great wind of love and hate.
> When shall the stars be blown about the sky,
> Like sparks blown out of a smithy, and die?
> Surely thine hour has come, thy great wind blows,
> Far-off, most secret, and inviolate Rose?
> [27–32]

In "The Book of the Great Dhoul" one comes at last on what seems to
be the "mighty memory" so elaborately remade by the fictive recollec-

tions of "The Tower." It is an account of the dream by which the poet is enchanted, that is to say, of the seduction of the poet by the Muse, and it defines his creativity as a response to destructive impulses produced by sexual excitement: the imagination dwells on the "woman lost" because it cannot tolerate the presence of the woman won. For the "old lecher" whose poems are now Yeats's poems, creativity is, as Yeats would put it later, a matter of "lust and rage":

> You think it horrible that lust and rage
> Should dance attention upon my old age;
> They were not such a plague when I was young;
> What else have I to spur me into song?
> ["The Spur"]

This way of putting it is already familiar from the last stanza of "The Circus Animals' Desertion," and its ironies seem, from the point of view of "The Book of the Great Dhoul," accurate enough. Yet its bitterness (as well as its complacency, which suggests that we are once again in the presence of the "remade" self) also registers the way in which the formula is genuinely reductive. The sexual analogy explains away more than it explains or, to put it more charitably, does not explain enough. What it leaves unexplained, in particular, is the origin of a feeling so massive in its quantity and apocalyptic in its quality that its recurrence, in both "The Secret Rose" and "The Tower," threatens to blot out the day and blow the stars about the sky. It is this implicit threat to the integrity of the mind, if not of reality itself, that pricks the poet on to even his most ironic self-inventions. The excitement over which the Muse presides is in this respect analogous to, but significantly different from, sexual excitement. Hence in Yeats the merely sexual—the mistress or woman won—is characteristically represented ironically, as the raving slut rather than the faery bride.

Hanrahan's misfortune (and, by implication, Yeats's) was to be enchanted by the latter rather than the former, and this above all else distinguishes his story as the story of the poet. Yet is precisely this immensely significant accident that a formulation like that of "The Spur" leaves unexplained and (except as ironic loss, "What else have I?") unexpressed. Nor is the 1905 version of Hanrahan's story, with its "symbolic" plot and spare, formulaic "Gaelic" prose style, any more helpful in establishing its context. The language and events of the earlier version, however, are both less artful and more suggestive about the source of Cleena/Echtge's mysterious power over Hanrahan's mind. "You have always loved me," she says to him in *The Secret Rose*, "better than your own soul, and you have sought me everywhere and in everything, though without knowing what you sought."

Her description of herself can of course be read as a hyperbolical way of pointing the irony of Hanrahan's rejection of her sexualized "mortal" presence; he cannot see that what angers him most is what he loves best. But her language also suggests that something more than an ironic splitting of the beloved object into two—the woman desired and the woman loved—is at issue in the conundrum of the "woman lost." It suggests that the encounter between Hanrahan and his fairy mistress is a metaphor for his mind's encounter with an aspect of itself, and in particular with the part of itself that defines the quality of its feelings about itself. She is the embodiment of his deep and pervasive sense of incompleteness and his longing to be more than he is, to unite himself with something idealized, omniscient, and omnipotent, to become something "intended, complete." At its extreme, it is the wish to transcend objectivity and be swallowed up in the delusional reality in which the self finds itself "everywhere and in everything," the triumph of madness where "moon and sunlight seem / One inextricable beam." This is Cleena/Echtge in her aspect as the terrifying and labyrinthine water-worm of "The Twisting of the Rope," and it is in this sense that her offer to "surround him with peace" is so hyperbolically overexciting: she is the solipsistic labyrinth from which he must turn aside. It is in this sense, moreover, that as the rejected "woman lost" she presides over the creative effort to remake the defective self into something that serves both as a defense against the feelings her absence excites and as a temporary satisfaction of their demands for omniscience and perfection.

The conclusion that the "mighty memory" of the poet in "The Tower" is something more than the recollection of a conflictful encounter between affection and sexuality is further supported by the evidence of the earliest version of Hanrahan's story, "The Devil's Book." Although the hero is here called "O'Sullivan" rather than Hanrahan, the events described are the same as those of *The Secret Rose*. The passage corresponding to that in "The Book of the Great Dhoul" quoted earlier, however, has both a different outcome and a different tone:

> And he opened his eyes, and Cleona was looking at her own foot-marks in the ashes.
> "Look at me," she went on; "I have a mortal body like your own. I saw the sorrowful dhrames o' the world dhriftin' above it, like a say as it slept in the night, and I skimmed the foam o' them in a noggin, and made mesel' a body, and it was love for your love o' me that made me do it, Owen."

He started up and cried out, everything turning round about him, fierce and sudden anger in his breast. "Had I not sorrow and trouble enough along wid ye?" he said. "Did I not lose three schools wid ye? I tell you that it was not you, but the Fairy Woman that I loved. . . . O, I have lost the Woman o' the Shee!"

"Do not drive me away" she said, clinging to his knees and sobbing. "I have loved ye ever since I saw ye lyin on the Rath of Cruchan and saw ye turnin' from side to side, for the fire in yer heart would not let ye rest. I love ye, for ye are fierce and passionate, now good and now bad, and not free and dim and wave-like as are the Sheogues. I love ye as Eve loved the Serpent."

"I hate ye!" he cried. "I hate ye—for I hate everybody, and I hate the world, and I want to be out of it."

"Do not drive me away, Owen: becaze o' ye, I left all my own people weepin' for me. Owen, I have always been good to yer family, and did me best to keep the good luck among ye. And ye were a hard family to help and I done it, Owen O'Sullivan."

"Begone from me!" he cried and strode out into the darkness.[32]

The most noticeable difference between this and the later versions is that of language. The characters have neither the grace and simplicity of speech Yeats would copy from Synge's and Lady Gregory's imitations of Gaelic in 1905 nor the elaborate Paterian cadence and "twilight" diction of *The Secret Rose*. They speak instead in the dialect of the music hall, and the effect is satirical. The difference, however, is more than one of tone. While Cleona's description of herself and O'Sullivan's response imply both the subjectivity (she is the stuff of his dreams) and the apocalyptic quality of feeling ("I hate the world") described in "The Book of the Great Dhoul," it is clear that here both are being interpreted reductively. What O'Sullivan discovers is that the woman of his dreams is no better than she should be. The metaphorical content of Cleona's mortality is not the ideal but the real, and her transformation promises not a redemptive "peace" but a repetition of the Fall:"I love ye as Eve loved the Serpent." The reduction of their encounter to the merely sexual, moreover, is followed by the other most noticeable difference between this and the later versions of Hanrahan's story. After striding out into the darkness, O'Sullivan does not return until dawn, "very drunk," to find his cabin has been thrown down by a whirlwind "such as the peasants ever associated with the Fairies"; then the following Sunday he is denounced from the pulpit, taken at night by some men of the neighborhood and "beaten soundly," sprinkled with holy water, and "dropped . . . over the boundary of the next county."[33]

The story of "lust and rage," in short, is not the story of the poet. But it should also be observed that here, as in "The Spur," what is being expressed is not an enlightened acknowledgment of the real but a bitterly ambivalent acceptance of the absence of the ideal, the loss of "the Woman o' the Shee." This loss, and not that of a sexual object, distinguishes O'Sullivan's story from Hanrahan's, and it is reconstituted in the latter as the "curse" of creativity. Insofar as it is the story of the poet, consequently, the story of the "woman lost" is the story of ambivalence rooted in a demand for omniscient perfection that is expressed by, but not limited to, the desire aroused by objects. The poet's burden is not the burden of unrequited love for a particular woman but the generalized excitement that his overstimulated fantasy finds everywhere and in everything: "In the noggin, in woman's eye, in drifting phantoms ... , it shall waken a fire in your heart, and in your feet, and in your hands. A sorrow of all sorrows is upon you, Owen Hanrahan the Red."

<hr>

The Woman Won

Of all the "unremembered" things about himself Yeats may have been responding to in the labyrinth of images and memories unfolded by Hanrahan in "The Tower," the most obvious is his relationship to Maud Gonne. "What is immensely moving" in the last lines of part II, says one recent critic, "is Yeats's clear self-condemnation, for he implicitly states a failure of desire on his part for Maud Gonne. Like Hanrahan, he turned aside, and could not give all for love."[34] The observation, while undoubtedly quite true as far as it goes, reflects in an interesting way our willingness to accept Yeats's characteristically hyperbolical estimate of what the appropriate limits of desire might be. Even in the case of a woman as lovely and charismatic as Maud Gonne undoubtedly was, "all for love" would have been too much for anyone else long before it was enough for Yeats. By 1917, the year he finally turned aside from her to marry Georgie Hyde-Lees, he had endured "that monstrous thing / Returned yet unrequited love" for more than twenty-five years.[35] "I was twenty-three years old when the troubling of my life began," he wrote in his draft memoirs in 1916.

> I had never thought to see in a living woman so great beauty. It belonged to famous pictures, to poetry, to some legendary past. A complexion like the blossom of apples, and yet face and body had

the beauty of lineaments which Blake calls the highest beauty because it changes least from youth to age, and a stature so great she
seemed of a divine race. Her movements were worthy of her form,
and I understood at last why the poet of antiquity, where we would
but speak of face and form, sings, loving some lady, that she paces
like a goddess.[36]

Their first meeting was in January 1889; they met again, and in 1891
Yeats mustered the courage to propose to her for the first of many times.
She refused, saying "there were reasons—she would never marry; but in
words that had no conventional ring she asked for my friendship."[37]

Her reasons as they emerged over the years were manifold. In 1889 she
had already been the mistress of the French journalist Lucien Millevoye
for some two years, and by 1891 she had been for three years the mother
of a son, whom she represented to Yeats at the time as her "adopted
daughter." After her son's death she had a daughter, Iseult, by Millevoye,
though by the time the child was born in 1895 they had agreed to separate. Yeats himself knew nothing of the affair until 1898, when Maud
confessed it to him in one of their moments of renewed intimacy. She
continued, however, to refuse his proposals, now on the grounds of her
"horror and terror of physical love."[38] There was, besides, always her
obsession and constant involvement in the cause of Irish nationalism, the
full extent of which was also kept from the notoriously indiscreet Yeats.
In 1889, for example, his offer to take her away from politics and "make
a beautiful life for her among artists and writers who could understand
her" was rejected on the grounds of her interest in "the work she had
chosen"—that is to say, in French anti-British intelligence activities during the Boer War.[39] In 1903 her devotion to the cause swept her into an
ill-advised but very patriotic marriage to Major John MacBride, who had
recently returned from leading an Irish brigade against the English in
South Africa. In 1904 a son, Seán, was born, but by 1905 she was
separated from her husband, charging cruelty. She could not seek a divorce and marry Yeats, she said, because she was now a Roman Catholic,
an argument that remained unassailable until MacBride became one of
the sixteen men the British shot after the Easter Rising in 1916.

Maud Gonne's refusal to become Yeats's temporal wife, however, did
not prevent their unconventional friendship from blossoming twice into
the emotional intensity of what Yeats called their "spiritual marriages."
The first occurred in 1898 and grew out of their work together on the
development of "Irish Mysteries." "An obsession more constant than
anything but my love itself was the need of mystical rites—a ritual system

of evocation and meditation—to reunite the perception of the spirit, of the divine, with natural beauty," he wrote in his 1916 memoir.

> My own seership was, I thought, inadequate; it was to be Maud Gonne's work and mine. . . . I, who could not influence her actions, could dominate her inner being. I could therefore use her clairvoyance to produce forms that would arise from both minds . . . there would be, as it were, a spiritual birth from the soul of a man and a woman. . . . I believed we were about to attain a revelation.
>
> Maud Gonne entirely shared these ideas, and I did not doubt that in carrying them out I should win her for myself. . . . At every moment of leisure we obtained in vision long lists of symbols. . . . [They] took their places gradually in a symbolic fabric that had for its centre the four talismans of the Tuatha de Danaan, the sword, the stone, the spear and the cauldron. . . .[40]

Ultimately Yeats was no more successful in winning Maud for himself than was Hanrahan, into whose story the "four talismans" found their way in 1905, in winning Echtge. The work on the rituals was at its height in 1898, when, Yeats recalls in his memoir, he and Maud met after breakfast in the Nassau Hotel in Dublin:

> She said, "Had you a strange dream last night?" I said, "I dreamed this morning for the first time in my life that you kissed me." She made no answer, but late that night when dinner was over and I was about to return home she said, "I will tell you now what happened. When I fell asleep last night I saw standing at my bedside a great spirit. He took me to a great throng of spirits, and you were among them. My hand was put into yours and I was told that we were married. After that I remember nothing." Then and there for the first time with the bodily mouth, she kissed me.[41]

The next day, however, he found that she regretted what had been said and done. "'I should not have spoken to you in that way,' she said, 'for I can never be your wife in reality.'" In the days that followed, "she was . . . always very emotional, and would kiss me very tenderly, but when I spoke of marriage on the eve of her leaving said, 'No, it seems to me impossible.' And then, with clenched hands, 'I have a horror and terror of physical love.'"[42] Their work on the "Irish Mysteries" continued until about 1901 and produced, in draft, two sets of initiation rituals.[43] But in the end it too was to prove a "vain attempt,"[44] and after 1899 Yeats was to lose Maud first to the revolutionary excitement of the Boer War and, at last, to Major MacBride.

The second "spiritual marriage" did not occur until after Maud's marriage had been over for several years. In June 1908 Yeats wrote in his journal, "At Paris with [Maud Gonne]. On Saturday evening (20th), she said something that blotted away the recent past and brought all back to the spiritual marriage of 1898. On Sunday we talked more plainly. She believes that this bond is to be recreative and to be the means of spiritual illumination between us. It is to be a bond of the spirit only and she lives from now on, she said, for that and for her children."[45] Over the next few months their renewed "marriage" produced recurrent moments of ecstatic "astral" union, usually in sleep, often when they were far apart, and "always," Yeats noted, "where desire is unthinkable—desire in the ordinary sense."[46] On July 26, for instance, she wrote to him in Ireland that she had

> had such a wonderful experience last night that I must know at once if it affected you and how? . . . Last night . . . I thought I would go to you astrally. (It was not working hours for you & I thought by going to you I might even be able to share with you some of my vitality and energy. . . .) . . . We met somewhere in space, I don't know where—I was conscious of starlight and of hearing the sea below us. You had taken the form, I think, of a great serpent. . . . As I looked into your eyes . . . your lips touched mine. We melted into one another till we formed only *one being, a being greater than ourselves,* who felt all and knew all with double intensity.[47]

On October 20, she recorded on a page of his journal, he came to her suddenly while she was reading it "with an ecstasy I cannot describe. The intensity of the spiritual union prevents. . . ."[48]

Yeats's own ecstasies were less intense. He felt what Maud felt only in "phantom" or "shadowy" forms, a defect he attributed to a decrease in his visionary powers since 1898. Nevertheless he too became adept at "becoming one" with her spirit and "looking into her being."[49] Late in 1908, however, they began to quarrel over politics again, and by January 21, 1909, Maud had again decided that they "must be apart," partly because her Catholicism prevented her from divorcing MacBride and partly because her feelings for Yeats were again becoming something more than spiritual. "The old dread of physical love has awakened in her."

> What end will it all have? I fear for her and for myself. She has all myself. I was never more deeply in love, but my desires must go elsewhere, if I would escape their poison. I am in continual terror of some entanglement parting us, and all the while I know that she

made me and I her. . . . Always since I was a boy I have questioned
dreams for her sake—and she herself always a dream and deceiving
hope. . . . She would be cruel if she were not a child who can always say, "You will not suffer because I will pray." [50]

In fact, Yeats had begun to send his desires elsewhere as early as 1896
when, perhaps partly in response to rumors he had heard about Maud
and Millevoye in France, he was for a year the lover of the woman he
delicately referred to in his memoirs as "Diana Vernon." There had been
possibly one other affair (ca. 1903)[51] before 1909 when, hoping to escape what was poisoning his relationship with Maud, he took a mistress in London, "an unmarried woman past her first youth." The affair
lasted, "without great conviction on either side," until 1913, when she
announced that she was pregnant by him.[52] Yeats had "all but decided"
to marry her when he was dissuaded by the mediums he consulted in the
matter; it was, they said, a "deception," which proved to be the case.[53]
They did, however, urge him to marry someone, and their advice was
seconded by the efforts of his friend Lady Gregory, who subjected Yeats
to a barrage of eligible acquaintance in the winter of 1913–14.[54] But by
then the most likely candidate appears to have been Georgie Hyde-Lees,
whom Yeats had met in 1912. They shared an interest in the occult and in
spiritual research, and she was young, handsome, and enthusiastic; there
is some evidence that they discussed marriage prior to 1917. Nevertheless
Yeats remained indecisive about her until after he had renewed his suit to
Maud after MacBride's death in 1916. He was refused a final time, first
by Maud and then the following summer by her daughter Iseult, who had
been carrying on an adolescent flirtation with him since 1910.[55] But by
this time Yeats appears to have made up his mind, with some more
urging from his mediums and astrologers, to marry. Immediately after
receiving Iseult's refusal, he proposed a third time, to Georgie, and was
accepted. The banns were published in London on October 1, 1917, and
the ceremony performed on October 21; Yeats was fifty-two and his
bride twenty-six.

Undoubtedly, then, Yeats like Hanrahan did finally turn aside. Yet it is
difficult to see here, as it is in the 1905 "Red Hanrahan," how the
admission is also an indictment. If anything was obvious about his relationship with Maud Gonne, it was her resolute turning aside from him
and the "physical love" he aroused, rather than the other way round.
Nevertheless, it is equally clear that Yeats did interpret his marriage
to Georgie as treason. During the first days of their honeymoon he became withdrawn and deeply depressed and began writing poetry which

showed that his imagination still dwelled on the events of the summers just past at Maud's house in Normandy:

> A strange thing surely that my Heart, when love had come un-
> sought
> Upon the Norman upland or in that poplar shade,
> Should find no burden but itself and yet should be worn out.
> It could not bear that burden and therefore it went mad.
>
> The south wind brought it longing, and the east wind despair,
> The west wind made it pitiful, and the north wind afraid.
> It feared to give its love a hurt with all the tempest there;
> It feared the hurt that she could give and therefore it went mad.
>
> I can exchange opinion with any neighbouring mind,
> I have as healthy flesh and blood as any rhymer's had,
> But O! my Heart could bear no more when the upland caught the
> wind;
> I ran, I ran, from my love's side because my Heart went mad.
> ["Owen Aherne and His Dancers," 1–12]

Under the circumstances, it is difficult not to interpret this poem as if it were, like the 1897 version of Hanrahan's story, an account of the latent rather than the manifest content of events. Here, as in "The Tower" version of the 1905 story, the poet persists in interpreting his own failure to "awaken" what slept in Maud and Iseult as if it were an expression of his own terrified and angry rejection of them. The hypothesis becomes more plausible when one reminds oneself that the poem is being written on his honeymoon; in fact, there is no need to look as far away as Normandy for the most likely source of the emotional tempest that threatens the Heart with madness. Something of the sort is implicitly acknowledged in the remaining section of the poem, which gains considerably in complexity of reference when one recalls that the twenty-two-year-old Iseult was not the only "young child" whose love had come into his life unsought:

> The Heart behind its rib laughed out. "You have called me mad," it
> said,
> "Because I made you turn away and run from that young child;
> How could she mate with fifty years that was so wildly bred?
> Let the cage bird and the cage bird mate and the wild bird mate in
> the wild."
>
> "You imagine lies all day, O murderer," I replied.
> "And all those lies have but one end, poor wretches to betray;

I did not find in any cage the woman at my side.
O but her heart would break to learn my thoughts are far away."

"Speak all your mind," my Heart sang out, "speak all your mind;
        who cares,
Now that your tongue cannot persuade the child till she mistake
Her childish gratitude for love and match your fifty years?
O let her choose a young man now and all for his wild sake."
[13–24]

In fantasy, it is Maud and Iseult from whom the Heart runs; in fact, it is
Georgie. As in the earlier versions of the poet Hanrahan's story, the
substance of the accusation of the "woman lost" is most recognizable
(but least notorious) in the poet Yeats's response to the "woman at his
side," the woman won. Besides his wife and his anonymous London
mistress, there had been in Yeats's Muse-haunted life only one other
such, Georgie's stepaunt and the mother of her close friend Dorothy
Pound, Olivia Shakespear. Yeats called her "Diana Vernon" after the
heroine of *Rob Roy*.

Olivia Shakespear and Yeats met in the spring of 1894 through her
cousin Lionel Johnson. She was married but estranged from her husband;
by the summer of the following year she and Yeats had resolved to "come
away" together.[56] In the fall of 1895 Yeats left his family's home in
Bedford Park for rooms in the Temple with Arthur Symons; then, in
March of 1896, he moved on to the greater privacy of the rooms in
Woburn Buildings that were to be his London residence until his marriage. There, at the age of thirty-one, he consummated his first love affair:

At last she came to me ... and I was impotent from nervous
excitement.... A week later she came to me again, and my nervous
excitement was so painful that it seemed best to sit over our tea and
talk.... She understood instead of, as another would, changing
liking for dislike—was only troubled by my trouble. My nervousness did not return again and we had many days of happiness. It
will always be a grief to me that I could not give the love that was
her beauty's right, but she was too near my soul, too salutary and
too wholesome to my inmost being. All our lives long, as da Vinci
says, we long, thinking it is but the moon that we long [for], for our
destruction, and how, when we meet [it] in the shape of a most fair
woman, can we do less than leave all others for her? Do we not
seek our dissolution upon her lips?

My liaison lasted but a year.... I had a struggle to earn my
living, and that made it harder for me, I was so often preoccupied

> when she came. Then Maud Gonne wrote to me; she was in London and would I come to dine? . . . And at last instead of reading much love poetry, as my way was to bring the right mood round, I wrote letters. My friend found my mood did not answer hers and burst into tears. "There is someone else in your heart," she said. It was the breaking between us for many years.[57]

The scene is proleptic. Yeats is recalling in his 1916 memoir a past that was to repeat itself in the early days of his honeymoon less than a year later. Moreover, his reminiscence is in effect identical with the fictive memoir of "The Tower" in 1925, and in particular with the version of the poet's story published in *The Secret Rose* only a month after the end of his "liaison" in 1897.[58] On the whole, it seems reasonable to conclude that although Yeats had begun to remake the ironic O'Sullivan into the poetic Hanrahan as early as 1892 (when the first version of "The Twisting of the Rope" appeared),[59] his conception of the latter's encounter with Cleena owes much to Olivia's wholesome and salutary presence. This observation, however, only makes his rejection of her offer of an enlightened and affectionate sexual partnership ("I will surround you with peace") all the more unaccountable, unless one assumes that here too something more than sexuality (or, for that matter, affection) was at issue.

This assumption is supported by the fact that here, as in "The Book of the Great Dhoul," the poet's rejection of the woman at his side is associated with a constellation of feelings that endows sexuality with a characteristically apocalyptic meaning. Their relationship is more than that of one person to another; instead, it once again suggests something having to do with the relationship of the self to itself and the "transcendent" issues of subjective wholeness and dissolution: "She was too near my soul, to salutary and too wholesome to my inmost being. All our lives long . . . we long . . . for our destruction." The fact that Yeats is here nominally referring to two different women makes it only slightly more difficult to appreciate the way in which he is registering two different versions of the same response. To fear what one longs for ("too wholesome") is to long for what one fears ("our destruction"). What he desires in the frigid and capricious Maud Gonne, in short, is what he shuns in the warm and loving Olivia: the labyrinthine folding up of the inmost self in another's being that is also the solipsistic dissolution of the objective consciousness. In "Owen Aherne and His Dancers" this overexciting quality in the "woman won" is expressed in the hypochondriacal apprehension of madness, the feeling of being blown to the four winds by the inner tempest that is the occasion for both the creative remaking of the self in poetry and the withdrawal of feeling from the "woman at my side" to the "woman lost."

The underlying character of the anxieties that dictated Yeats's consistent choice of the "woman lost" is also suggested by the quality of feeling mobilized by the cycle of spiritual marriage and divorce that characterized his relationship with Maud Gonne. It has already been observed, for example, that the "astral unions" in which they became transcendentally "greater than themselves" by "becoming one," "melting," or "looking into one another's being" could occur only when "desire was unthinkable." It is even more significant, however, that at such times the combination of sexual frustration and "spiritual" excitement produced symptoms that Yeats attributed to nervous exhaustion or "breakdown." The summer that followed the end of his affair with Olivia Shakespear and the beginning of the rapprochement that led to his first "spiritual marriage," for example, was the beginning of what he was tempted to call "the most miserable time of my life."

> It was a time of great personal strain and sorrow. Since my mistress had left me, no other woman had come into my life, and for nearly seven years none did. I was tortured by sexual desire and disappointed love. Often as I walked in the woods at Coole it would have been a relief to have screamed aloud. When desire became an unendurable torture, I would masturbate, and that, no matter how moderate I was, would make me ill. It never occurred to me to seek another love. I would repeat to myself again and again the last confession of Lancelot, and indeed it was my greatest pride, "I have loved a queen beyond measure and exceeding long." I was never before or since so miserable as in those years that followed my first visit to Coole. In the second as during the first visit my nervous system was worn out. The toil of dressing in the morning exhausted me, and Lady Gregory began to send me cups of soup when I was called.[60]

That Yeats should have been unhappy, even quite miserable, under such circumstances is understandable; that the consequences of his sexual initiation should have been so debilitating for so long is less so. During the first summers, at least, he could do no work at all, and there is the suggestion that he was on the verge of going mad and roaming the woods like Lancelot. However this may be, it is clear that his apprehensions were a response to an excitement that was only partly sexual in its objectives. In his exhausted state he lived, as he recalls in his 1916 memoir, "amid mystery," amid intimations of transcendence and spiritual ecstasy. He was in this state of mind when he began a "great collection of faery belief" with Lady Gregory among the cottages around Thoor Ballylee, of which he recalls in particular the stories of "change-lings" that were to find their way into "Red Hanrahan" in 1905:

> It seemed as if these people possessed an ancient knowledge. Ah, if we could but speak face to face with those they spoke to. "That old man," Lady Gregory said to me ... "may have the mystery of the ages." I began to have visions and dreams full of wisdom and beauty. Much of my thought since is founded upon certain sentences that came in this way. Once I asked when going to sleep what was the explanation of those curious tales of people "away," of which [we] had so many. In all these tales some man, woman, or child was believed to be carried off bodily by the faery world, a change-ling ... being left instead. I awoke enough to know that I lay in bed and had the familiar objects round, but to hear a strange voice speaking through my lips: "We make an image of him who sleeps, and it is not him who sleeps but it is like him who sleeps, and we call it Emmanuel."
>
> I was crossing one afternoon a little stream, and as I leaped I felt an emotion strange to me—for all my thoughts were pagan—a sense of utter dependence on the divine will. It was over in an in-stant, and I said to myself, "That is the way Christians feel." That night I seemed to wake in my bed to hear a voice saying, "The love of God for every soul is infinite, for every soul is unique; no other soul can fill the same need in God." ...
>
> Sometimes as I awoke marvellous illuminated pages seemed to be held before [me], with symbolic pictures that seemed profound, but when I tried to read the text all would vanish or but a sentence remain. I remember, "The secret of the world is so simple that it could be written on a blade of grass with the juice of a berry"; and "The rivers of Eden are in the midst of our rivers."[61]

What Yeats had to gain from such states of mind, which were also, as we have seen, those associated with his work on the "Irish Mysteries" with Maud Gonne, was the beatitude of the "completed" soul. What he had to fear from the nervous exhaustion they induced was, as he intui-tively realized, the psychotic dissolution of the self that produced the symptoms of the "changeling." It is not surprising to find, consequently, that the termination of his second "spiritual marriage" by Maud's "old dread of physical love" immediately brought on a "breakdown" that left him unfit for work for four months.[62] "I begin to wonder," he wrote in a journal entry dated January 31, 1909,

> Whether I have and always have had some nervous weakness in-
> herited from my mother. (I have noticed my own form of excitability
> in my sister Lolly, exaggerated in her by fits of prolonged
> gloom. . . .) In Paris I felt that if the strain were but a little more I
> would hit the woman who irritated me . . . The feeling is always the
> same: a consciousness of energy, of certainty, and of transforming
> power stopped by a wall, by something one must either submit to
> or rage against helplessly. It often alarms me; is it the root of mad-
> ness? So violent it is, and all the more because I seldom lose my
> temper in the ordinary affairs of life. . . . Then, too, I notice that
> my old childish difficulty of concentration is as great as ever. . . . I
> should learn to exclude this irritation from my conversation at any
> rate, as certainly I have learned to exclude it from my writings and
> my formal speech. In one way it has helped me, for the knowledge
> of it has forced me to make my writings sweet-tempered and, I
> think, gracious. There was a time when they were threatened by it;
> I had to subdue a kind of Jacobin rage. I escaped from it all as a
> writer through my sense of style. Is not one's art made out of the
> struggle with one's soul? Is not beauty a victory over oneself?[63]

The crisis of 1909 was also, as "Owen Aherne and His Dancers" indicates, the crisis of 1917; the "escape" in the latter case, however, was as
much the victory of his wife's art as of his own. Her offer to "surround
him with peace" had been met during the first few days of their honeymoon by withdrawal and depression; like Olivia Shakespear before her,
Georgie Yeats found that the "woman won" had the "other in his heart"
to contend with. Unlike Olivia, however, she did not insist on the point.
Instead, she decided to see what she could do to distract him by faking
automatic writing. But to her surprise, "the loosely held pencil scribbled
out fragments of sentences on a subject of which she was ignorant."[64]
Yeats was galvanized; it was the beginning of the work published in *A
Vision* that, with interpretation and revision, was to occupy him for the
last twenty years of his life. "On the afternoon of October 24th 1917,
four days after my marriage," he says in the introduction to the 1937
edition, "my wife surprised me by attempting automatic writing. What
came in disjointed sentences, in almost illegible writing, was so exciting,
sometimes so profound, that I persuaded her to give an hour or two day
after day to the unknown writer, and after some half-dozen such hours

offered to spend what remained of life explaining and piecing together those scattered sentences. 'No,' was the answer, 'we have come to give you metaphors for poetry.'"

They spent, he goes on, "much of 1918 at Glendalough, at Rosses Point, at Coole Park, at a house near it, at Thoor Ballylee, always more or less solitary, my wife bored and fatigued by her almost daily task and I thinking and talking of little else."[65] It was not much of a life for a young wife, who might have imagined better ways of spending her time alone with her husband. But under the circumstances her intuitive grasp of the need to redirect the "spiritual" excitement that threatened their marriage amounted to conjugal inspiration. Its effect on Yeats's poetry was of course pervasive, but it was also fairly successful in more practical terms. Yeats was, it is true, to remain "excitable" and apprehensive about the "root of madness" in his art for the rest of his life. His "breakdowns," however, cease to be much recorded after his marriage.[66] "My wife," he wrote to Lady Gregory on December 16, 1917, "is a perfect wife, kind, wise, and unselfish. I think you were such another young girl once. She has made my life serene and full of order."[67]

In the end, then, Yeats was reconciled to the woman at his side and found in marriage some of the sense of coherence and graciousness he had previously thought to find only in artifice. Yet the sort of perfection he alludes to suggests, at the moment of its realization, something that goes beyond the story of the women won and lost. His graceful compliment to his young wife and aging friend is more than a way of praising the present; it is a way of recalling the home he had found at Coole during the "most miserable time of his life" and the woman who, like Georgie, had successfully imposed order on the tempests of the mind. Lady Gregory had not only sent him up cups of soup in the morning but also, in the years that followed, bought furniture for his rooms, worried about his health, sent him hampers of food and wine, and lent him money or given it outright.[68] "Nobody has ever shown me such kindness," he wrote her in November 1897. "Everybody tells me how well I am looking, and I am better than I have been for years in truth. The days at Coole passed like a dream, a dream of peace."[69] By 1902 she had become his "dear friend,"[70] and when during his breakdown in 1909 he received word of her critical illness, he wrote in his journal,

> Feb. 4. This morning I got a letter telling me of Lady Gregory's illness. I did not recognize her son's writing at first, and my mind wandered, I suppose because I am not well. I thought my mother

was ill and that my sister was asking me to come at once: then I
remembered that my mother died years ago and that more than kin
was at stake. She has been to me mother, friend, sister and brother.
I cannot realize the world without her—she brought to my wavering thoughts steadfast nobility. All day the thought of losing her is
like a conflagration in the rafters. Friendship is all the house I
have.[71]

The house of friendship was for Yeats as different from the sort of
house he had grown up in as Lady Gregory herself was from the mother
who had passed on nothing to her children but weakness of the nerves.
His praise of the home his wife made for him, consequently, implicitly
recalls other houses and other women, and specifically something having
to do with the relationship between children and the women to whom
they are only "kin." On September 16, 1909, during a recurrence of the
symptoms of his breakdown, Yeats wrote in his journal,

> Head not very good. Two days ago Lady Gregory said, when they
> spoke of her grandchild's going to Harrow in 1921, "Where will his
> grandmother be then?" I thought of this house, slowly perfecting
> itself and the life within it in ever-increasing intensity of labour, and
> then of its probably sinking away through courteous incompetence,
> or rather sheer weakness of will, for ability had not failed in young
> Gregory. And I said to myself, "Why is life a perpetual preparation
> for something that never happens?"[72]

His thoughts about the decline and fall of the sons of ancestral houses
were, as the close association between his recollection of them and his
apprehensions about his "bad" head indicates, also thoughts about himself. "For some months now," he wrote six years later in the concluding
paragraph of his *Reveries over Childhood and Youth,*

> I have lived with my own youth and childhood, not always writing
> indeed but thinking of it almost every day, and I am sorrowful and
> disturbed. It is not that I have accomplished too few of my plans,
> for I am not ambitious; but when I think of all the books I have
> read, and of the wise words I have heard spoken, and of the anxiety
> I have given to parents and grandparents, and of the hopes that I
> have had, all life weighed in the scales of my own life seems to me a
> preparation for something that never happens.[73]

In passages like these, a second version of the story of the poet begins
to emerge, a version in which the origin of the feeling of depression and
excitement that is the curse of the aging man is located not in the feelings

men and women have about each other, but in the feelings a child has about himself. The scenario for this inner drama was not, as George Russell observed, to penetrate the "externalities" of *Reveries*. Indeed, it was not to find any very complete expression until, a few months after he had finished "The Tower" in 1925, Yeats found himself "among school children" and, sorrowful and disturbed, began to elaborate the story of the "woman lost" again.

Two

SONS AND MOTHERS

"Among School Children"

Soon after the publication of the first edition of A *Vision* in 1925, Senator W. B. Yeats began to take an interest in the problems of public education. He was now, after all, the father of a six-year-old daughter and a four-year-old son; in 1926, having first fortified himself for the task by consulting his friend Joseph O'Neil, secretary of the Department of Education, he embarked on an official tour of inspection of the primary schools. "I went to study a very remarkable convent school," he wrote Lady Gregory later.

> Waterford is becoming the centre of Irish school reform and will remain so if it can be protected from the old-fashioned ideas of the inspectors. It is having the fight we have all had. Our work is being embodied in the programme and I was amused in one class when a child, on being asked to give the "narratives" last learned (my visit was unexpected), repeated my biography "out of *Who's Who*"— poor intellectual diet—and another child, Sigerson's—disgusting diet. The children had no idea who I was. This, however, was not typical. The literary work, prose and verse, was very remarkable.[1]

In private, his feelings about his sudden confrontation with his own past and Ireland's literary future at St. Otteran's were more complex. He had only recently been preparing the latest edition of *Reveries over Childhood and Youth* (the sixth volume of the Macmillan *Collected Edition*) and a selection of his 1909 journals (*Estrangement*) for the press.[2] By March his visit to Waterford had become, amid the echoes of other memories, feelings, and thoughts about other children, the topic for a poem: "School children and the thought that live [life] will waste them perhaps that no possible life can fulfill our dreams or even their teacher's hope. Bring in the old thought that life prepares for what never happens."[3] By September, the poem was well under way. On September 24 he wrote to Olivia Shakespear, with whom he had been reconciled now for at least a decade,

> Here is a fragment of my last curse upon old age. It means that even the greatest men are owls, scarecrows, by the time their fame has come. Aristotle, remember, was Alexander's tutor, hence the taws (form of birch)
>
> Plato imagined all existence plays
> Among the ghostly images of things;
> Solider Aristotle played the taws
> Upon the bottom of the King of Kings;
> World famous, golden thighed Pythagoras
> Fingered upon a fiddle stick, or strings,
> What the star sang and careless Muses heard.—
> Old coats upon old sticks to scare a bird.
>
> Pythagoras made some measurement of the intervals between notes on a stretched string. It is a poem of seven or eight similar verses.[4]

The subject of "Among School Children," like that of "The Tower," is the feeling of depression and decrepitude Yeats associated with the "rage . . . against old age." Yet in its final form it is—again like "The Tower"—also an expression of the beatitude of the remade self. The eighth stanza of the finished poem is the famous apostrophe to the possibility of an unwasted life,

> Labour is blossoming or dancing where
> The body is not bruised to pleasure soul,
> Nor beauty born out its own despair,
> Nor blear-eyed wisdom out of midnight oil.
> O chestnut-tree, great-rooted blossomer,
> Are you the leaf, the blossom or the bole?

> O body swayed to music, O brightening glance,
> How can we know the dancer from the dance?

The artifice through which the speaker is remade is an elaboration of images and memories; and once again the train of association begins with a "stare" ("I pace the battlements and stare") that registers not the outer but the inner landscape:

I   I walk through the long schoolroom questioning:
          A kind old nun in a white hood replies;
          The children learn to cipher and to sing,
          To study reading-books and history,
          To cut and sew, be neat in everything
          In the best modern way—the children's eyes
          In momentary wonder stare upon
          A sixty-year-old smiling public man.

          I dream of a Ledaean body, bent
          Above a sinking fire, a tale that she
          Told of a harsh reproof, or trivial event
          That changed some childish day to tragedy—
          Told, and it seemed that our two natures blent
          Into a sphere from youthful sympathy,
          Or else, to alter Plato's parable,
          Into the yolk and white of the one shell.
          [1–16]

The content and function of the poet's dream are complex. In the first place, and most obviously, it expresses how an old man begins to feel when children stare at him. He remembers "youthful sympathy" and goes on,

III   And thinking of that fit of grief or rage
          I look upon one child or t'other there
          And wonder if she stood so at that age—
          For even daughters of the swan can share
          Something of very paddler's heritage—
          And had that colour upon cheek or hair,
          And thereupon my heart is driven wild:
          She stands before me as a living child.

IV   Her present image floats into the mind—
          Did Quattrocento finger fashion it
          Hollow of cheek as though it drank the wind

> And took a mess of shadows for its meat?
> And I though never of Ledaean kind
> Had pretty plumage once—enough of that,
> Better to smile on all that smile, and show
> There is a comfortable kind of old scarecrow.
> [17–32]

What drives the speaker "wild" is a particularly vivid and poignant vision of the decay and death of all things: an old man is grieving for himself, for the beloved "Ledaean" companion of his youth, and for all living children. There can be no doubt that this is what Yeats intended to say when he thought of writing the poem, and no doubt that it is part of what he says in the poem he wrote. But it is important to notice that once again "old age" is a state of mind as well as a time of life and that, once again, it is associated with the excesses of the imagination. The sixty-year-old man begins to feel like a "scarecrow" after, not before, his heart has been driven wild. Here, as at the critical point in his reconstruction of Hanrahan's story in "The Tower," he has almost said too much. Something frightening and uncomfortable has begun to intrude into his nostalgic dream of childhood and youth:

> . . . —enough of that,
> Better to smile on all that smile, and show
> There is a comfortable kind of old scarecrow.

The image that the poet dwells on most as he walks in the schoolroom is, as we might expect, the image of the "woman lost": "I dream of a Ledaean body." Part of the "unremembered" content of recollection, apparently, is "lust and rage"; Helen, the "daughter of the swan" who betrays all living hearts in "The Tower," is Yeats's most familiar metaphor for Maud Gonne. His deliberate alteration of Plato's parable in the second stanza, however, should also remind us that there is more at stake in the remaking of the self than the sexualized ironies of an "old lecher." His memory of youthful sympathy is a memory of spiritual, not corporeal, union: here the perfect being Zeus split "as you might divide an egg with a hair" to create the sexes is reunited with itself by fusion and incorporation rather than physical contact.[5] Like the delusional blending of subjective and objective "moon and sunlight" apostrophized in "The Tower," inner and outer, yolk and white, are inextricably bound up in the transcendently perfect "sphere" of the one shell. The Maud Gonne of "Among School Children," in short, is a version of Hanrahan's Muse. The wildness she excites has apocalyptic overtones; the decrepitude the poet feels suggests that more than the body is in danger of falling apart. Her most "present" threat is to the "mind":

> Hollow of cheek as though it drank the wind
> And took a mess of shadows for its meat.

But the complexities of recollection in "Among School Children" do not end (or, for that matter, begin) with the story of the "woman lost." The poet's dream recalls not one but two times past: his memory of "youthful sympathy" is itself a way of remembering something else. The man who walks in the schoolroom is remembering what it felt like to remember "childish tragedy": hers ("a tale that she / Told") and, implicitly, his ("our two natures blent"). It is his memory of *that* "fit" which accounts for the sympathy he felt once and the wildness and decrepitude he feels now; the story of the Muse has become part of the story of childhood. "And thinking of that fit of grief or rage ... my heart is driven wild ... I ... had pretty plumage once—enough of that, better to smile."

"That," like the story of Red Hanrahan, is the poet's own story, the "unremembered" content of the images and memories stirred by the children. What he almost allows himself to remember at the end of stanza IV is the story a depressed, anxious, and overexcited poet could tell about the humiliation, grief, and rage he felt as a child schooled in "harsh reproof and trivial event." But memory does not recur. Here, as at other critical moments in other autobiographical meditations, the poet is suddenly evasive; his need to recall the beauty imagination dwells on most is equaled by his need to dissociate himself from its terror. After reproving himself for dwelling even briefly on his own "pretty plumage," he takes the matter up again in stanza V in a way that is both more impersonal and more specific:

> What youthful mother, a shape upon her lap
> Honey of generation had betrayed,
> And that must sleep, shriek, struggle to escape
> As recollection or the drug decide,
> Would think her son, did she but see that shape
> With sixty or more winters on its head,
> A compensation for the pang of his birth,
> Or the uncertainty of his setting forth?
> [33–40]

The poet speaks, with our tacit assent, for all the sons of man. Youth and beauty are displaced by age and decrepitude; life seems to prepare for what never happens. His way of putting it, however, also suggests a more personal grievance. When I try to express how I feel when I feel old, he says, I think of how a mother feels about her son. I feel the way the son would feel if he knew he had become something she did not love; the limits of my affection for myself are the limits of her affection for him. In effect, the underlying conviction that makes the poet's question about "youthful mothers" rhetorical is a memory: I know how she would feel about me now because I knew how she felt about me then. The sorrow and disturbance of the aging man among school children, to paraphrase Yeats's manuscript book, recalls the wildness, shame, grief, and rage of the son whose first lesson in life was that he could never fulfill his mother's hope.

The story of sons and mothers that is being remembered in stanza V is, like the story of Homer and Helen in "The Tower," a story of seduction and betrayal, though who is being betrayed, and by what, is not immediately clear. What is clear when one unravels its difficult syntax is that the poet is trying to say two things at once. The main clause ("What youthful mother ... would think her son ... a compensation ... ?") is a self-accusation that expresses the content of his depression. The dependent clauses ("... a shape upon her lap / Honey of generation had betrayed, / And that must sleep, shriek, struggle to escape / As recollection or the drug decide") suggest that a son's betrayal of a mother is in turn caused by "honey of generation." Apparently the poet is referring to the indirect effect of the mother's sexual weaknesses on the son; had she not been tempted by the sweetness of copulation, he need never have been born.

This, however, is only one of several things the poet has in mind. His source for "honey of generation," he says in a note to the *Collected Poems,* is Porphyry's *On the Cave of the Nymphs,* where we are told that the symbolism of honey is "indicative of the pleasure which draws souls down to generation"; the infant son's "struggle to escape" being, in this case, the soul's struggle to return to what it remembers as a state of "pre-natal freedom."[6] The effect of the "honey" on the son's soul is direct; the loss of freedom is the result of its own weakness. Moreover, the honey's sweetness, Porphyry goes on to say, "signifies, with some theologists, the same thing as the pleasure arising from generation, by which Saturn being ensnared, was castrated."[7] Apparently the implicit story of stanza V includes not only the weakness of mothers for fathers and sons for mothers but also the murderous rivalry of fathers and sons.

Yeats's reference to Porphyry, then, suggests that the "freedom" he regrets corresponds to the condition that, in both Greek "theology" and more recently psychoanalytic theory, precedes the event that accounts for the repressive institutions and harsh reproofs of human culture. According to Hesiod, the privileged and innocent Golden Age ruled by Earth's (Gaia's) husband-son Saturn (Kronos) ended when he was overthrown by their son Jupiter (Zeus). According to Freud, the unconscious wish to do as Jupiter did accounts, in both individuals and societies, for the institution of a repressive superego.[8] The "shape" the poet mentions is in this sense the psychological rather than the biological shape, whose burden of grief and rage—which here seems associated with patricidal fantasies—defines it as an individual, separated by its inner guiltiness from the unambivalent freedom of its "Saturnian" age.

All this, of course, would suggest to either a Greek "theologist" or a modern psychoanalyst no more than the sort of tragedy anyone might expect to encounter in life. A psychoanalyst in particular might say that the repression of a child's incestuous impulses and patricidal (or matricidal) fantasies and the formation of the superego are not only inevitable but desirable. Thus if on one hand the internalization of harsh parental reproof gives the superego an arbitrary and irrational quality that reflects its infantile and traumatic origins, on the other it also provides the child with a psychic structure that enables him to begin to "be his own parent" and ultimately to become a parent in his turn. In a mature individual the painful but appropriate defeat of the child's "Saturnalian" delusions of incestuous grandeur manifests itself in the reasonableness and realism of his estimate of and demands on himself and others, and the "passing of the oedipus complex" into the real, if diminished, pleasures of genital love.[9]

But whether one is inclined to this (or any other) sort of rational optimism or to a more Grecian fatalism, the account of "honey of generation" that has suggested itself so far does little to distinguish the poet's story from the story of other men. It does not in particular give any account of the "spiritual" resonance of the hypochondria and depression that are the occasion of creativity: the solipsistic quality and the apocalyptic quantity of feeling that underlies the need to remake the self. For the poet of "Among School Children" as for Hanrahan after his encounter with Cleena in "The Book of the Great Dhoul," life is cursed, a betrayal greater than any possible compensatory achievement. "Even the greatest men are owls, scarecrows, by the time their fame has come," he had written to Olivia Shakespear; and in stanza VI here he continues,

> Plato thought nature but a spume that plays
> Upon a ghostly paradigm of things;
> Solider Aristotle played the taws
> Upon the bottom of a king of kings;
> World-famous golden-thighed Pythagoras
> Fingered upon a fiddle-stick or strings
> What a star sang and careless Muses heard:
> Old clothes upon old sticks to scare a bird.
> [41–48]

The poet's catalog of "greatest men" is a recapitulation of his own successes, and their "scarecrow" humiliation is his own: speculative philosopher (in *A Vision*), practical philosopher (as Free State senator), and philosopher-poet (honored by the Nobel Prize). Once again, terror, grief, and rage are disarmed by irony ("Old clothes upon old sticks to scare a bird") before being followed, in stanza VII, by a resumption of the theme of sons and mothers:

> Both nuns and mothers worship images,
> But those the candles light are not as those
> That animate a mother's reveries,
> But keep a marble or a bronze repose.
> And yet they too break hearts. . . .
> [49–53]

Up to this point in the poem, the version of the poet's story told in "Among School Children" has only suggested, in an indirect and unsatisfactory way, the story of mothers, fathers, and sons that, in both myth and medicine, is part of the common inheritance of humanity. One way of accounting for what makes the poet uncommon, of course, would be to observe, as a psychoanalyst would, that the conflict between fathers and sons can take both more and less appropriately traumatic forms. The passing of the oedipus complex can be correspondingly incomplete, producing in the extreme the symptoms of painful and chronic psychic conflict that psychoanalysis calls the "transference neuroses."[10] To the extent that Yeats's poet feels himself at best a man apart from other men and at worst a man "touched" by madness, one might suppose that the story of the "woman lost" was an expression of, or a defense against, a paternal reproof that was too harsh or, perhaps, not harsh enough. Hanrahan's mysterious paralysis in Echtge's "great shining house" could be a physical symptom of the anxieties aroused by incestuous "overexcitement." The tongue could be a metaphor for the genitals and its paralysis an expression of the "castrating" severity of a superego that reproduces a father's excessive severity or, conversely, compensates for his failure to be severe enough.[11]

Yet to infer so much from the single reference to Greek "theology" in stanza V is to overlook the fact that here, as in the case of "Plato's parable," Yeats is altering his sources to fit the requirements of the self-invented man. The story of poet and Muse, as we have already observed, is not the story of a conflict involving the self and its sexual objects but, in some "transcendent" sense we have not yet been able to understand, the integrity of the self per se and the vicissitudes of the "spiritual" side of life with which first the Muse and now, in stanza VII, the mother is identified: "Both nuns and mothers worship images." Furthermore, it has become clear in stanza VII that the seduction and betrayal of the son by "honey of generation" as Yeats imagines it is not the story of paternal intervention at all but of the intervention of the idealized "image" of the son himself. Strictly speaking, the "theology" associated with the aging poet's excited and apprehensive "decrepitude" locates the origin of the psychological "shape" not in the conflicts of fathers and sons but in the heartbreaking indifference of mothers.[12]

The story of the son who became a poet, then, is the story of the phase of psychological development that determines not the quantity of maternal affection—the "harsh reproof" of the father internalized as the superego—but its quality. It is in this "pre-oedipal" phase that the "spiritual" or what psychoanalysis would call the "narcissistic" issues of personality are defined, as the poet suggests, by the image of the self reflected in the mirror of a mother's love. What is at stake is precisely the sense of wholeness that Yeats found "no natural thing." In the early stages of psychic development, "inner" and "outer" stimuli have not yet been differentiated into "self" and "other." Consciousness, like Hanrahan's Rose, is "everywhere and in everything" and consequently finds in the response of its as yet undifferentiated objects the quality of its response to itself. The most available and therefore most significant of these objects is the mother. In the normal course of events, maternal response is appropriately sympathetic and loving, and as more and more objects are differentiated from the self, it is gradually internalized as the basis for an inner assurance of integrity and self-esteem that is capable of surviving the vicissitudes of later phases of development.[13]

Like the oedipal period, however, the narcissistic period can take inappropriate and traumatic forms. Maternal response may be more or less ambivalent or, in extreme cases, absent. The consequences range from petty egoism to psychosis. The "narcissistic" personality suffers, to a greater or lesser degree, from chronic or acute feelings of emptiness and fragmentation; it may seek compensation for its unfulfilled need for a "spiritual" union of self and other in its relationships with objects and persons, or it may find a final refuge in withdrawal and delusion.[14]

> ... the tragedy began
> With Homer that was a blind man,
> And Helen has all living hearts betrayed.
> O may the moon and sunlight seem
> One inextricable beam,
> For if I triumph I must make men mad.

The dramatis personae of the story of "childish tragedy" recalled in the first part of the seventh stanza of "Among School Children"—mother, image, and son—suggest a similar scenario of seduction and betrayal. The tragedy of life begins with the conviction that mothers love sons in a way that seems both excessive (as if they were images of God) and radically defective (sons are not images). "O Presences," the poet goes on,

> That passion, piety or affection knows,
> And that all heavenly glory symbolise—
> O self-born mockers of man's enterprise. . . .
> [53–56]

The enterprise that expresses man's devotion to his best self is impaired by the underlying suspicion that its subjective "presence" is the vestige of a mother's response not to a son but to the image of a son. The mockery of the "self-born" symbol of heavenly glory is an expression of the son's humiliated sense of the disparity between a mother's passionate "worship" of the son she imagines and her profound indifference to the son she bore. It is in effect the disparity between the smiling "public" and despairing "private" selves elaborated in the first four stanzas as the memory of the "woman lost," and its origin, as the poet puts it in stanza V, is the self-image of the shape "Honey of generation had betrayed."

Up to the end of stanza VII, the poet's only response to the "mockery" of the maternal image has been irony, the rigid "schooling" of the self in the acceptance of its divided nature. It is something we have come across before—in "The Circus Animals' Desertion," in the first part of "The Tower," and in the earliest version of the story of Red Hanrahan—and will come across again. At this point it is only necessary to recall that irony is only one of two possible endings for the story of the poet and his muse, the other being the ecstatically "remade" self apostrophized in part III of "The Tower." Parkinson's study of the manuscripts of "Among School Children" has led him to conclude that in writing it Yeats experimented with both. The poem "of seven or eight stanzas" announced to Olivia Shakespear, Parkinson says, may have originally concluded with a version of the last four lines of stanza VII that "suggests a completeness, a full stop to the experience of the poem":

> And yet they too break hearts—the Presences
> That love, or piety or affection knows
> And dead or living statuary symbolize
> Mock every great man and his enterprize.

"If Yeats," Parkinson adds, "had held to his original intention of writing a poem on naturalistic disappointment, this would have been a sorrowful and fitting ending, though the poem would have been considerably less."[15]

Whether or not Yeats ever thought of these lines as the poem's conclusion, Parkinson is certainly correct when he says that it would have been fitting if he had. He is also right in implying that the poem we now have is considerably different from (and probably more than) the poem about the curse of old age Yeats set out to write from his "old thought" and that this difference only becomes noticeable in the fifth line of the seventh stanza. "The Presences" is now "O Presences," and the tone of the poem's conclusion not one of ironic defeat but of defiant assertion:

> Labour is blossoming and dancing where
> The body is not bruised to pleasure soul. . . .

The alternative to irony in stanza VIII is a quality of feeling—variously characterized by critics as "exaltation," "ecstasy," "triumph," and "adoration"—whose aesthetic effect is almost universally admired by Yeats's readers.[16] What it amounts to in terms of the narcissistic "theology" of "Among School Children" is a rhetorical intimation of an idealized and ecstatic reunion of self and other that relieves the poet of the shameful burden of self-consciousness imposed by the maternal "image." When he asks, "How can we know the dancer from the dance?" he implies not only that objects are true and beautiful when they are "known" as a whole but also that to know objects to be true and beautiful is to feel merged in an unknowable otherness that is greater and more perfect than the self. This sort of knowing becomes, at the moment of apprehension, a quality of the relation of self and object that feels as if it were a quality of the relation of the self to itself. To perceive that the tree and the dancer are true and beautiful is to feel, in a sudden, ecstatic flow, that the sorrowful and disturbed "I" that walks the long school-room has become, however briefly, a community of loved and loving selves, a "we" that is wise, beautiful, and perfect,

> . . . blossoming and dancing where
> The body is not bruised to pleasure soul,
> Nor beauty born out its own despair,
> Nor blear-eyed wisdom out of midnight oil.
> O chestnut-tree, great-rooted blossomer,
> Are you the leaf, the blossom or the bole?
> O body swayed to music, O brightening glance,
> How can we know the dancer from the dance?
> [57–64]

Among Pollexfens

If the compensatory "labour" to restore what was so poi-gantly absent from Yeats's way of recalling the story of sons and mothers is the work of art in "Among School Children," it was also, as he implies in the final stanza, the labor and the art of living. "Some violent bitter man," he wrote, recalling Lady Gregory's "house of friendship" at Coole,

> some powerful man,
> Called architect and artist in, that they,
> Bitter and violent men, might rear in stone
> The sweetness that all longed for night and day,
> The gentleness none there had ever known;
> . . . .
> O what if gardens where the peacock strays
> With delicate feet upon old terraces,
> Or else all Juno from an urn displays
> Before the indifferent garden deities;
> O what if levelled lawns and gravelled ways
> Where slippered Contemplation finds his ease

And Childhood a delight for every sense,
But take our glory with our violence?

What if the glory of escutcheoned doors,
And buildings that a haughtier age designed,
The pacing to and fro on polished floors
Amid great chambers and long galleries, lined
With famous portraits of our ancestors;
What if those things the greatest of mankind
Consider most to magnify, or to bless,
But take our greatness with our bitterness?
["Ancestral Houses," 17–40]

The "greatness" of the prosperous and titled Irish upper class was not, as his erstwhile friend and collaborator George Moore was fond of pointing out, Yeats's past.[17] The ancestral houses of the poet who liked to think "that if he had his rights he would be Duke of Ormonde" were the houses of the middle-class Yeatses, not the aristocratic Butlers, and their greatness was the pride of mercantile success rather than of blood. William Butler Yeats's father, John Butler Yeats, was the eldest son of a Church of Ireland clergyman whose family, if still quite respectable and moderately well-off, had come down in the world since the late eighteenth century, when their ancestor Benjamin Yeats had been wealthy enough to marry a Butler. That fortunate union had brought a silver cup with the Ormonde crest on it into the family, as well as the lands in County Kildare that the poet's father inherited from his father in November 1862. But the encumbrance on the property was by then large and the income small. When John Butler Yeats had announced his engagement to Susan Mary Pollexfen a few months before, his real prospects had been his expectations as a law student at the King's Inns in Dublin. Susan was the eldest daughter of William Pollexfen, a newly rich Sligo ship and mill owner. J. B. Yeats had met her there that summer while he was on holiday with her brother George, his old schoolfellow. They were married at Sligo on September 10, 1863.

Susan Pollexfen Yeats liked to be near the sea, and their first home, Georgeville, was in Sandymount, a suburb of Dublin that looks north across the bay to Howth. It was, Joseph Hone says, "a recently-built, six-roomed, semi-detached house at the head of Sandymount Avenue . . . the most genteel house on the avenue, with stone steps up to the hall door and plate-glass windows."[18] Its solid aspirations were somewhat dwarfed, however, by the vicinity of the establishment of Robert Corbet, J. B. Yeats's uncle. Corbet was rich enough to afford a castle,

Sandymount Castle, amid whose "levelled lawns and gravelled ways" J. B. Yeats had spent many happy childhood days and had later lived, in contemplation and slippered ease, during his years at Trinity. It was at Georgeville, at 10:40 P.M. on June 13, 1865, that William Butler Yeats was born, the first of four surviving children, and it was to the grounds of the castle that little Willie's nurse took him for his first walks. His impression of the place, however, seems to have been mostly secondhand. "When I was a child," he wrote in 1902,

> I often heard my elders talking of an old turreted house where an old great-uncle of mine lived, and of its gardens and its long pond where there was an island with tame eagles; and one day [my father] read me some verses and said they made him think of that old house where he had been very happy. The verses ran in my head for years and became to me the best description of happiness in the world, and I am not certain that I know a better even now. They were those first dozen verses of [William Morris's] *Golden Wings* that begin:—

> Midways of a walled garden,
>   In the happy poplar land,
>   Did an ancient castle stand,
> With an old knight for a warden.

> Many scarlet bricks there were
>   In its walls, and old grey stone;
>   Over which apples shone
> At the right time of the year.

> On the bricks the green moss grew,
>   Yellow lichen on the stone,
>   Over which red apples shone;
> Little war that castle knew.[19]

In 1866 a second child, Susan Mary (Lily), was born, and J. B. Yeats completed his terms and was called to the Irish Bar. But whatever pleasure he may have had in his achievement or in living near the seat of his former happiness was abruptly interrupted by the bankruptcy and suicide of Robert Corbet that same year. "Of business," J. B. Yeats recalls in his memoir, "he know little or nothing, and probably neglected it, but he did not neglect his gardens."[20] The memory of those gardens passed on to the poet by his father, and particularly of the island with its chained eagles, would be preserved in *The Wanderings of Oisin* and echoes, no doubt, in his later tributes to "ancestral houses" and grounds like Lady Gregory's

Coole Park. But there would be no real castle in the Yeats family again until he bought Thoor Ballylee, and it is this, perhaps, that accounts for the otherwise puzzling fervency of the passage in "The Tower" that recalls

> A figure that has grown so fabulous
> There's not a neighbour left to say
> When he finished his dog's day:
> The ancient bankrupt master of this house.

It soon became clear, at any rate, that much of Robert Corbet's impractical and unlucky spirit lived on in his nephew John. After his uncle's death, J. B. Yeats found little either to hold him in Dublin or make a barrister's life palatable; in 1867, therefore, he decided to abandon the security of the law for the uncertainty of a career in the arts. He had always had a talent for sketching—he often spent his hours in court drawing the heads of his colleagues—and now he proposed to train himself as a painter in the English art schools. His wife, who wanted neither her husband to leave the bar nor her family to leave Ireland, opposed the idea. But J. B. Yeats was resolute and that year moved his establishment to 23 Fitzroy Road, Regent's Park, London, and became a student at Heatherleigh's Art School and later at the Academy School. There three more children were born to share his dwindling income: Elizabeth Corbet (Lollie) in 1868, Robert Corbet (Bobbie) in 1870, and John Butler (Jack) in 1871. The family's financial uncertainties were compounded by Susan Yeats's unhappiness in London. She took the children to Sligo as often as she could for extended holidays by the sea, and after Jack's birth she refused to come back at all. For the next two years J. B. Yeats was left to live and study alone in London.

With the exception of some brief and fragmentary impressions of Ireland (probably of Sandymount) and London, all of the earliest memories Yeats records in his *Reveries over Childhood and Youth* are of Sligo; and most of these are of his grandfather and grandmother, William and Elizabeth Pollexfen, of his numerous aunts and uncles (Susan Yeats was one of ten surviving children), and of the large gray family house, Merville. It was to Merville that his mother brought him home most frequently between his second and sixth years; it became, during his seventh and eighth years, his permanent residence. At this time he had, he says in *Reveries,* no memory of his father at all, and little interest in the Yeats side of the family.

William Pollexfen was a self-made man at the height of his mercantile success, an eminence he had achieved after running away to sea as a boy. "I could see my grandfather's ships come up the bay or the river, and his sailors treated me with deference, and the ship's carpenter made and mended my toy boats and I thought nobody could be so important as my grandfather."[21] Yet despite the glow shed on him by the commercial glories of his grandfather's house, Yeats's memory of his life at Merville was one of chronic "misery." Some of it, he says in *Reveries,*

> was loneliness and some of it was fear of old William Pollexfen my grandfather. He was never unkind, and I cannot remember that he ever spoke harshly to me, but it was the custom to fear and admire him. He had won the freedom of some Spanish city, for saving life perhaps, but was so silent that his wife never knew it until he was near eighty.... He had a violent temper and kept a hatchet at his bedside for burglars and would knock a man down instead of going to law, and once I saw him hunt a party of men with a horsewhip.... I think I confused my grandfather with God, for I remember in one of my attacks of melancholy praying that he might punish me for my sins.

As for his "grown-up uncles and aunts, my grandfather's sons and daughters," Yeats remembers that they "came and went, and almost all they said or did has faded from my memory, except a few harsh words that convince me by a vividness out of proportion to their harshness that all were habitually kind and considerate." Nevertheless, as in the case of the grandfather who was "never unkind," he found himself "always afraid of my uncles and aunts." Once an uncle "found me eating lunch which my grandmother had given me and reproved me for it and made me ashamed. We breakfasted at nine and dined at four and it was considered self-indulgent to eat anything between meals; and once an aunt told me that I had reined in my pony and struck it at the same moment that I might show it off as I rode through the town, and I, because I had been accused of what I thought a very dark crime, had a night of misery. Indeed I remember little of childhood but its pain."

In *Reveries* the sum of such harsh reproofs and trivial events is an impression of a dour and authoritarian patriarchy ruled by William Pollexfen. But the quality of his authority as Yeats describes it is not without its ambiguities. Indeed Yeats's inability to see any direct connection between his own unhappiness and a grandfather who was "never unkind" or aunts and uncles who impressed him as being "habitually kind and considerate" leads him to state at the outset that "there was no reason for my unhappiness" and later to suppose that his miseries were "not made by others but were a part of my own mind": "Nobody was unkind, and my grandmother has still after so many years my gratitude and my reverence. The house was so big that there was always a room to hide in, and I had a red pony and a garden where I could wander, and there were two dogs to wander at my heels."

His terrifying grandfather, moreover, was feared more in spirit and "custom" than in deed. Immediately after saying that he "confused his grandfather with God," for instance, Yeats goes on to remember that

> for all my admiration and alarm, neither I nor any one else thought it wrong to outwit his violence or his rigour; and his lack of suspicion and something helpless about him made it easy while it stirred our affection. When I must have been still a very little boy, seven or eight years old perhaps, an uncle called me out of bed one night, to ride the five or six miles to Rosses Point to borrow a railway-pass from a cousin. My grandfather had one, but thought it dishonest to let another use it, but the cousin was not so particular. I was let out through a gate . . . and rode delighted through the moonlight. . . .
> I was home again by two or three in the morning. . . . My grandfather would not have thought such an adventure possible, for every night at eight he believed that the stable-yard was locked, and he knew that he was brought the key. . . . He never knew, what everybody else in the house knew, that for all the ceremonious bringing of the key the gate was never locked.[22]

The contradiction between the terrifying irascibility and endearing helplessness of the grandfather described in *Reveries* is partly the result of Yeats's characteristic tendency toward nostalgic idealization of his "old fathers" and partly an example of the pervasive discretion that makes his memoir such an "external" work. In retrospect the Pollexfens seemed "something grand like the figures of Stonehenge in the moonlight" to him,[23] and family loyalty prevented him from dwelling on the one Pollexfen trait that explained both their puritanical gloom and what J. B. Yeats called their "awesome helplessness." His wife's brother George, he says in *Early Memories,* "was because of his family and their traditions puritanic, but his puritanism was of a peculiar sort; he wasn't in the least aggressive like the Belfast man, nor was he conceited nor inquisitorial as the Scotch are; it was merely that he saw human nature sorrowfully, and with little hope."[24] If, he once told his son, George had ever been sentenced to death, "on the morning of his execution he would have been the only calm person present": " . . . Since he was by nature without any capacity for sympathy he would not have appealed to anyone. No relief in sight, he would have looked for none. That's what I mean by the awesome helplessness of human nature."[25]

In George, this self-centered and hopeless "sorrowfulness" was accompanied by chronic hypochondria.[26] In his father and in his brothers and sisters it was the symptom of chronic and often acute depression. Indeed the contradiction in William Pollexfen's "patriarchal" presence can be explained by the fact that it depended not on any real omniscience or repressive rigor but on his response to the same pervasive melancholy that his grandson experienced as if it were "part of his mind." His grim silence and grumbling irritability and his violent and trivial furies were, as everyone in the household tolerantly acknowledged, the expression not so much of his efforts to enforce a puritanical creed as of his own obsessive inner turmoil, to which the objects and persons around him had only a passing relationship. "Grandpapa Pollexfen," Lily Yeats wrote in her scrapbook,

> we liked, admired, and avoided. He never talked to anyone. He grumbled, complained, and ejaculated all day long. The past and the future had no interest for him at all. He was in such a state of irritation with the present moment that he could think of nothing else. He was quite unsuspicious so it was only what he saw that irritated, so there was everything to be said for "keeping out of the master's way." We grandchildren did it, only seeing him at meals, and then sitting if possible on the same side of the table so that he could not be driven mad by seeing us take too much sugar. He had an alarming way of stopping grumbling and eating and looking at us in silence while we carried two sugar spoons from the bowl to our plates.[27]

At best there was something slightly silly about the grandfather that Yeats confused with God; at worst there was in him something that verged on, and may indeed have sometimes become, real madness. In February 1873, when Willie was seven, his father wrote to his wife from London, "I hope when you write again you will have something better to tell of your father. All your family's ailments begin in the mind. A sort of nightmare takes possession of them and then they lose their appetite and get ill."[28] And thirty-five years later, remembering his father-in-law, he wrote to his brother Isaac that "a great doctor here, Dr. Spitzka, says mind and digestion are closely connected. He has cured several cases of insanity of *long standing,* simply by attending to their digestion.... It was by treating his digestion that old Wm. Pollexfen was cured."[29]

If the extent of the pathology is sketchily attested to in the case of the father, the existence of psychosis in his children was explicitly, if not openly, acknowledged by the family. His father's namesake, William (the second of that name, the first having died in childhood), is the only case mentioned in *Reveries*. He was an engineer and had designed the Sligo quays but was when Willie knew him "going mad."[30] He was institutionalized until his death in 1913.[31] Two others (still unnamed in any published source) were, as J. B. Yeats put it, "in Asylums," one for a "morbid depression" that followed the death of his parents in 1892 and the other for what Murphy calls in his *Yeats Family and the Pollexfens of Sligo* "'a series of severe emotional breakdowns' through a long life." These three were the only members of the Merville household who required "special care," but there were also, Murphy says, "other depressives... (and a couple of manics as well)."[32]

In regard to such matters Yeats himself was discreet to the point of mendacity throughout his autobiographies.[33] Nowhere is this more true than in his description of his mother, Susan Yeats, in *Reveries*. "WBY tells us remarkably little of her, " Murphy says, and he adds, "Students have not had much factual material to work with. At the time of the pioneer studies of W. B. Yeats's life there were surviving children of hers and it would perhaps not have been kind to speak fully of a life that had been, to put it frankly, so unhappy."[34]

Some of what made Susan Yeats's life particularly unhappy can be attributed to J. B. Yeats's failures as a husband. But it is clear that it was also, as in the case of her son, a "part of her own mind," a "nervous weakness" that she shared with her brothers and sisters and bequeathed to her children. "I can see now, Yeats wrote in *Reveries*, "that she had great depth of feeling, that she was her father's daughter."[35] The picture of her there is meager. Yeats remembers her "sewing or knitting in spectacles and wearing some plain dress" or "talking over a cup of tea in the kitchen with our servant, the fisherman's wife."[36] She was, he remembers, self-effacing and (not unreasonably, in the years after 1867) preoccupied by "financial worries." "My memory of what she was like in those days has grown very dim, but I think her sense of personality, her desire of any life of her own, had disappeared in her care of us and in much anxiety about money.... Yet ten years ago when I was in San Francisco, an old cripple came to see me who had left Sligo before her marriage; he came to tell me, he said, that my mother 'had been the most beautiful girl in Sligo.'"[37]

Her "depth of feeling" showed itself most strongly in the quality of her inner rather than her outer life. It was she, Yeats says, who kept alive in her children the "instinctive" longing for Sligo during their years in London that he later expressed in "The Lake Isle of Innisfree" and at the same time taught them to "laugh at all displays of emotion." She considered such displays the characteristic "vulgarity" of (of all people) the English: "My mother had shown them to me kissing in railway stations, and taught me to feel disgust at their lack of reserve."[38] She appears to have impressed most people as a "quiet, gentle, and sweet" but "silent and flitting" figure who "never seemed to stand up for herself."[39] Her family, however, found something more in her than restraint. "She had always, my father would say," Yeats recalls in *Reveries*, "intensity, and that was his chief word of praise; and once he added to the praise, 'No spendthrift ever had a poet for a son, but a miser might.' "[40]

John Butler Yeats's second thoughts about his wife's "intensity" suggest, like stanza VII of "Among School Children," that there was a side to the sort of mother a poet might remember that never fully emerges from the nostalgic and discretion-softened portrait of *Reveries*. If J. B. Yeats accepted his wife, as he felt a husband should, with "all her limitations, her want of intellect, even her want of heart,"[41] he also realized that she was her father's daughter in more than her melancholy "depth of feeling." Her anxiety about money and her emotional austerity were both Pollexfen traits, and J. B. Yeats saw in them cause and effect. "Their canons did not permit them to indulge in an affection for their children, so they clung the more to houses and lands."[42] His daughter Lily was impressed in particular by the contrast between her life at Merville and a visit to her father's mother:

> I was never so happy before. Grandmama Yeats was demonstrative, called me pet names, caressed me. I followed her about. She gave me feathers to stuff a doll's mattress.... I was put in bed by several merry aunts. They all ran about, laughed, played....
>
> The Pollexfen grandparents' house—all was serious, silent. There was no merry talk there. People walked soberly about. There were no pet names or caresses. Life was serious and silent, no merry talk at meals, no running to and fro.[43]

With the Pollexfens, J. B. Yeats told his son, "feelings, especially the affections and sympathies, were put under a ban ... married people might like each other ... [but] they must never give expression to the feeling in public or private."[44] In this context the dignified reserve of the mother in *Reveries* becomes recognizable as the mother whom Lily Yeats remembered as being "prim and austere." Sharing her brother George's hopeless stoicism, she "suffered all in silence. She asked no sympathy and gave none. . . . When we were children and were ill she always said, 'Grin and bear it,' and so she did. She endured and made no moan."[45] "I often said to her these words," J. B. Yeats wrote John Quinn:

> "You know I have to take your affection for granted," for I never saw the slightest sign of it, except once, and here was [*sic*] the manner of that "once": I had left the house and been gone a few moments when, remembering something, I returned and found her where I left her, and she showed so much pleasure that I was surprised and gratified—that was the "once." . . . She was not sympathetic. The feelings of people about her did not concern her. She was not aware of them. She was always in an island of her own. Yet had you penetrated to her inner mind you would have found it all occupied with thoughts of other people and of how to help them. . . . I used to tell her that if I had been lost for years and then suddenly presented myself she would have merely asked, "Have you had your dinner?"[46]

The effect of Susan Yeats's personality on her eldest son was, in her husband's opinion, a marked one. "There is a good deal of his mother," he told Quinn in the same letter, "in Willie." The legacy of her emotional austerity was in part the "aristocratic" fussiness, restraint, and hauteur affected by the man; but it was also, though less obviously to the world at large, patent in the "nervous weakness" she passed on to at least her three eldest children. If the "strain of depressive melancholia" in the Pollexfens was something Yeats began to take seriously in himself only in the middle of his fifth decade, it was something his father had feared from the beginning. "When his own children were growing up," Murphy says, J. B. Yeats "saw signs of it in them and feared it might strike one or more of them beyond redemption. . . . JBY often worried about Lily, but it was Lollie who cracked under the strains of her life and showed the classic symptoms of persecution complex, mania, and depression from about 1910 until 1915."[47] In 1911, Lollie took a therapeutic tour of Italy and wrote her father letters that were "quite crazy. . . . When she is a Pollexfen she makes the worst of things."[48] Nor was Lily exempt. She "never speaks of it to anyone," J. B. Yeats confessed to his brother in 1912, "and to me always speaks of it as nerves, as I to her—but it is depressive mania, and it affected more or less most of the Pollexfens. Three of them were in Asylums."[49]

In his eldest son the earliest signs of what later became "breakdowns" were, by Yeats's own testimony in *Reveries,* exaggerated and chronic feelings of loneliness and depression. "Willie," J. B. Yeats wrote in his unpublished memoirs, "was a curious little elf, extraordinarily nervous and sensitive, yet detached and undemonstrative. He had solemn eyes and arched eyebrows and would remain for a long time quite silent and then ask such questions as 'Is it only wicked mothers who give their children bones to eat?' What hobgoblin fancies were going through his mind no one troubled to ask. We were all too busy for such investigations."[50] But his father was not too busy to worry, particularly after the child's mother had taken him to live among Pollexfens. "I am very anxious about Willy," J. B. Yeats wrote Susan from London in November 1872; "he is never out of my thoughts. I believe him to be intensely affectionate, but from shyness, sensitiveness and nervousness, difficult to win and yet he is worth winning. . . . Willy is sensitive intellectual and emotional, very easily rebuffed and continually afraid of being rebuffed so that with him one has to use sensitiveness so rare at Merville."[51]

To both father and son, the prepsychotic Pollexfen character seemed, as it would seem to some psychologists today, a kind of genetic defect, something "in the blood."[52] Yet there is much in both what is now known about the Merville household and what the poet recalls about sons and mothers in "Among School Children" to suggest that in his case the apprehension of madness was "rooted" elsewhere. The imaginary "ancestral houses" affected by the poet years later, and to a certain extent reconstituted in the houses of affection built round him by Lady Gregory and his wife, express above all his hunger not so much for status or luxury as we usually understand them as for an integrity and richness in the quality of experience, a "sensitiveness" unknown at houses like Merville:

> The sweetness that all longed for night and day,
> The gentleness none there had ever known.

What the rest of the inhabitants of the great grey house at Sligo may have longed for and perhaps found in varying degrees of madness can only be conjectured, though Yeats's guess seems as good as anyone else's. What he longed for and never (or rarely) knew during his years there can be more reliably surmised. The atmosphere of his grandfather's house was not, as we have already observed, so much one of overt repression as of depressed indifference. "Nobody was unkind" was Yeats's way not of saying everyone was kind but of registering his profound sense of isolation from human response. Among Pollexfens, the deadliest sins were not those of rebellion against authority but those of self-love; anyone, even the smallest child, who showed signs of self-assertion, self-regard, or self-indulgence was guilty of a "very dark crime." The little boy who liked to show off on his pony and sometimes ate between meals was trying to be "somebody," and his punishment was to be treated as if he were nobody at all. If in his melancholy the child to whom "no one was unkind" sometimes wished that his grandfather would punish him for his "sins," it was perhaps because he longed above all, for better or worse, to find that other "somebody" who might also care enough to praise.

Another child might have felt such humiliations less keenly or recovered from them more quickly. But Willie was, his father says, "a curious little elf," who seemed to demand far more and expect far less in the way of affection than other children his age. Some of his "nervous weakness" could have been, one might suppose, a vague intuition of what the special burdens and privileges of genius might some day be, an inner intimation of a talent that set him constitutionally apart from others and was indeed "part of his mind." At this point in his life, however, it would be very difficult to distinguish the effects of the as yet unrealized giftedness that he may (or may not) have inherited from the Pollexfens from the influence of the particular Pollexfen whose presence had been coeval with consciousness itself.[53] The tragedy of the life that prepared for what never happened began, as Yeats would see clearly fifty years later, with the generation of a heartbroken "shape" from its conflict with the outer coldness and inner "intensity" of a self-absorbed and unempathic "youthful mother." The deep, inexplicable melancholy of the seven-year-old and the hypochondria and depression that the mature poet would make the occasion of so much beautiful verse both express a sense of betrayal—a sense that in its deepest form is the conviction of having been unaccountably denied what one was once most entitled to: the mysterious, magical "brightening glance" of recognition and reassurance bestowed on the nascent self by the emerging maternal other. In the lonely struggles to come, that glance is the sustenance of the spirit, its absence an impoverishment.[54]

The son of a mother who reserved the full measure of her sweetness for the images of her "inner mind" might well feel like an outcast from the feast of life, emptier, lonelier, and more like "nobody" than most; he might well wonder bitterly, as a sixty-year-old man would after him, whether one generation ever has anything to offer another but public smiles and "bones to eat." Nor would it be strange if he were to feel in his turn profoundly isolated and self-absorbed or if, in the years to come, he should often seem too preoccupied with both the outward signs of integrity and self-esteem and the inward apparatus of "spiritual" regeneration. The unalloyed and unimpaired correspondence between life's outermost forms and its innermost fountains was for Yeats, as we observed at the beginning, the least natural of all things, a self-delighted richness that at best seemed imaginable only as the privilege of the few fortunate enough to be born in houses built by someone else's ancestors. "Surely," he would write in the opening lines of "Ancestral Houses,"

> among a rich man's flowering lawns,
> Amid the rustle of his planted hills,
> Life overflows without ambitious pains;
> And rains down life until the basin spills,
> And mounts more dizzy high the more it rains
> As though to choose whatever shape it wills
> And never stoop to a mechanical
> Or servile shape, at others' beck and call.
>
> Mere dreams, mere dreams! Yet Homer had not sung
> Had he not found it certain beyond dreams
> That out of life's own self-delight had sprung
> The abounding, glittering jet. . . .
> [1–12]

———

The Stirring of the Beast

It was with the remaking of such refreshing certainties that, Yeats felt, the artist had his business. The shape he sought was the shape of "self-delight," the outward form of the overflowing, abounding, self-enhancing inner resource that sustains all mere dreams and ambitious pains. In finding it he would reaffirm—and, I think, in his best lyrics does reaffirm—our trustful sense of the fundamental goodness and integrity of life in a world in which we all, and Yeats more than most, once had reason to feel the uncertainty of our setting forth. At such moments art restores, in what psychoanalysis would call "secondary" or "transitional" forms, something of the undifferentiated sense of self and not-self lost in the passing of the "primary" narcissism of the infant: "to know" is once again "to be."

In someone more afflicted by "nervous weakness" than Yeats, the recovery of self-delight might have bordered on, or have become, psychotic delusion; in someone less talented, it would probably have ended with eccentricity and affectation. Yeats was never wholly the one or merely the other; yet what he was, and particularly what he was able to make of his unique verbal gifts, had something in common with both. One can observe, for instance, that in both Yeats's poetry and in psychoanalytic clinical observation the narcissistically "remade" self can take either of two structurally antithetical but affectively identical forms. One, that of part III of "The Tower," is the solipsistic incorporation of objects by the omniscient and perfected self (the grandiose "I"); the other, that of the last stanza of "Among School Children," is the incorporation of the self into an omniscient and perfected object (the ecstatic "we").[55]

In both cases, the underlying metaphor or, to put it in a more psychological way, "mode" is oral and reflects an infant's earliest and least differentiated experience of inner and outer realities, that of the swallowed and the swallowing. The quality of maternal response that first forms or malforms our spiritual "shape" is experienced first in the vicissitudes of hunger and satiety, and in Yeats's poetry the alternation of the images of decrepitude and self-delight routinely suggests that unmerited deprivation (the "old scarecrow") has at last been rewarded by unforeseen abundance (the "abounding jet"). Taken together with irony, which will be discussed more fully later on, the "I" and the "we" that the poet feels he has become at such moments define the affective range of the Yeatsian lyric, the dialectic, as he put it in a poem written two years after "Among School Children," between "My Soul" and "My Self":

My Soul.   Why should the imagination of a man
              Long past his prime remember things that are
              Emblematical of love and war?
              Think of ancestral night that can,
              If imagination scorn the earth
              And intellect its wandering
              To this and that and t'other thing,
              Deliver from the crime of death and birth.

My Self.   Montashigi, third of his family, fashioned it
              Five hundred years ago, about it lie
              Flowers from I know not what embroidery—
              Heart's purple—and all these I set
              For emblems of the day against the tower
              Emblematical of the night,

> And claim as by a soldier's right
> A charter to commit the crime once more.

My Soul. Such fullness in that quarter overflows
> And falls into the basin of the mind
> That man is stricken deaf and dumb and blind,
> For intellect no longer knows
> *Is* from the *Ought,* or *Knower* from the *Known*—
> That is to say, ascends to Heaven;
> Only the dead can be forgiven;
> But when I think of that my tongue's a stone.
> ["A Dialogue of Self and Soul," 17–40]

Despite their nominal differences of opinion, the interlocutors of "A Dialogue of Self and Soul" are both, as Bloom points out, equally lonely and self-absorbed.[56] The Soul's emblem is the tower, and like the "I" of "The Tower" it represents the divine solipsism that finds everything within itself and is stricken "deaf and dumb and blind" by its own overflowing abundance. Its tone is as characteristic as its metaphysics and belongs to the group of Yeats's lyrics that end, to use one of his favorite phrases, on a "cold and passionate" note. Generally speaking, the manner is cold, imperious, withdrawn, scornful, and "proud";[57] the matter asserts the triumph of subjectivity over mere objects, "this and that and t'other thing"; and in both respects the Soul echoes the last will and testament that introduces the poet's effort to "make his soul" in part III of "The Tower":

> It is time I wrote my will;
> I choose upstanding men
> That climb the streams until
> The fountain leap, and at dawn
> Drop their cast at the side
> Of dripping stone; I declare
> They shall inherit my pride,
>
> . . . .
> And I declare my faith:
> I mock Plotinus' thought
> And cry in Plato's teeth,
> Death and life were not
> Till man made up the whole,
> Made lock, stock and barrel
> Out of his bitter soul,
> Aye, sun and moon and star, all,
> And further add to that

> That, being dead, we rise,
> Dream and so create
> Translunar Paradise.
> [121–56]

Most readers find the rhetoric of such "ascensions to heaven" the less attractive of the two forms of self-delight in Yeat's poetry. This is so not because of the "philosophy" involved or, for that matter, because of the speaker's apparent inability to communicate his beatitude ("When I think of that my tongue's a stone"). Yeats's Soul is if anything too eloquent, and it is to its tone rather than its metaphysics that the majority of us respond most strongly and most negatively. There is, to be sure, something in its haughty and scornful overestimation of itself that we might find tolerable, and even charming, in a stage of life that, like adolescence, precedes or accompanies the development of more realistic self-esteem.[58] But when it is presented, as it is here, as the wisdom of maturity, its pose of invulnerable egotism suggests transitions unmade and demands unmet: the grief and rage of the depressed and humiliated child have found a secondary elaboration in the rigid arrogance and defensive hostility of the "superhuman" Soul. Its claims, of course, are not always so strident. In some of Yeats's poems the sheer need implicit in the Soul's declarations of pride and faith have a touching and even beatific effect similar to that of the final lines of "Among School Children." In the famous peroration of "A Prayer for My Daughter," for example, the poet finds relief from the "great gloom that is in my mind" in an apostrophe to what he calls the Soul's "radical innocence":

> Considering that, all hatred driven hence,
> The soul recovers radical innocence
> And learns at last that is self-delighting,
> Self-appeasing, self-affrighting,
> And that its own sweet will is Heaven's will;
> She can, though every face should scowl
> And every windy quarter howl
> Or every bellows burst, be happy still.
> [65–72]

In the equally well known and much admired conclusion of "A Dialogue of Self and Soul," however, the final beatitude is that of the Self, which, like the poet of "Among School Children," finds its salvation from the "crime of death and birth" in the communal "we":

My Self.   A living man is blind and drinks his drop.
        What matter if the ditches are impure?

What matter if I live it all once more?
Endure that toil of growing up;
The ignominy of boyhood; the distress
Of boyhood changing into man;
The unfinished man and his pain
Brought face to face with his own clumsiness;

The finished man among his enemies?—
How in the name of heaven can he escape
That defiling and disfigured shape
The mirror of malicious eyes
Casts upon his eyes until at last
He thinks that shape must be his shape?
And what's the good of an escape
If honour find him in the wintry blast?

I am content to live it all again
And yet again, if it be life to pitch
Into the frog-spawn of a blind man's ditch,
A blind man battering blind men;
Or into that most fecund ditch of all,
The folly that man does
Or must suffer, if he woos
A proud woman not kindred of his soul.

I am content to follow to its source
Every event in action or in thought;
Measure the lot; forgive myself the lot!
When such as I cast out remorse
So great a sweetness flows into the breast
We must laugh and we must sing,
We are blest by everything,
Everything we look upon is blest.
[41–72]

Here, as in "Among School Children," the flow of "sweetness" un-
locked by creativity is associated with diffusion rather than solipsistic
incorporation. The "defiling and disfigured shape" of self-consciousness
has been swallowed up in the transcendent other, the "blest" and blessing
"everything we look upon." This is the Yeats that most of us like best,
and it is certainly the Yeats most extravagantly admired by his critics.[59] It
is important to realize, however, that in terms of the narcissistic defects of
the "remade" poet it is in effect identical with the grandiose solipsism
that, with a few exceptions, is the pompous and silly Yeats most of us
would like to forget. Worse still, both selfless ecstasy and solipsistic gran-

diosity are also characteristic of a group of poems in which many find
what is least sympathetic and most dubious about the Yeatsian aesthetic,
the quality he referred to as "passion." "We have all," he wrote to
Dorothy Wellesley in 1936, "something within ourselves to batter down
and get our power from this fighting. I have never 'produced' a play in
verse without showing the actors that the passion of the verse comes from
the fact that the speakers are holding down violence or madness—'down
Hysterica passio.' All depends on the completeness of the holding down,
on *the stirring of the beast underneath*. . . . Without this conflict we have
no passion only sentiment and thought."[60]

The "passion" in conflict Yeats describes here is peculiar to the
"apocalyptic" forms of self-delight that, in the later poetry in particular,
are perhaps the most familiar of Yeats's voices:

> The Second Coming! Hardly are those words out
> When a vast image out of *Spiritus Mundi*
> Troubles my sight: somewhere in sands of the desert
> A shape with lion body and the head of a man,
> A gaze blank and pitiless as the sun,
> Is moving its slow thighs, while all about it
> Reel shadows of the indignant desert birds.
> The darkness drops again; but now I know
> That twenty centuries of stony sleep
> Were vexed to nightmare by a rocking cradle,
> And what rough beast, its hour come round at last,
> Slouches towards Bethlehem to be born?

Whatever its moral ambiguities may be, "The Second Coming" is undoubtedly one of Yeats's most effective fictions. Like "Among School
Children"—a poem it seems to resemble in no other way—it ends in an
ecstatic adoration, and once again the form is that of the rhetorical final
question in which the awful merger of the self and the idealized other is
expressed as the knowing of the unknowable ("But now I
know . . . what . . . ?"). What troubles those readers who do not, in the
words of "Ancestral Houses," feel obliged to "take our greatness with
our violence" is that here the reconstitution of aesthetic delight invites us
to participate in a kind of excitement that is so manifestly related to the
feeling that things are falling apart. Whitaker, for instance, sees in the
poem a meditation on "the nature of every man's conscious or unconscious complicity" in the destructive horrors of history; Bloom adds, "We
must see that our horror is his ecstasy."[61]

But the ecstatic horror of "The Second Coming" also reminds us of something about the issues at stake in the remaking of the self that is less obvious in poems that are easier to like (or, for that matter, to dislike). Creativity is, as Yeats disdainfully observed to Dorothy Wellesley, a matter not merely of unlocking the inner sources of sweetness and "sentiment" that are the contents of self-delight but also of reconstituting its forms. The most heartbreaking legacy of mothers who worship images is the extent to which their lack of empathy is internalized as a defect not only in a son's self-esteem but also in his sense of the integrity and fundamental wholeness of consciousness itself. The deepest anxiety expressed in his later efforts to find secondary fulfillments of the unresolved demands of primary narcissism is the fear of dissolution of consciousness and a return of the prenarcissistic isolation of physical and mental functions that characterizes what psychoanalysis calls the "autoerotic" phase.[62] The threat presented by "the stirring of the beast," as Yeats would put it, is that falling apart at the very center of things in which even the solipsistic "ceremony of innocence is drowned" in the archaic chaos from which it emerged. The function of the artifice that holds the beast at bay is in this respect, as Yeats always suspected, analogous to the function of psychotic delusion, and its purposes are cogently illustrated in "The Second Coming" by the eerie and hysterical quality of the "great beast" itself. It is, as Yeats describes it, literally the "remade" form of something strange not only to us but to itself,

> A shape with lion body and the head of a man,
> A gaze blank and pitiless as the sun.

Insofar as this incipient sense of being something that does not belong together underlies the "passionate" artificing of the self-invented man, it can be argued that the discomfort many readers feel about poems like "The Second Coming" betrays a preference not for a different aesthetic content but for a more acceptable form of that content. The difference between the opening lines of that poem and those of "The Tower" or "Among School Children," for example, is primarily the degree to which essentially identical anxieties have been elaborated: whether, in other words, narcissistic excitement and autoerotic fragmentation are being presented in the (relatively) direct form of apocalyptic metaphor or have been converted into the depression and hypochondria that are the "symptoms" of the creative "I."

Similarly, the disturbing apostrophe to the idealized and omniscient "shape" of the beast at the end of "The Second Coming" is more explicit about the sort of excitement and anxiety it resolves than are Yeats's other versions of selfless ecstasy. In the "ceremonious" and urbane complexity of his ottava rima meditations, such feelings often become, in the labyrinth of the remembered and the half-remembered, something of which the aesthetically recreative feelings of "innocent" awe and adoration are the only conscious vestige. The body swayed to music, the blossoming tree, and the beast are functionally identical. Each seems true and beautiful to the extent that it eases our common burden of "childish tragedy" by drawing on the secondary compensations of *Spiritus Mundi*. Each is passionate to the extent that it expresses and defends us from the terror that is ultimately the archaic nightmare of the cradle from which the birth of the conscious "shape" delivers us all.

> The darkness drops again; but now I know
> That twenty centuries of stony sleep
> Were vexed to nightmare by a rocking cradle,
> And what rough beast, its hour come round at last,
> Slouches towards Bethlehem to be born?

The manifestations of the "beast" in Yeats's poetry are manifold and as diverse as are the subjects of his lyrics. In general, they are identified by the "overexcited" quality of feeling associated with them: the Muse in "The Tower," the "living child" in "Among School Children," the sphinx in "The Second Coming." One of its most pervasive images, however, is that of the wind. In "A Prayer for My Daughter," for instance, the occasion of the poet's famous apostrophe to the "radical innocence" that is "self-delighting,"

> Self-appeasing, self-affrighting,
> . . .its own sweet will is Heaven's will,

is a familiar state of emotional tumult and depression that brings together the tower, the living child, the rocking cradle, and the fury of the outer weather. The poet begins,

> Once more the storm is howling, and half hid
> Under the cradle-hood and coverlid
> My child sleeps on. There is no obstacle
> But Gregory's wood and one bare hill
> Whereby the haystack- and roof-levelling wind,
> Bred on the Atlantic, can be stayed;
> And for an hour I have walked and prayed
> Because of the great gloom that is in my mind.

> I have walked and prayed for this young child an hour
> And heard the sea-wind scream upon the tower,
> And under the arches of the bridge, and scream
> In the elms above the flooded stream;
> Imagining in excited reverie
> That the future years had come,
> Dancing to a frenzied drum,
> Out of the murderous innocence of the sea.
> [1–16]

The "haystack- and roof-levelling wind" is, among other things, reminiscent of the "whirlwind" that lays Hanrahan/O'Sullivan's cabin flat in the 1892 version of the "mighty memories" of "The Tower." As such it is a metaphor for the subjective power of the "woman lost" who becomes a "living child" in "Among School Children" and is elaborated in "The Secret Rose" as

> The hour of thy great wind of love and hate.
> When shall the stars be blown about the sky,
> Like the sparks blown out of a smithy, and die?
> Surely thine hour has come, thy great wind blows,
> Far-off, most secret, and inviolate Rose?
> [28–32]

The wind is probably most familiar to readers of the early poetry, however, as what, in a more general way, the "peasants ever associated with the Fairies," the "Host of the Air." Used in this sense it appears both in the title of what is probably the best volume of Yeats's early work, *The Wind among the Reeds* (1899), and in its introductory poem, "The Hosting of the Sidhe":

> The host is riding from Knocknarea
> And over the grave of Clooth-na-Bare;
> Caoilte tossing his burning hair,
> And Niamh calling *Away, come away:*
> *Empty your heart of its mortal dream.*
> *The winds awaken, the leaves whirl round,*
> *Our cheeks are pale, our hair is unbound,*
> *Our breasts are heaving, our eyes are agleam,*
> *Our arms are waving, our lips are apart;*
> *And if any gaze on our rushing band,*
> *We come between him and the deed of his hand,*
> *We come between him and the hope of his heart.*
> The host is rushing 'twixt night and day,

> And where is there hope or deed as fair?
> Caoilte tossing his burning hair,
> And Niamh calling *Away, come away.*

And finally, in the latest as well as the earliest poetry, there is the adumbration of the "hour of hours" in the wind "bred on the Atlantic" that screams once again upon the defiant solipsism of "The Black Tower" (1939):

> Say that the men of the old black tower,
> Though they but feed as the goatherd feeds,
> Their money spent, their wine gone sour,
> Lack nothing that a soldier needs,
> That all are oath-bound men:
> Those banners come not in.
>
> *There in the tomb stand the dead upright,*
> *But the winds come up from the shore:*
> *They shake when the winds roar,*
> *Old bones upon the mountain shake.*
> [1–10]

The most familiar of all of Yeats's ways of representing his fears of fragmentation, however, is the image not of the wind itself but of the creatures who ride the wind. In "The Second Coming" the multitudinous, whirling otherness of "The Hosting of the Sidhe" becomes the gyring flight that carries the falcon beyond the circumference of recall,

> Turning and turning in the widening gyre
> The falcon cannot hear the falconer;
> Things fall apart; the centre cannot hold;
> Mere anarchy is loosed upon the world. . . .

Generally speaking, the avian image is Yeats's favorite apocalyptic symbol, both in poems that, like "The Second Coming," conclude in an ecstatic merger and, as we shall see in discussing the "Byzantine" poems, in those that end in solipsistic "gaiety." In the former group the image of the swan is the most common, and here as elsewhere there is a considerable variation in the manifest content of the poet's "passion." At one extreme, the apostrophe to the beauty of the drifting swans whose "clamorous" and "broken" flight haunts the mirrored and brimming silence of October twilight in "The Wild Swans at Coole" suggests a final event that is intensely numinous but benign:

The trees are in their autumn beauty,
The woodland paths are dry,
Under the October twilight the water
Mirrors a still sky;
Upon the brimming water among the stones
Are nine-and-fifty swans.

The nineteenth autumn has come upon me
Since I first made my count;
I saw, before I had well finished,
All suddenly mount
And scatter in great broken rings
Upon their clamorous wings.

. . . . ,

But now they drift on the still water,
Mysterious, beautiful;
Among what rushes will they build,
By what lake's edge or pool
Delight men's eyes when I awake some day
To find they have flown away?
[1–30]

In an earlier version, "The Wild Swans at Coole" had expressed the poet's sense of ironic decrepitude after he had been refused by Maud Gonne for the last time in the summer of 1916; in this version (a rearrangement of the original stanzas probably completed in October 1917), it is his prothalamion.[63] The mysterious beauty of their "wildness" is thus a premonition of the gusty outbreak of the honeymoon poems,

But O! my Heart could bear no more when the upland caught the
    wind;
I ran, I ran, from my love's side because my Heart went mad.

And six years later still, the swan has become the apocalyptic alter ego of the "rough beast" in "Leda and the Swan":

How can those terrified vague fingers push
The feathered glory from her loosening thighs?
And how can body, laid in that white rush,
But feel the strange heart beating where it lies?

A shudder in the loins engenders there
The broken wall, the burning roof and tower
And Agamemnon dead.

> Being so caught up,
> So mastered by the brute blood of the air,
> Did she put on his knowledge with his power
> Before the indifferent beak could let her drop?
> [5–14]

Here the swan's flight, like the flight of the falcon, is associated with "spiritual" excitement, tragic rage, and the hysterical feeling of autoerotic "strangeness" of body parts (whose body? whose heart?) that threatens consciousness when it is "mastered" by the idealized and omniscient otherness, the indifferent "brute blood of the air."

Besides these poems, all of which conclude with one version or another of the Yeatsian adoration or ecstasy, there is also a group of poems in which "passion" is characterized by the sort of grandiose and solipsistic withdrawal that first impressed us in the third part of "The Tower." Once again, we are dealing primarily with a kind of poem that elicits the most ambiguous responses from its readers, even from those who might be inclined to praise a "Leda and the Swan" or a "Second Coming." In the third section of "Nineteen Hundred and Nineteen" for instance, the swan is the image of "the solitary soul" the poet sees in the "troubled mirror" of the Black and Tan War, its "breast thrust out in pride / Whether to play, or to ride / Those winds that clamour of approaching night" (59–68).[64] He concludes,

> The swan has leaped into the desolate heaven:
> That image can bring wildness, bring a rage
> To end all things, to end
> What my laborious life imagined, even
> The half-imagined, the half-written page.
> [79–83]

The apocalyptic anxiety underlying the solitary "pride" of the self-mirroring soul is most familiar, however, in the "cold and passionate" paradoxes of the "Byzantine" poems. Byzantium is Yeats's imaginary city of the Soul; in "Sailing to Byzantium" (1927), the poet explains that he has "sailed the seas and come" there because the natural world

> I   is no country for old men. The young
> In one another's arms, birds in the trees
> —Those dying generations—at their song,
> The salmon-falls, the mackerel-crowded seas,
> Fish, flesh, or fowl, commend all summer long
> Whatever is begotten, born, and dies.

> Caught in that sensual music all neglect
> Monuments of unaging intellect.

II   An aged man is but a paltry thing,
    A tattered coat upon a stick, unless
    Soul clap its hands and sing, and louder sing
    For every tatter in its mortal dress,
    Nor is there singing school but studying
    Monuments of its own magnificence;
    And therefore have I sailed the seas and come
    To the holy city of Byzantium.
    [1–16]

The poem, as so often elsewhere, is about how it feels to feel old, and this is, despite the poet's references to his "tattered mortal dress," a feeling of overwhelming excitement and anxious inner "strangeness." His heart, he goes on to explain in his prayer to the Byzantine sages "standing in God's holy fire" is so "sick with desire...it knows not what it is," and the remedy he prays for is that he may come to know only the mirror-resembling "study" of his own singing:

III   O sages standing in God's holy fire
    As in the gold mosaic of a wall,
    Come from the holy fire, perne in a gyre,
    And be the singing-masters of my soul.
    Consume my heart away; sick with desire
    And fastened to a dying animal
    It knows not what it is; and gather me
    Into the artifice of eternity.

IV   Once out of nature I shall never take
    My bodily form from any natural thing,
    But such a form as Grecian goldsmiths make
    Of hammered gold and gold enamelling
    To keep a drowsy Emperor awake;
    Or set upon a golden bough to sing
    To lords and ladies of Byzantium
    Of what is past, or passing, or to come.
    [17–32]

The imaginary golden bird on the Virgilian golden bough in "Sailing to Byzantium" is probably Yeats's best-known version of the grandiose "I" that subsumes all things "past, or passing, or to come." Despite its explicit rejection of "any natural thing" it is also, like the "self-delight" of "A Prayer for My Daughter," one of his most moving images. This poem is a prayer too: the poet is on the threshold of his holy solipsism, but not yet (as he is in the third part of "The Tower") within its precincts. His longing to be "out of nature" bears, as Yeats would surely have admitted, the inner stirring of a "rage to end all things"; the apocalyptic terror implicit in his wish to find a haven in "the artifice of eternity" is suggested by echoes of "The Second Coming" ("perne in a gyre") and by the "holy fire" that consumes the heart. But both rage and terror have been elaborated into a kind of "passion" that, like the feeling that moves us in many of Yeats's most successful poems, has the masochistic sweetness and the hypochondriacal pathos of "old age":

> Consume my heart away; sick with desire
> And fastened to a dying animal
> It knows not what it is; and gather me
> Into the artifice of eternity.

"Byzantium," which was written two years later, is too explicit about how it might feel to be "out of nature" not to be profoundly disconcerting. The poet imagines the city's deserted streets and courts at midnight ("The Emperor's drunken soldiery are abed") and finds in the gold mosaics of their walls and floors images of the "superhuman" state he seeks:

> Miracle, bird or golden handiwork
> More miracle than bird or handiwork,
> Planted on the star-lit golden bough,
> Can like the cocks of Hades crow,
> Or, by the moon embittered, scorn aloud
> In glory of changeless metal
> Common bird or petal
> And all complexities of mire and blood.
>
> At midnight on the Emperor's pavement flit
> Flames that no faggot feeds, nor steel has lit,
> Nor storm disturbs, flame begotten of flame,
> Where blood-begotten spirits come
> And all complexities of fury leave,
> Dying into a dance,
> An agony of trance,
> An agony of flame that cannot singe a sleeve.
>
> Astraddle on the dolphin's mire and blood,
> Spirit after spirit! The smithies break the flood,

> The golden smithies of the Emperor!
> Marbles of the dancing floor
> Break bitter furies of complexity,
> Those images that yet
> Fresh images beget,
> That dolphin-torn, that gong-tormented sea.
> [17–40]

It is difficult, perhaps impossible, to say exactly what the poet is seeing as he gazes at the images of bird and "dolphin-torn" mosaic sea. The ambivalence of "Sailing to Byzantium" has given way to a deeper, more disturbing kind of estrangement. He reminds us in the first line, "The unpurged images of day recede," and as they do the language of the poem reverts to the private, unelaborated idiom of delusion. The extended oxymoron of the last two stanzas—cold fires, dancing deaths, agonized trances—comes as close as anything Yeats wrote to conveying the mind's agonized struggle to maintain its integrity in the face of its own overwhelming excitement. As we enter the "artifice of eternity," the manic exaltation that makes all things new increases with, and becomes less distinguishable from, the sadistic "fury" that destroys them utterly; the solipsistic "miracle" of the created thing is its ability to isolate us from what we see and feel. The mosaics of "Byzantium" are in this respect the most appropriate emblem Yeats ever found for his creative enterprise. The tiny, glittering fragments that give back the image of his "mirror-resembling dream" in the marbles of the dancing floor are the rigid forms of shattered stone, broken and breaking, remaking and remade:

> Those images that yet
> Fresh images beget,
> That dolphin-torn, that gong-tormented sea.[65]

The manic rage of "Byzantium" is the characteristic mode of Yeatsian "passion" in the later poetry. In the posthumous *Last Poems* in particular, it is familiar as the "gaiety" and "tragic joy" that, in the introductory poem, bid the poet "rejoice":

> Irrational streams of blood are staining earth;
> Empedocles has thrown all things about;
> Hector is dead and there's a light in Troy;
> We that look on but laugh in tragic joy.
> ["The Gyres," 5–8][66]

The two best-known examples of this final variation of the remade self, however, are probably "Lapis Lazuli" (1936) and "Under Ben Bulben"

(1938). In the first of these, as before in "The Second Coming," history and the events of the outer world become the metaphorical occasion of the initiation of an inner struggle with the stirring of "Hysterica passio" that begins,

> I have heard that hysterical women say
> They are sick of the palette and fiddle-bow,
> Of poets that are always gay,
> For everybody knows or else should know
> That if nothing drastic is done
> Aeroplane and Zeppelin will come out,
> Pitch like King Billy bomb-balls in
> Until the town lie beaten flat,
> [1–8]

and ends with the famous evocation of the tragic "gaiety" that transfigures "all that dread":

> Two Chinamen, behind them a third,
> Are carved in lapis lazuli,
> Over them flies a long-legged bird,
> A symbol of longevity;
> The third, doubtless a serving man,
> Carries a musical instrument.
>
> Every discoloration of the stone,
> Every accidental crack or dent,
> Seems a water-course or an avalanche,
> Or lofty slope where it still snows
> Though doubtless plum or cherry-branch
> Sweetens the little half-way house
> Those Chinamen climb towards, and I
> Delight to imagine them seated there;
> There, on the mountain and the sky,
> On all the tragic scene they stare.
> One asks for mournful melodies;
> Accomplished fingers begin to play.
> Their eyes mid many wrinkles, their eyes,
> Their ancient, glittering eyes, are gay.
> [37–56]

The "gaiety" apostrophized in "Lapis Lazuli," like the strange ecstasy of the speaker of "The Second Coming," is premised on the hysterical conviction that things are falling apart in an apocalyptic "last scene." Here, however, the process of creative "transfiguration" is the process of elaborating "all that dread" into an idealized image of solipsistic withdrawal that is the "artifice of eternity." As in the Byzantium poems, the feeling of grandiose exaltation that accompanies the reconstitution of narcissistic omnipotence is expressed by the changeless glories of art itself, into which the poet "delights to imagine" that he has been vicariously gathered.

Finally, there is the poem that concludes the *Last Poems,* "Under Ben Bulben," the source of the epitaph that now appears over Yeats's grave in Drumcliff churchyard. The poem, like the third section of "The Tower," is testamentary, and its legacy, once again, is the grandiose "pride" of a speaker whose solipsistic conviction is that man—that is, the artist—"made up the whole":

> Poet and sculptor, do the work,
> Nor let the modish painter shirk
> What his great forefathers did,
> Bring the soul of man to God,
> Make him fill the cradles right.
> [37–41]

> Irish poets, learn your trade,
> Sing whatever is well made,
> Scorn the sort now growing up
> All out of shape from toe to top,
> Their unremembering hearts and heads
> Base-born products of base beds.
>
> . . . .
> Sing the lords and ladies gay
> That were beaten into the clay
> Through seven heroic centuries;
> Cast your mind on other days
> That we in coming days may be
> Still the indomitable Irishry.
> [68–83]

In the end the poem, which is little more than a redaction of an academic prose "creed" Yeats had written out earlier, is saved from long-winded eccentricity by its concluding lines.[67] The sixth section was developed as **an afterthought from notes he had made in the margin of a book on Rilke:**

> Under bare Ben Bulben's head
> In Drumcliff churchyard Yeats is laid.
> An ancestor was rector there

Long years ago, a church stands near,
By the road an ancient cross.
No marble, no conventional phrase;
On limestone quarried near the spot
By his command these words are cut:

> Cast a cold eye
> On life, on death.
> Horseman, pass by!

[84–94]

The solipsistic passion of the poet who is, for readers of the *Collected Poems,* Yeats's final version of himself, is perhaps his most grandiose rhetorical triumph. Yeats speaks to us, or seems to speak to us, from beyond the grave in the characteristically cold but passionately solicitous "gaiety" of stone; death itself, the thought of which is the closest most of us ever come to acknowledging the absolute molecular chaos from which we have all emerged and to which we must someday return, has been overcome.

It is probably because the apprehensions stirred by the anticipation of our own biological dissolution are so universal and so deep that we are willing to accept an element of rather puerile vanity ("no *conventional* phrase") that we might find less appealing elsewhere. As it is, the lines are deeply moving. Yet I cannot help wondering whether Yeats is really addressing himself to what most of us would mean by either life or death. I suspect that what his artifice redeemed him from was not the dread of final unconsciousness but the fear that death would perpetuate the state of whirling, fragmented, dissolving consciousness that threatened him in life. If, as his language suggests, our experience must be measured in the end, as his was in the beginning, by the "cold eye" of a mother's indifference, then indeed there can be little felt difference between living and as much of dying as the living can imagine. Without the assurance of inner wholeness vouchsafed by that loving, empathic "brightening glance," consciousness can only be, or threaten to become, increasingly rigid and withdrawn or fragmented and dispersed. Yeats's epitaph, in this respect, is no more than a grim (or grimly humorous) acceptance of an old fear: for the sake of keeping *some* "shape," "my tongue's a stone" has become "my stone's a tongue."[68]

However this may be, the power of Yeats's artifice in "Under Ben Bulben" is reflected by our willingness to read it as if it really were his last poem. It was not, nor was it his intention that it seem to be.[69] His own ordering of the *Last Poems and Two Plays* that are now the second half of his "last poems" was quite different from the one adopted by his posthumous editors in the *Collected Poems*. It begins rather than ends with the testament of "Under Ben Bulben"; it concludes (as it were, posthumously) with the "foul rag-and-bone shop of the heart" in "The Circus Animals' Desertion" and the "wild old wicked man" of "Politics."[70] The last three lines of "Under Ben Bulben" have been cut above the poet's grave in Drumcliff churchyard; the table of contents of the *Last Poems and Two Plays* suggests that Yeats might have preferred

> But O that I were young again
> And held her in my arms!
> ["Politics," 11–12]

The Inner Self and the Other Self

A discussion of the vicissitudes of "passion" in Yeats's work cannot be complete without some reference to the first fruits of his temporal marriage, *A Vision*. In the introduction to the 1937 edition, Yeats says that the "unknown writer" his wife gave her hours to day after day

> took his theme at first from my just published *Per Amica Silentia Lunae*. I had made a distinction between the perfection that is from a man's combat with himself and that which is from a combat with circumstance, and upon this simple distinction he built up an elaborate classification of men according to their more or less complete expression of one type or another. He supported his classification by a series of geometrical symbols and put these symbols in an order that answered the question in my essay as to whether some prophet could not prick upon the calendar the birth of a Napoleon or a Christ. A system of symbolism, strange to my wife and to myself, certainly awaited expression, and when I asked how long that would take I was told years.[71]

The first part of the work, the struggle to communicate accurately with "unknown instructors" who often seemed to be deliberately keeping him from "mastering their conception" and who were sometimes opposed by beings called "Frustrators," "always ingenious and sometimes cruel" in their attempts to "confuse us and waste time," came to an end in 1920.[72] There followed five years of compilation and interpretation; finally, in January 1926, the first edition of *A Vision: An Explanation of Life*

Founded upon the Writings of Giraldus and upon Certain Doctrines Attributed to Kusta Ben Luka was issued by private subscription. "The first version of this book," Yeats later wrote,

> except the section on the twenty-eight Phases and that called "Dove or Swan" which I repeat without change, fills me with shame. I had misinterpreted the geometry, and in my ignorance of philosophy failed to understand distinctions upon which the coherence of the whole depended, and as my wife was unwilling that her share should be known, and I to seem sole author, I had invented an unnatural story of an Arabian traveller which I must amend and find a place for some day because I was fool enough to write half a dozen poems that are unintelligible without it.[73]

Under the influence of renewed reading in philosophy and fresh communications from the "instructors," the work of revision was begun again. This time, the period consumed in the work was almost a dozen years; the *Vision* we now have, including the revised text and all its new and old prefatory matter, was published by Macmillan in 1937.

Reading Yeats's verse in the context supplied by the plan of universal history and psychology he so painstakingly elaborated over the last twenty-odd years of his life is for most—barring a compulsiveness equal to his own—a tedious and distracting exercise. But both the tedium and the distraction, and even some of the compulsion are now for better or worse an integral part of the Yeats everyone knows, if only by hearsay, and all can be in this respect genuinely enlightening. I suspect, in fact, that to read *A Vision* through with the kind of attention it demands is to understand, if nothing else, something of what it might have felt like to be Yeats. On one hand it is the record, unchecked by aesthetic considerations, of his hunger for structure, for the artifice that would render as something "intended, complete" not just the lyric moment but the whole of experience. On the other hand it accurately reproduces, in its bewildering proliferation of distinctions and "geometrical" relationships, something of the incipient chaos of that experience. What is memorable about *A Vision* is its grand design, the "Great Wheel"; what escapes memory and even, from moment to moment in reading, understanding is precisely the detailed mastery of events that the possession of such a design seems to imply. "Some will ask," Yeats wrote in concluding his introduction to the 1937 edition,

> whether I believe in the actual existence of my circuits of sun and moon. . . . To such a question I can but answer that if sometimes,

> overwhelmed by miracle as all men must be when in the midst of it,
> I have taken such periods literally, my reason has soon recovered;
> and now that the system stands out clearly in my imagination I
> regard them as stylistic arrangements of experience comparable to
> the cubes in the drawing of Wyndham Lewis and to the ovoids in
> the sculpture of Brancusi. They have helped me to hold in a single
> thought reality and justice.[74]

The essential connection between philosophical and aesthetic artifice in
his own case was of course something Yeats had always insisted on. "I
put *The Tower* and *The Winding Stair* into evidence," he asserted in the
first paragraph of the 1937 introduction, "to show that my poetry has
gained in self-possession and power."[75] By the power that put him in
aesthetic possession of himself he meant, as we have seen, the power that
came from overcoming the rough, stirring beast whose source in "The
Second Coming" is identified with the *Spiritus Mundi,* the spirit or, as he
had called it in *Per Amica Silentia Lunae,* the *Anima* or soul of the world.
In *Per Amica,* Yeats (relying on the Platonist Henry More) describes the
world-soul as a kind of divine solipsism, an omnipotent and omniscient
presence that contains, and is contained by, all objective and subjective
forms of experience.[76] "If all our mental images no less than apparitions
(and I see no reason to distinguish)," Yeats says, "are forms existing in the
general vehicle of *Anima Mundi,* and mirrored in our particular vehicle,
many crooked things are made straight. I am persuaded that a logical
process, or a series of related images, has body and period, and I think of
Anima Mundi as a great pool or garden where it moves through its
alotted [sic] growth like a great water-plant or fragrantly branches in
the air."[77]

The image of the blossoming world-soul suggests a transcendent "we"
familiar from the "benign" ecstasies of "Among School Children." In
the decade that followed the publication of *Per Amica* in 1917, however, the "instructors" that spoke through his wife brought Yeats
images of the activities *Anima Mundi* that were both more terrifying
and more "passionate." In *A Vision,* the "body and period" of
its vicissitudes are described in the chapters that also supply the "metaphors" for poems like "The Second Coming" and "Leda and the Swan."
Both poems are, in fact, a part of the text, the first appearing at the
end of chapter 4 ("The Great Year of the Ancients") and the second
at the beginning of chapter 5 ("Dove or Swan").

The subject of both chapters is the historical hypothesis Yeats called
the "non-temporal vision" of the Eternal Return. His doctrine (or

"myth," as he would have preferred to call it) is that the movement of time is circular as a whole and in its parts. His object is first to establish the size of its largest "period" (in "The Great Year of the Ancients") and then to apply this period directly to the analysis of the eras of recorded Western history (in "Dove or Swan"). With respect to the former, he lists a number of possibilities: there is the "Platonic Year" of Ptolemy (36,000 years), the "Etruscan cycle" (11,000), and the equinoctial year (26,000). But in the end it becomes clear that he has cited these only as precedents. The period he is most interested in is the Great Year defined by the completion of the movement of the "Four Principles," a period of 4,000 years lying between the beginning of what he calls the *"antithetical* influx" and the end of the *"primary* influx" that follows it.

Though some of Yeats's structural terminology is unavoidable even for our purposes here, we need not concern ourselves with understanding it in detail. The important thing about his Great Year is that, as far as he was concerned, it was the period that had to pass before any given set of underlying historical influences in the *Anima Mundi* could recur in exactly the same relationship. It was the highest possible abstraction, the hypothesis beyond which there were no further hypotheses, the end of speculation and the beginning of knowledge, the final determinism. To achieve its "vision" was to achieve the "non-temporal" withdrawal from the tragic scene implicit in both the grandiose exaltation of the "artifice of eternity" of "Sailing to Byzantium" and the solipsistic "gaiety" of "Lapis Lazuli," both of which imply a merger of the pattern of all experience "past, or passing, or to come" into the speaker's perfected self-possession.

It is the quality of cold withdrawal in Yeats's doctrine of the Eternal Return that critics often find the most "inhuman" strain in his philosophy, particularly since they suspect him, with a great deal of justice, of emphasizing its destructive rather than constructive aspects.[78] Yeats's Great Year is a schematization of human experience premised on eternal conflict and punctuated by repeated disasters from which there is neither redemption nor appeal. It is, in effect, his most complexly and anxiously protracted elaboration of the narcissistic rage against which he feared "the centre could not hold," and by the end of chapter 4 his mystical terminology has become the language of apocalypse that here, as elsewhere, is a "metaphor for poetry":

> The approaching *antithetical* influx and the particular *antithetical* dispensation for which the intellectual preparation has begun will

reach its complete systematisation at the moment when, as I have
already shown, the Great Year comes to its intellectual climax.
Something of what I have said it must be, the myth declares, for it
must reverse our era and resume past eras on itself; what else it
must be no man can say, for always at the critical moment the
Thirteenth Cone, the sphere, the unique intervenes.

> Somewhere in the sands of the desert
> A shape with lion body and the head of a man,
> A gaze blank and pitiless as the sun,
> Is moving its slow thighs, while all about it
> Reel shadows of the indignant desert birds.[79]

It is not really necessary to penetrate the obscurities of *"antithetical
influx"* and *"Thirteenth Cone"* to get a sense of what the issues at stake
in such passages might be. In the end, what communicates itself most
vividly about Yeats's Great Year is his conviction that his phase of its
"body and period" is the last. His "philosophy" assures him that the
release of a destructive force unequaled in intensity in the whole preceding 4,000 years—for Yeats, the whole memory of Western man—is imminent and inevitable. *A Vision* bears witness to the visionary's civiliza-
tion; the "we" of which he declares himself the spokesman is the historical
equivalent of the poet's "passionate" individuality. Culture, like "style,"
was for Yeats locked in a perpetual struggle against its own disintegration, and in "Dove or Swan," which returns to the beginning of the Great
Year and the "sudden blow" that, Yeats says, was the "annunciation that
founded Greece," the vicissitudes of *Anima Mundi* are compared with
the effects of "Hysterica passio" on a single, collective personality:

> A civilization is a struggle to keep self-control, and in this it is
> like some great tragic person, some Niobe who must display an
> almost superhuman will or the cry will not touch our sympathy.
> The loss of control over thought comes towards the end; first a
> sinking in upon the moral being, then the last surrender, the irra-
> tional cry, revelation—the scream of Juno's peacock....
>   I imagine the annunciation that founded Greece as made to
> Leda....[80]

I have tried to suggest that *Anima Mundi,* the collective or historical
"personality," is another elaboration of the apprehensive sense of incipient fragmentation implicit in Yeats's own "nervous weakness." But it
should also be observed that it is in this respect distinct from the dynamic
of the entity to which he assigned the psychic economy of the individual

"personality," the *Anima Hominis*. Although both are based on the analytic framework of the "Great Wheel" that perpetually brings all things round from *antithetical* to *primary* and back again in "every completed movement of thought or life,"[81] *Anima Hominis* differs from *Anima Mundi* in its emphasis on the dynamic of "opposition," or of self and antiself, within each of its twenty-eight phases, rather than on the apocalyptic threat embodied by its movement as a whole. The vicissitudes of *Anima Hominis,* in other words, express a relationship not with a terrifying, hidden "inner" self but with a heartbreaking "other" self. In *Anima Hominis* Yeats's conviction that life prepares for what never happens has become the doctrine of "estrangement" that, like the "topic" for "Among School Children," found its earliest expression in his 1909 diaries.[82] It reappears in *Per Amica Silentia Lunae* and finds its most complex formulation in the chapter of *A Vision* called "The Great Wheel."[83] Here again particular terms are obscure, but the general situation clear:

> When I wish for some general idea which will describe the Great Wheel as an individual life I go to the *Commedia dell' Arte* or improvised drama of Italy. The stage-manager, or *Daimon,* offers his actor an inherited scenario, the *Body of Fate,* and a *Mask* or rôle as unlike as possible to his natural ego or *Will,* and leaves him to improvise through his *Creative Mind* the dialogue and details of the plot. He must discover or reveal a being which only exists with extreme effort. . . .[84]

The doctrine that the individual life is the sum of the struggle to be that which is "of all things not impossible the most difficult" is reminiscent in its "extremity" of the heartbreaking relationship of the son and the maternal "image" described in "Among School Children." What Yeats calls the "antiself" suggests not the hidden, archaic demands of the unappeased narcissistic "beast" but an internalized version of the ideal "worshipped" by an unempathic mother.[85] In discussing the attributes of the *Daimon* that was to become the presiding spirit or "stage-manager" of *Anima Hominis* in *A Vision,* Yeats remarks in *Per Amica Silentia Lunae* that he is

> persuaded that the Daimon delivers and deceives us, and that he wove that netting from the stars and threw the net from his shoulder. Then my imagination runs from Daimon to sweetheart, and I divine an analogy that evades the intellect. I remember that Greek antiquity has bid us look for the principal stars, that govern enemy

> and sweetheart alike, among those that are about to set . . . and that
> it may be "sexual love," which is "founded on spiritual hate," is an
> image of the warfare of man and Daimon; and I even wonder if
> there may not be some secret communion, some whispering in the
> dark between Daimon and sweetheart.[86]

The analogy that evades the intellect here is the implicit "communion"
between the *Daimon* and the seductive but treacherous archaic presence,
the nunlike mother that, in its sexualized form, is the "woman lost" of
"The Tower." The antiself is the vestige of her will and, more
significantly, of her self-absorbed indifference to her son's "natural ego."
The "self-born" demands of the antiself reflect the grandiosity not of a
son's but of a mother's fantasies, and the effort to fulfill them is fundamentally at odds with his real narcissistic needs. To feel as Yeats does
about *Anima Hominis* is to feel that being "somebody" is like being
imagined by somebody else, and that the somebody you might yourself
imagine being is nobody at all.[87]
The conflict between this "other" self and the unappeased "inner" self
represented by the "stirring of the beast" is the implicit scenario of
Yeats's way of imagining the story of that somebody of somebodies, the
hero, in his plays about Cuchulain. In the Yeatsian lyric it is most obvious in his consistently ironic interpretation of the meaning of individual
life and "man's enterprise." The poem that introduces *Per Amica Silentia
Lunae,* "Ego Dominus Tuus," for example, elaborates the doctrine of the
antiself into a complex system of "mockery" that suggests both the hollow "otherness" of the public image and the underlying sense of oral
deprivation, the "bitter" unreliability of maternal supply, that determines
the ideals of even the greatest men, here particularly the greatest poets.
The poem is a dialogue. The first speaker, "Hic," argues rather half-
heartedly that the aim of man's enterprise is to find the "self and not an
image" and gives Dante and Keats as examples. "Ille," who prefers to
"call on his own opposite, " replies that Dante's "hollow face" was a
mask:

> And did he find himself
> Or was the hunger that had made it hollow
> A hunger for the apple on the bough
> Most out of reach? and is that spectral image
> The man that Lapo and that Guido knew?
> . . . .
> Being mocked by Guido for his lecherous life,
> Derided and deriding, driven out

> To climb that stair and eat that bitter bread,
> He found the unpersuadable justice, he found
> The most exalted lady loved by man.
> [22–37]

And in reply to Hic's description of Keats's "deliberate happiness" he adds,

> His art is happy, but who knows his mind?
> I see a schoolboy when I think of him,
> With face and nose pressed to a sweet-shop window,
> For certainly he sank into his grave
> His senses and his heart unsatisfied,
> And made—being poor, ailing, and ignorant,
> Shut out from all the luxury of the world,
> The coarse-bred son of a livery-stable keeper—
> Luxuriant song.
> [54–62]

Ultimately, then, Yeats's deepest sense of the possibilities of individual life, of the lives of others and of his own, is an intuition of the pervasive narcissistic deprivation, the "unpersuadable justice" that denies satisfaction to both the senses and the heart. The story of the poet always, in one way or another, leads back to the unresolvable story of sons and mothers and the vicissitudes of shame, depression, and hypochondria. Yet insofar as the antiself suggests the scope of man's enterprise, it also reminds us of the other image in which sons see themselves or despair of seeing themselves: the image of the father. Indeed the story of the poet is most familiar to readers of Yeats's *Autobiography* as the story of fathers and sons: what he had hoped to become and what he became is there interpreted, when it is interpreted at all, in terms of his struggle to escape his "father's influence." Becoming himself was a matter not only, as he put it in "The Tower," of "turning aside" from the archaic, inner world of the "woman lost" but also of turning toward the outer world of men and things. If his best work still seems to us, as it did to the Nobel Prize committee in 1923, to be somehow "private" and lyrical, it should be kept in mind that his enterprise as a whole was profoundly (if ambivalently) public and communal. "I have got into the habit," he wrote in the journal he kept on his journey to Stockholm to receive the prize in 1924, "of recommending or commending myself to general company for anything rather than my gift of lyric writing, which concerns such a meagre troop," and later added, "On the other hand, if I give a successful lecture, or write a vigorous, critical essay, there is immediate effect; I am confident that on some one point, which seems to me of great importance, I know more than other men, and I covet honour."[88]

The part of the poet's story that suggests the heroic competitor for "honour" is the subject of the second half of this study. Psychologically speaking, it can be restated in terms of the transformation of the illusory pre-oedipal fantasy of unlimited power and glory into a post-oedipal acceptance of the diminished satisfactions offered by real objects and capabilities. It is in this sense the story of the poet's successful efforts to overcome solipsism and to put fantasy into the service of the relatively social and object-oriented purposes of art. Yet to the extent that it is also, in Yeats's case, the story of a transformation that was never fully made, it is also the story of defeat; the conquest of fantasy was itself obsessive, debilitating, and life diminishing.[89] This was so partly, as I have argued, because of his overwhelming sense of "spiritual" or narcissistic defectiveness, and partly, as I shall go on to say, because of an equally debilitating ambiguity in his experience of the oedipal event itself. Yeats's way of imagining the best a man might do in the world tended throughout his life to be the object of either sentimental overvaluation or ironic undervaluation, and nowhere is the conflict between the two more fully expressed than in the epic figure he chose as the speaker of the poem in which he announced his artistic coming of age, the poet-hero of the Ossianic cycle, Oisin:

> First that sea-rider Oisin led by the nose
> Through three enchanted islands, allegorical dreams,
> Vain gaiety, vain battle, vain repose,
> Themes of the embittered heart, or so it seems,
> That might adorn old songs or courtly shows;
> But what cared I that set him on to ride,
> I, starved for the bosom of his faery bride?

Three

FATHERS AND SONS

Sea-Rider Oisin

If *The Wanderings of Oisin* is not much read any more, the irony in terms of the poet's own ambitions is clear. Of all the *Collected Poems,* those that Yeats once hoped would be the most popular—*Oisin, Baile and Aillinn, The Old Age of Queen Maeve*—now command the meagerest troop. The narrator of Oisin's story and the other stories of the Irish heroic age is the poet Yeats was least successful at being; yet throughout his career he remained committed, first in narrative verse and later in the drama, to the idea of reviving, and if necessary reinventing, what he conceived to be the Irish national culture.

To be concerned, as we will be from now on, with the story of the poet as a "public man" is consequently to be concerned primarily with works that have no public and whose failure to attract one is often, unfortunately, the most interesting thing about them. One might wonder, for example, whether there is any implicit connection between the aesthetic and psychological vicissitudes of the self-invented man: whether, to put it another way, Yeats's inability to become a certain kind of poet had anything to do with his inability to tell a certain kind of story. The

"vanity" of the "epic" version of man's enterprise he tried to imagine in
Oisin may reflect, as he would later suggest himself, not just the mawkishness of youth but also the limits of the imaginable:

> But what cared I that set him on to ride,
> I, starved for the bosom of his faery bride?[1]

The Wanderings of Oisin is also interesting for a more obvious reason,
for it is with this poem that the story of the "public" Yeats begins, in both
fact and fiction. *The Wanderings of Oisin and Other Poems,* which
appeared only a few months before his twenty-fourth birthday in 1889,
was the book of verse that, with only slight inaccuracy, Yeats liked to
remember as his "first," and as such it was also his first version of the
story of the poet. Indeed it is in this respect that the scope of his early
ambition is, if not explicit, obvious, though perhaps not so obvious now
as it once was. In 1889 Yeats could assume that an Anglo-Irish audience
would know what an Anglo-American audience almost a century later is
less likely to know: that in *Oisin* his persona is nothing less than the
"greatest poet of the Gael."[2]

According to legend, Oisin (or Ossian) was the son of Finn Mac-
Cumhaill (MacCool), the Irish hero who led the Fianna Éireann, a band
of warriors sworn to protect Ireland from invasion in the late third
century. Oisin is their chief bard; centuries later, after a magically pro-
longed sojourn in Tír na nÓg, the Land of the Young, he is supposed to
have returned to Ireland to record the deeds of the Fianna in a cycle of
"Ossianic" narrative poems. In *Oisín i dTír na nÓg,* which Yeats read in
translation in the *Transactions of the Ossianic Society,* Oisin is represented as an immensely old man telling Saint Patrick about the "wanderings" that account for his supernatural longevity.[3] "You who are
bent, and bald, and blind," Patrick says to Oisin in the opening lines of
Yeats's version,

> With a heavy heart and a wandering mind,
> Have known three centuries, poets sing,
> Of dalliance with a demon thing.
> [I.1–4]

The "greatest poet of the Gael" imagined by the poet in his twenties is
in many ways remarkably like the "public man" who at sixty was not
without real pretensions to the title, the "Yeats" we imagine when we
read "The Tower" or "Among School Children." Once again we are
invited to attend to the reminiscences of a passionate and depressed old

man, and once again the "decrepit age" that spurs him into song is closely associated with the memory of a supernatural "woman lost" or, as Patrick censoriously puts it, "demon thing." But there is also something unfamiliar about the context of the familiar. Oisin is not the ironically isolated lyricist who speaks the opening lines of "The Tower," "Among School Children," or "The Circus Animals' Desertion"; a part of the fiction here is an idealized, heroic past, a prior relationship not only with a "spiritual" love but also with the poet's beloved comrades and his father, Finn. In retelling Oisin's story, Yeats is implicitly identifying his voice with the communal voice of Irish nationalism past and present: the glories of the Fianna with whom Oisin rode and of the Fenian Irish Republican Brotherhood into which John O'Leary had introduced Yeats shortly before.[4] Oisin replies to the saint,

> Sad to remember, sick with years,
> The swift innumerable spears,
> The horsemen with their floating hair,
> And bowls of barley, honey, and wine,
> Those merry couples dancing in tune,
> And the white body that lay by mine;
> But the tale, though words be lighter than air,
> Must live to be old like the wandering moon.
>
> Caoilte, and Conan, and Finn were there,
> When we followed a deer with our baying hounds,
> With Bran, Sceolan, and Lomair. . . .
> [I.5–15]

One way of describing the difference between this version of the poet's story and that told later in much more successful poems, then, is to observe that it is an account of the loss not only of the "white body that lay by mine," but also of the heroic companionship of men, of the "horsemen with their floating hair." The epic poet's version of the lyric poet's question in "The Tower," in other words, is whether the imagination dwells the most on the woman or the man lost, and Oisin's final speech at the end of book III makes it clear that of all the things he is "sad to remember," it is the latter that affects him most. Patrick has heard his tale of the "demon thing" through with saintly patience and exhorts Oisin to penitence and thoughts of heaven. Finn and his companions are now, he says, tortured in the flames of hell. Oisin answers in a way that suggests both the depressive symptoms of poetic inspiration we have found expressed in the works of Yeats's "real" old age and an unfamiliar heroic nostalgia:

> Ah me! to be shaken with coughing and broken with old age and
>   pain,
> Without laughter, a show unto children, alone with remembrance
>   and fear;
> All emptied of purple hours as a beggar's cloak in the rain,
> As a hay-cock out on the flood, or a wolf sucked under a weir.
>
> It were sad to gaze on the blessèd and no man I loved of old there;
> I throw down the chain of small stones! when life in my body has
>   ceased,
> I will go to Caoilte, and Conan, and Bran, Sceolan, Lomair,
> And dwell in the house of the Fenians, be they in flames or at
>   feast.
> [III.217–24]

Briefly, the story that Patrick has heard in the intervening 850 lines is this. One day, Oisin says, as he is riding with his father and the Fianna near the seashore, they suddenly come upon a fairy woman, Niamh, who says she is the daughter of the deities Aengus and Edain. She has fallen in love with "Oisin's name," and seeing her, he too falls in love. She invites him to mount her horse and ride with her to a land where death and sorrow are unknown; he accepts and leaves the Fenians mourning by the shore to begin his 300 years of wandering. In Yeats's version, however, the theme of Oisin's wanderings is not his pursuit of Niamh—her home is only the first of the "three enchanted islands" they visit—but his chronic nostalgia for Ireland and the Fenians. He tells Patrick that his stay on the first island, for instance, ends in this way:

> When one day by the tide I stood,
> I found in that forgetfulness
> Of dreamy foam a staff of wood
> From some dead warrior's broken lance:
> I turned it in my hands; the stains
> Of war were on it, and I wept,
> Remembering how the Fenians stept
> Along the blood-bedabbled plains,
> Equal to good or grievous chance:
> Thereon young Niamh softly came
> And caught my hands, but spake no word
> Save only many times my name,
> In murmurs, like a frighted bird.
> We passed by woods, and lawns of clover,
> And found the horse and bridled him,
> For we knew well the old was over.
> [I.364–79]

Each time Oisin feels what he calls the "ancient sorrow of men," he and Niamh mount the magical horse and travel over the sea to another island. Finally, after two more islands have been visited, he insists on seeing Ireland again. Niamh reluctantly agrees but tells him that if he so much as touches the earth there he will "come no more to [her] side." Oisin rides to Ireland but finds it much changed: his companions have been dead for centuries, and there is now only "a small and feeble populace stooping with mattock and spade." The old gods have been driven out by the Christianity of Patrick. Oisin is overwhelmed by pity and grief and longs to return to Niamh; but as he turns to go he sees two men staggering under a heavy sack of sand:

> Leaning down from the gem-studded saddle, I flung it five yards with my hand,
> With a sob for men waxing so weakly, a sob for the Fenians' old strength.
>
> The rest you have heard of, O croziered man; how, when divided the girth,
> I fell on the path, and the horse went away like a summer fly;
> And my three hundred years fell on me, and I rose, and walked on the earth,
> A creeping old man, full of sleep, with the spittle on his beard never dry.
> [III.187–92]

At first glance there seems to be as much in the poet Oisin's story as in his character to remind us of Yeats's later lyric versions of himself. Oisin's tale is in many ways like that of the poet Hanrahan, in which, as we have seen, Yeats took up the matter of the origins of creativity as early as 1892 and as late as 1925. In both cases the characteristic decrepitude of the poet is related to the loss of a supernatural "spiritual" companion, the "faery bride"; in both cases this loss is the result of a "treacherous" action that expresses his profound ambivalence toward the sort of feelings she excites. In Oisin's case, however, the matter is further complicated by the fact that his love for Niamh is opposed not so much by his apprehensions about her "spiritual" seductiveness—though this is perhaps the undertone of the apocalyptic apostrophe to the Fenians at the end of the poem—as by his nostalgia for the world of his father.

The scenario of Oisin's reminiscence, in other words, suggests that the issues at stake for the epic poet are not exclusively narcissistic: the effect of the idealized image of the son worshiped by the mother has been replaced, or modified, by the image of the father worshiped by the son. Oisin's dissatisfied "wanderings" in the "Land of the Young" suggest not, as we might expect, an archaic longing to become a mother's child but a child's longing to exchange the unconditional demands of a mother's love for what he perceives as the obligations and privileges—the freedom and the risk, "equal to good or grievous chance"—of being a father's son. Oisin is undone at last not simply by the vicissitudes of self-love represented by Niamh as she appears in "The Hosting of the Sidhe,"

> . . . Away, come away,
> Empty your heart of its mortal dream,

but more complexly by a conflict between her demands and the "heroic" bond that unites him with his mortal comrades and his fellowman: "With a sob for men waxing so weakly, a sob for the Fenians' old strength."

Oisin's story, then, seems to be a way of recalling relationships and events that are, in terms of the archaic "theology" of poems like "Among School Children," relatively late in Yeats's way of imagining the genesis of man's "shape." The epic poet's subject is not the "apocalyptic" anxiety associated with the vicissitudes of self-love but the guilt and glory associated with the transformation of the way we love ourselves into the way we care for others. His story is most like what a psychoanalyst would call the "oedipal" story: the change from "boyhood into man" that begins with the father's traumatic interruption of the son's "Saturnalian" self-absorption and ends with the establishment of the superego and the "passing" of incestuous love and filial revolt into conjugal affection and paternal authority.

And in fact there is a good deal about the way in which the story Yeats's imagination dwells on most is presented that seems to justify such an interpretation. One could argue, for example, that in telling his story Yeats's poet-hero is engaging in a dialogue between two conflicting versions of paternal authority: Saint Patrick, the repressive "father confessor" whose solicitation of Oisin's account of guilty "dalliance" opens the poem, and Finn, the idealized father whose glory inspires the apostrophe that ends it. In this context, Yeats's version of Oisin's past suggests how a son might attempt to express and resolve conflicting feelings of rage and admiration; in this interpretation, Patrick and Finn represent the dual origin and function of the superego.

Yet if this much is true, it is also true that putting it this way overemphasizes something that seems peripheral to, or at best only one aspect of,

the story Yeats actually tells. The "oedipal" analogy is more appropriate
to Yeats's Gaelic source than to his retelling of it; in this respect what I
have just described is the poem Yeats wanted to write, not the one he
wrote. But it should already be apparent that there is even in the sort of
story he chose an intimation of how ambiguous the outcome of a poet's
version of "man's enterprise" might be. The end of Oisin's journey is
after all not a reunion with the community of men but the familiar lyric
"touch" of narcissistic isolation, depression, and decrepitude. And besides, even if we choose to ignore this and see in his wanderings only the
story of fathers and sons, we would also have to allow that as an "oedipal" fantasy it has a number of features peculiar to itself.

The most obvious of these is that Oisin's real father, Finn, is present in
a decisive way only as nostalgia: as what might be called the "father
lost." Moreover, even in his idealized form as the heroic father that
nostalgia recalls, Finn is curiously powerless in the face of the seductive
claims of his son's "faery bride." Thus in describing Niamh's wooing in
book I (which I quote at length to give the reader some feeling for the
verse), Oisin tells Patrick that

> [We] found on the dove-grey edge of the sea
> A pearl-pale, high-born lady, who rode
> On a horse with bridle of findrinny;
> And like a sunset were her lips,
> A stormy sunset on doomed ships.
>
> . . . .
>
> "O pleasant woman," answered Finn,
>
> . . . .
>
> " . . . where are your noble kith and kin,
> And from what country do you ride?"
>
> "My father and my mother are
> Aengus and Edain, my own name
> Niamh, and my country far
> Beyond the tumbling of this tide."
>
> "What dream came with you that you came
> Through the bitter tide on foam-wet feet?
> Did your companion wander away
> From where the birds of Aengus wing?"
>
> Thereon did she look haughty and sweet:
> "I have not yet, war-weary king,
> Been spoken of with any man;

Yet now I choose, for these four feet
Ran through the foam and ran to this
That I might have your son to kiss."

"Were there not better than my son
That you through all that foam should run?"

"I loved no man, though kings besought,
Until the Danaan poets brought
Rhyme that rhymed upon Oisin's name,
And now I am dizzy with the thought
Of all that wisdom and the fame
Of battles broken by his hands,
Of stories builded by his words
That are like coloured Asian birds
At evening in their rainless lands."

O Patrick, by your brazen bell,
There was no limb of mine but fell
Into a desperate gulph of love!
"You only will I wed," I cried.
. . . .

"O Oisin, mount by me and ride
To shores by the wash of the tremulous tide,
Where men have heaped no burial-mounds,
And the days pass by like a wayward tune,
Where broken faith has never been known,
And the blushes of first love never have flown;
. . . .

And you shall know the Danaan leisure;
And Niamh be with you for a wife."
Then she sighed gently, "It grows late.
Music and love and sleep await,
Where I would be when the white moon climbs,
The red sun falls and the world grows dim."

And then I mounted and she bound me
With her triumphing arms around me,
And whispering to herself enwound me;
But when the horse had felt my weight,
He shook himself and neighed three times:
Caoilte, Conan, and Finn came near,
And wept, and raised their lamenting hands,
And bid me stay, with many a tear;
But we rode out from the human lands.
[I.19–114]

Such passages are likely to leave us impatient and, perhaps, a little puzzled. The verse seems so gratuitously mawkish, overripe, and self-caressing in its diction and rhythm; the events it describes seem so obscure and unrealized. Like the exchange among Hanrahan, Echtge, and the three old women in "Red Hanrahan," that among Finn, Niamh, and Oisin is dreamlike—"'What dream came with you?'" Finn asks—because it, like many dreams, gives us the impression that what is happening is happening for some other reason than the one we are given. The instinctive antipathy between Finn and Niamh ("Were there no better than my son / That you through all that foam should run?") seems as fortuitous as Niamh's need to have his son "to kiss" or Oisin's sudden fall into "a desperate gulph of love." The quantity and quality of feeling expressed, in other words, seems to have an unconscious (or, to put it in a more Yeatsian way, a "symbolic") determination and resonance.

The format of the encounter, as we have already observed, suggests that the resonance is oedipal. Even if we had no other reasons for assuming that Niamh represented maternal forces, the distinctly infantile quality of Oisin's relationship to her ("and whispering to herself enwound me") would be enough for the sake of argument. And yet if this seems true, it is also true that Yeats is imagining not the defeat of fathers by sons (much less of sons by fathers) but the defeat of both by the mother: "Then I mounted and she bound me / . . . Finn came near, / And wept, . . . / And bid me stay." In *Oisin* the father and son are not rivals for the mother; *the father and mother are rivals for the son*. The encounter that opens the poet-hero's reminiscences is a drama not of paternal power but of paternal weakness. Its "oedipal" content is the way fathers fail to preserve their sons from their helpless infatuation with mothers.[5]

It is this failure, and not incestuous passion alone, that precipitates Oisin into the Land of the Young and accounts for his subsequent wanderings in search of his idealized "father lost." In this respect, Oisin's recollections are a Telemachy, although the analogy between his wanderings and the first four books of the *Odyssey* only emphasizes what is different about Yeats's way of imagining the story of fathers and sons. Unlike Odysseus, Finn never rejoins his son to affirm the continuity of the heroic communal and conjugal order: he never becomes the "father found." In his absence, his son's willingness to abandon the privileged but too absorbing love that "enwinds" him becomes not an act of obedience leading to autonomy and adulthood but an act of treachery leading to narcissistic decrepitude. Oisin's journey, unlike that of Telemachus, is not the long way home but a short cut to the land of the very old, Patrician Ireland, the land of nuns and mothers, where the only vocations for a man are prayer and poetry. Finn's *nostos* begins and ends in his son's nostalgia; in "Holy Ireland" only those who have chosen "second best," like Oisin and the "wild old wicked man" of the *Last Poems,* prefer to recall what Saint Patrick says are "the bad old days." As Yeats would put it years later in a bitterer mood and a more contemporary metaphor, mourning the loss of O'Leary, the old Fenian whose "noble head" he had so admired in his youth,

> What need you, being come to sense,
> But fumble in a greasy till
> And add the halfpence to the pence
> And prayer to shivering prayer, until
> You have dried the marrow from the bone?
> For men were born to pray and save:
> Romantic Ireland's dead and gone,
> It's with O'Leary in the grave.
> ["September 1913," 1–8]

The ironical tone of the lyric poet in "September 1913" and the other poems like it that appeared in *Responsibilities* in 1914 ("The Grey Rock," "To a Wealthy Man," "Paudeen," "The Dolls," and "A Coat," among others) is not, of course, the tone of the epic poet-hero of *Oisin*. Oisin remains to the end incapable of even the most ambivalent conspiracy with fate. "When life in my body has ceased," he tells Patrick,

> I will go to Caoilte, and Conan, and Bran, Sceolan, Lomair,
> And dwell in the house of the Fenians, be they in flames or at feast.

The passionate nostalgia that preserves Oisin from ironic despair is something found nowhere else in Yeats's poetry, except perhaps in his aesthetic canonization of the martyrs of the Rising in "Easter 1916." But his predicament is common to all the Yeatsian speakers who identify themselves as men among men and whose subjects are "public": those, that is, who align themselves with the communal and dramatic world of history rather than the lyric, obsessive, and "eternal" world of the Muse. For Yeats, the hero was related to his community not redemptively but ironically, while the ironist often emerged, especially in *Responsibilities* and the later poetry, as the only possible model for "heroic" behavior. Thus in the ballads included in the *Last Poems,* many of which were written for a series of *Broadsides* meant to "get verse into circulation" among the Irish people,[6] the poet bitterly "sings" of men whose steadfast

nobility sets them apart from "Tom and Dick, and all that troop": of
Parnell, who "fought the might of England / And saved the Irish poor"
only to become the victim of English hypocrisy and Catholic bigotry
because he "loved a lass"; of Roger Casement, the Anglo-Irish public
servant who "died upon the gallows" for Ireland and suffered equally
from the slander aroused by his supposed "diaries"; or of the O'Rahilly,
leader of "the Kerry men" during the Rising who "went to great expense"
to keep them out of Dublin but felt it his duty to "travel half the night" to
get there himself:

> What remains to sing about
> But of the death he met
> Stretched under a doorway
> Somewhere off Henry Street;
> They that found him found upon
> The door above his head
> "Here died the O'Rahilly.
> R.I.P." writ in blood.
>   *How goes the weather?*
> ["The O'Rahilly," 28–36]

The bitter judgment of man's enterprise implicit in such poems (*"How
goes the weather?"*) is shared by a number of others in the *Last Poems*
and echoes in their refrains: *" 'What then?' sang Plato's ghost. 'What
then?' "* ("What Then?"); *"Daybreak and a candle-end"* ("The Wild Old
Wicked Man"); *"fol de rol de rolly O"* ("The Pilgrim"); *"The Colonel
went out sailing"* ("Colonel Martin"); *"What shall I do for pretty
girls / Now my old bawd is dead?"* ("John Kinsella's Lament for Mrs.
Mary Moore"); or, finally, in "The Curse of Cromwell," where the
ironies of "September 1913" blend with the idealistic nostalgia of *Oisin,*

> You ask what I have found, as far and wide I go:
> Nothing but Cromwell's house and Cromwell's murderous crew,
> The lovers and the dancers are beaten into the clay,
> And the tall men and the swordsmen and the horsemen, where are
>   they?
> And there is an old beggar wandering in his pride—
> His fathers served their fathers before Christ was crucified.
>   *O what of that, O what of that,*
>   *What is there left to say?*
> [1–8]

We have not yet arrived at a clear way of rendering the full complexity
of feeling expressed in the Yeatsian irony. What is clear at this point is

that the story of the "curse" that afflicts Yeats's public men is in part a story of an attempt to replace the "woman lost" with the idealization of, and identification with, an equally ephemeral paternal figure ("His fathers served their fathers . . . *O what of that*"). The sense of something gloriously "absent" from life that reduces such sons to ironic beggary is in turn related to the father's own narcissistic weaknesses. A whole complex of "heroic" and conjugal antagonisms is dramatized in the Cuchulain plays; but in *Oisin* it is expressed primarily as an aspect of the story of fathers and sons, of the poet-hero whose epic wanderings in search of his lost past have yet to be discussed in detail.

Three Enchanted Islands

In its least complicated sense, the sense that the narrative fiction invites us most strongly to entertain, Oisin's wanderings are a movement in time and space. But "wandering" can be used to describe the poem in another sense, that suggested by Patrick in the second line:

> You who are bent, and bald, and blind,
> With a heavy heart and a wandering mind,
> Have known three centuries, poets sing,
> Of dalliance with a demon thing.

In terms of the poem's narrative present—its "frame narrative," the conversation between Oisin and Patrick—Oisin's story is a representation of psychological movement; more specifically, of the sort of "wandering" that implies obsession, madness, and in this case poetic inspiration, for it is in the wanderings of his mind that Oisin finds the matter for his song. The "ancient" Oisin's retrospective wanderings are in this respect identical with the much more explicitly subjective geographical metaphor for the movement of the mind in time past elaborated by the decrepit speaker of "The Tower" thirty-five years later:

> I pace upon the battlements and stare
> On the foundations of a house, or where
> Tree, like a sooty finger, starts from the earth;
> And send imagination forth
> Under the day's declining beam, and call
> Images and memories
> From ruin or from ancient trees. . . .
> [17–24]

This is the stanza that introduces us to the many-layered and circuitous "wanderings" of the poet's mind that lead at last to the "labyrinth" presided over by the "woman lost." It is interesting to observe, consequently, that the threshold to her domain in book I of *Oisin* is identified by the same striking image, the "sooty finger." Oisin has mounted the magical horse and, wound in Niamh's white arms and lulled by her songs, has crossed the sea past certain mysterious "phantoms" to come in sight of the Land of the Young:[7]

> The horse . . . raced,
> Neighing along the lifeless waste;
> Like sooty fingers, many a tree
> Rose ever out of the warm sea;
> And they were trembling ceaselessly,
> As though they were all beating time,
> Upon the centre of the sun,
> To that low laughing woodland rhyme.
> And, now our wandering hours were done,
> We cantered to the shore, and knew
> The reason of the trembling trees:
> Round every branch the song-birds flew,
> Or clung thereon like swarming bees;
> While round the shore a million stood
> Like drops of frozen rainbow light,
> And pondered in a soft vain mood
> Upon their shadows in the tide,
> And told the purple deeps their pride,
> And murmured snatches of delight.
> [I.169–87]

The land of the vaguely onanistic "trembling trees," so strangely encrusted with multitudinous, jewel-like, self-absorbed "murmuring" life, is Niamh's country, the Tír na nÓg of Yeats's Ossianic source, which he variously referred to as the island of "the Living," of "Dancing," and of "gaiety."[8] It is, we are told, a land of joy, where there is no death, change, or sadness. It is thus the antithesis of the Ireland Oisin now inhabits, and he describes his sojourn there to Patrick as follows:

> O Patrick! for a hundred years
> I chased upon that woody shore
> The deer, the badger, and the boar.
> O Patrick! for a hundred years
> At evening on the glimmering sands,
> Beside the piled-up hunting spears,

These now outworn and withered hands
Wrestled among the island bands.
O Patrick! for a hundred years
We went a-fishing in long boats.

. . . .
O Patrick! for a hundred years
The gentle Niamh was my wife;
But now two things devour my life;
The things that most of all I hate:
Fasting and prayers.
[I.343–60]

The description, which immediately precedes Oisin's first attack of nostalgia for his father's "blood-bedabbled plains," suggests that except for the absence of death, change, and sorrow, Niamh's country is much like any other: a place where men hunt, fight, fish, and marry. Yeats's version is in this instance quite close to the spirit of the Gaelic original, in which Oisin not only marries Niamh but also has three children by her.[9] Yet the passage is in fact only a small part of the lines describing life in the Land of the Young in *Oisin,* most of which are given over to an untraditional and very Yeatsian elaboration of the traditional conception. Something of the quality of the elaboration has already been suggested by the "trembling trees" passage quoted above. Most of it—about 120 lines— consists of three lengthy "songs," two sung by the island's inhabitants and one by their king, Aengus.[10] Taken together, these songs, which Oisin says are accompanied by a kind of "rushing" choral dance, give the joys of Yeats's "Isle of the Living" an eerie and apocalyptic quality similar to that of "The Secret Rose" or, more aptly, of the "unbound" threat to consciousness of "The Hosting of the Sidhe":

The host is rushing 'twixt night and day,
And where is the hope or deed as fair?
Caoilte tossing his burning hair,
And Niamh calling *Away, come away.*
[13–16]

And indeed, if anything is clear about the sort of "joy" Oisin describes besides the sometimes overwhelming monotony of the verse he describes it in, it is that it is quite different from, and even opposed to, the sort of solid comforts that he tells Patrick he enjoyed "a hundred years." Thus, for example, when Oisin tries to entertain his new companions with a song of "human joy," they hear only "the saddest harp in all the world" and take him for enlightenment to where Aengus, their king, "dreams from sun to sun, / A druid dream of the end of days / When the stars are to wane and the world be done":

> And now, still sad, we came to where
> A beautiful young man dreamed within
> A house of wattles, clay, and skin;
> One hand upheld his beardless chin,
> And one a sceptre flashing out
> Wild flames of red and gold and blue,
> Like to a merry wandering rout
> Of dancers leaping in the air;
> And men and ladies knelt them there
> And showed their eyes with teardrops dim,
> And with low murmurs prayed to him,
> And kissed the sceptre with red lips,
> And touched it with their finger-tips.
> [I.247–59]

In response to their caresses their young dreaming king holds his scepter up and launches into a disquisition on "joy." Joy, he says, is the seminal principle of creation, which "wakes the sluggard seeds of corn" and "makes the little planets run." Without it,

> "There were an end of change and birth,
> And Earth and Heaven and Hell would die,
> . . . .
> Folded like a frozen fly;
> Then mock at Death and Time with glances
> And wavering arms and wandering dances."
> [I.270–75]

"Of old," he continues, men's hearts too were "drops of silver joy"; now they "are slaves, / And toss and turn in narrow caves." "But here," he reminds his subjects in conclusion, "there is nor law nor rule,"

> "And here there is nor Change nor Death,
> But only kind and merry breath,
> For joy is God and God is joy."
> [I.284–86]

Thus encouraged, Oisin and his companions begin "a wild and sudden dance" which sweeps them down to the seashore where, like the birds, they bend their "swaying bodies down"

> And to the waves that glimmer by
> That sloping green De Danaan sod

[Sing,] "God is joy and joy is God,
And things that have grown sad are wicked,
And things that fear the dawn of the morrow
And the grey wandering osprey Sorrow."
[I.298–303]

Such passages—and there are, as I have said, three rather lengthy ones in book I—are not made any easier to read by the manifest inconsistency of their metaphysics. How, for instance, does one reconcile the "joy" that is the source of "change and birth" with the "joy" extolled by those who live where there is no "Change"? But whatever difficulty we may have in understanding what they may think about it, it is at least fairly clear how they behave and feel when it possesses them. The swaying ecstasy, the "wavering arms" and "glances" of the multitudinous community of "wandering dancers" is reminiscent of the ecstatic "we" that unites dancer and dance in "Among School Children"; while the solipsistic grandiosity and self-absorption ("God is joy and joy is God") of the dancers themselves suggests the "mirror-resembling dream" apostrophized in "The Tower" and the "self-delighting" "radical innocence" of "A Prayer for My Daughter." Their beatitude, in short, is narcissistic, and it is represented in ways that suggest the overwhelming feeling of well-being associated with its complementary "secondary structures."

It is equally important to notice, however, that here the narcissistic content of what Yeats imagines—associated, once again, with the apocalyptic "dream of the end of days" that Aengus dreams in his "Druid swoon"—is elaborated in a context whose outer form, at least, suggests a preoccupation with issues and relationships from a later stage of psychic development. There is in particular the explicit opposition between the young dreaming god-king, Aengus, and the "Time and Fate and Change" which, we are told in a later choral song, are ruled by another force, the God who is *not* joy and who rules the stars "with an iron rod" and an "iron bond,"

"But we in a lonely land abide
Unchainable as the dim tide,
With hearts that know nor law nor rule,
And hands that hold no wearisome tool,
Folded in love that fears no morrow,
Nor the grey wandering osprey Sorrow."
[I.337–42]

The rhetoric is revolutionary, and so, it seems, is the intent:[11] the "rod" that enslaves is not the "flashing sceptre" that Aengus holds up to announce his dispensation. Yet in spite of the radical reformation of the nature of experience that it implies, the scepter of Aengus is not the instrument of revolution. As the song rather lamely concludes, there is no need for change in the "lonely" place where the repression of the "unchainable" will never comes. The God of Time and Fate and Change, who is presumably also the God of Patrick's Ireland, rules elsewhere; the "hearts that know nor law nor rule" hold themselves aloof and traffic not in revolution but in mockery. And this, as Yeats himself would observe years later in the aftermath of real revolution, is itself a mockery:

> Mock mockers after that,
> That would not lift a hand maybe
> To help good, wise or great
> To bar the foul storm out, for we
> Traffic in mockery.
> ["Nineteen Hundred and Nineteen," 108–12]

In fact the interests of the beardless young man who holds his flashing scepter up are not those of the oedipal revolutionary but, as the content of his "Druid dream" indicates, those of pregenital narcissism. Despite his outward show of phallic aggressiveness—his scepter defies the "iron rod" of God—he is content to abide in a lonely land, "folded in love" and dreaming of the apocalyptic end of days. That Aengus, who is nominally both Niamh's father and the Celtic god of love, represents some form of genital sexuality is undeniable; but at the same time everything about the way Yeats imagines him and the land he rules suggests that here, as in "Among School Children," the "parable" of genitality has been altered to express the more archaic, less differentiated, and consequently more "spiritual" and "apocalyptic" satisfactions and anxieties of narcissism. The Land of the Young is a place where the oedipal resolution of the conflicts of mothers and sons has not occurred and cannot occur. The paternal God of Time and Fate and Change, the infinitely powerful yet perpetually absent antagonist whom Yeats would ironically refer to as "the old man in the skies" in the *Last Poems*, is only rhetorically available. Significantly, it is Oisin's desire for real, confrontable opponents and the "blood-bedabbled plains" on which the companionship of men is forged "equal to good or grievous chance" that finally drives him from Aengus's "lonely land":

> We found the horse and bridled him,
> For we knew well the old was over.

The second episode in Oisin's wanderings, variously referred to in the poem as the "Island of Victories" and the "Isle of Many Fears,"[12] is, like the first, an elaboration of a passage in the Gaelic original, and as in the first episode, here also the details of the elaboration are a reinterpretation. In the Ossianic poem, Oisin's victorious battle with an evil Fomorian giant for the liberty of a captive maiden occurs on the way to the Land of the Young: after three days' fighting Oisin kills and buries him, and the maiden is set free. The narrative function of the episode in the original is that of a "labor" that must be performed before the goal of the journey—Niamh and eternal youth—can be reached. As such it is also, in a straightforwardly "heroic" way, an oedipal fantasy in which the object of ambivalence (the beloved but castrating father) is resolved into two "objects" (Niamh's father, who greets Oisin as his son-in-law in the Land of the Young, and the evil Fomorian).

Yeats's placing of this event after Oisin's visit to the country of Niamh consequently suggests that here too he felt the need to alter something to fit his conception of the sort of past a poet-hero might remember. In its new position, the episode is part of the story of Oisin's nostalgia and his ambivalent dissatisfaction with Niamh, not his desire for her. The Island of Victories leads not toward but away from the sort of resolution implied by the Ossianic version. The latent content of the fantasy expressed by the narrative transition from book I to book II is the wish not for the resolution but for the initiation of the oedipal conflict that frees sons from mothers, and it is interesting to note that it is precisely this role (initiation rather than resolution) that the "dusky demon" Yeats supplies in the place of the Fomorian giant fills best.

Oisin's antagonist in Yeats's version is a "shape-changer" reminiscent of the Old Man of the Sea Menelaus meets in his wanderings.[13] Unlike that monster, however, this demon is "unsubduable," the representation of an antagonism that is perpetually and unresolvably renewed. His home is an island of "dark towers," where Niamh and Oisin find, at the entrance to a huge and slimy hall built by Manannan, the god of the sea, a lady "with eyes like funeral tapers" chained to two "old eagles." Oisin engages himself as her deliverer and fights from dawn to dusk with the protean demon who holds her in thrall:

> ... He changed and ran
> Through many shapes: I lunged at the smooth throat
> Of a great eel; it changed, and I but smote
> A fir-tree roaring in its leafless top;
> And thereupon I drew the livid chop

> Of a drowned dripping body to my breast;
> Horror from horror grew; but when the west
> Had surged up in a plumy fire, I drave
> Through heart and spine; and cast him in the wave
> Lest Niamh shudder.
> [II.174–83]

Oisin and the two women feast and celebrate the demon's death for three days, singing "of loves and angers without sleep, / And all the exultant labours of the strong." But on the fourth morning he finds, revived and "dropping sea-foam on the wide stair, / That demon dull and unsubduable." The battle is rejoined and the demon again killed at sunset and thrown into the sea, and again he emerges "new healed" on the fourth day; so, year after year, Oisin occupies himself in "endless feast [and] endless war." Finally, at the end of a hundred years, Oisin sees a beech bough riding on the waves as he stands on the stairway of the hall:

> . . . And my heart grew sore,
> Remembering how I had stood by white-haired Finn
> Under a beech at Almhuin and heard the thin
> Outcry of bats.
>
>   And then young Niamh came
> Holding that horse, and sadly called my name;
> I mounted. . . .
> [II.226–31]

What is most striking about Oisin's battle with the demon is, as Yeats himself would put it in "The Circus Animals' Desertion," its "vanity." Psychologically there is a similarity between this expression of the magnificent meaninglessness of "heroic" oedipal conflict—an ambivalence toward male identity expressed elsewhere as irony—and the powerlessness of the "father lost," Finn, in his confrontation with Niamh at the beginning of book I. Both the obsessive renewal and the ultimate indecisiveness of the antagonism between Oisin and his demonic opponent reflect the unresolved aspect of the story of fathers and sons that condemns Oisin to a life of "wandering" in the maternal world. In neither of the versions of the triangular oedipal constellation—Oisin/Finn/Niamh and Oisin/demon/lady—is the nominal "father" ever able to establish what might be called the normal paternal relationship, whether of possession or antagonism, with either mother or son. Despite the rhetorical context of Oisin's battles—the songs of "loves and angers without sleep, / And all the exultant labours of the strong"—much of the verse in book II suggests something oddly antiheroic and even pitiful about the ruler of the Isle of Many Fears. These are Oisin's first impressions:

> ... When through the great door
> The dawn came in, and glimmered on the floor
> With a pale light, I journeyed round the hall
> And found a door deep sunken in the wall,
> The least of doors; beyond on a dim plain
> A little runnel made a bubbling strain,
> And on the runnel's stony and bare edge
> A dusky demon dry as a withered sedge
> Swayed, crooning to himself an unknown tongue:
> In a sad revelry he sang and swung
> Bacchant and mournful, passing to and fro
> His hand along the runnel's side, as though
> The flowers still grew there: far on the sea's waste
> Shaking and waving, vapour vapour chased,
> White high frail cloudlets, fed with a green light,
> Like drifts of leaves, immovable and bright,
> Hung in the passionate dawn. He slowly turned:
> A demon's leisure: eyes, first white, now burned
> Like wings of kingfishers; and he arose
> Barking.
> [II.151–70]

Or again, here is the "monotone" Niamh and Oisin hear him singing as they ride away from the island and its still captive lady after a hundred years:

> "I hear my soul drop down into decay,
> And Manannan's dark tower, stone after stone,
> Gather sea-slime and fall the seaward way,
> And the moon goad the waters night and day,
> That all be overthrown.
>
> "But till the moon has taken all, I wage
> War on the mightiest men under the skies,
> And they have fallen or fled, age after age.
> Light is man's love, and lighter is man's rage;
> His purpose drifts and dies."
> [II.235–44]

The protean power that gives Oisin's antagonist the final victory over "the mightiest men under the skies" is directly related to his ironic judgment of their "purpose." The rather unprepossessing demon who mourns and croons by the dry stream is powerful because he is unconfrontable, and unconfrontable because he refuses to acknowledge the significance of oedipal aspiration: he is finally victorious because he can tolerate an infinite number of defeats. The reason for this peculiarly ironic (and peculiarly Yeatsian) version of the event that otherwise would give meaning to the purposes of men is not yet clear, but it can be observed that the presence of this "protean father" is contextually related to the absence of power—the power that might have made it a different kind of story. One of the conditions of the soul's decay on the Island of Victories is the absence of its lord, Manannan, whom Oisin describes to Patrick as being (or having been) unimaginably powerful. After releasing the lady from her chains, Oisin and Niamh accompany her into a colossal hall:

> . . . We climbed the stair to a high door;
> A hundred horsemen on the basalt floor
> Beneath had paced content: we held our way
> And stood within: clothed in a misty ray
> I saw a foam-white seagull drift and float
> Under the roof, and with a straining throat
> Shouted, and hailed him: he hung there a star,
> For no man's cry shall ever mount so far;
> Not even your God could have thrown down that hall;
> Stabling His unloosed lightnings in their stall,
> He had sat down and sighed with cumbered heart,
> As though His hour were come.
> [II.101–12]

Oisin and Niamh cross the hall with the lady, who finds a torch, disappears for a moment through a "dim doorway," and returns "holding a second light / Burning between her fingers." She gives it to Oisin, who sees that he is holding "a sword whose shine / No centuries could dim" on which the name "Manannan" is written in Ogham letters:

> That sea-god's name, who in deep content
> Sprang dripping, and, with captive demons sent
> Out of the sevenfold seas, built the dark hall
> Rooted in foam and clouds, and cried to all
> The mightier masters of a mightier race;
> And at his cry there came no milk-pale face
> Under a crown of thorns and dark with blood,
> But only exultant faces.
> [II.129–36]

The tone of Oisin's description of the absent god who built the hall and his ecstatic apostrophe to the "exultant faces" of his "mightier race"—

not unlike, it should be noted, his way of describing the pagan exuberance of Finn's race—suggest an implicit similarity between the predicament of the son who wanders in search of the ideal lost father and that of the son whose father is "found" but unconfrontable. Indeed, despite the manifest differences and the apparent antagonism between the demon and Manannan, one has the impression that both are somehow manifestations of the same "protean" forces, metaphorically associated with the sea. This blurring of the absent and present proprietors of the gigantic hall is suggested not only by Oisin's references to the "captive demons" who built it but also by the captive maiden's way of describing her oppressor:

> "Neither the living, nor the unlabouring dead,
> Nor the high gods who never lived, may fight
> My enemy and hope; demons for fright
> Jabber and scream about him in the night;
> For he is strong and crafty as the seas
> That sprang under the Seven Hazel Trees,
> And I must endure and hate and weep,
> Until the gods and demons drop asleep,
> Hearing Aedh touch the mournful strings of gold."
> [II.79–87]

In a number of respects—apocalyptic associations (Aedh is the Celtic god of death), transcendent strength, mastery of "demons," and identification with the "springing" waters of the sea—the maiden might be repeating Oisin's description of Manannan. One might be led to wonder, in fact, whether Oisin (or Yeats) is the only one who cannot see the obvious: that his unnamed demonic opponent *is* the sea god who, according to Celtic tradition, was "the master of tricks and illusions."[14] This ironic possibility is, in this poem at least, never made explicit; but its existence suggests a corresponding conclusion about the psychological "springs" of the two "fathers" Oisin confronts in Manannan's dark tower. What Oisin imagines as he stands under the hall's vast dome and what he finds by the "little runnel" beyond "the least of doors" are both expressions of the same feeling of unfulfilled filial longing. What seems on one hand to be more than it is is also on the other less than it seems; the hyperbolically overvalued "father lost" (whose sword cannot bring victory) and the ironically undervalued "father found" (whose victories are not of the sword) are complementary versions of the felt discrepancy between the kind of father a son might wish for and the kind he gets.[15]

I have already commented on the relationship between the lost father and Yeats's characteristically ironic sense of "man's purpose" in general.

It is interesting to note, however, that the complementary images of the absent oedipal figure are also characteristic of Yeats's interpretation of his purpose as "poet-hero" in particular—that is, as the artist who "covets the honour" of his fellowmen. Something of this interpretation of Oisin's "vain battle" is already incipient in book II. As the poet-hero waits, Manannan's sword in hand, for the first encounter in his endless war with the protean demon, there is the intimation of an audience: he sees

> A dome made out of endless carven jags,
> Where shadowy face flowed into shadowy face,
> Looked down on me; and in the self-same place
> I waited hour by hour, and the high dome,
> Windowless, pillarless, multitudinous home
> Of faces, waited; and the leisured gaze
> Was loaded with the memory of days
> Buried and mighty.
> [144–51]

The sea of faces that fills the immeasurable vacancy of Manannan's dome ("No man's cry shall ever mount so far") and "looks down" on Oisin suggests an idealized audience associated with the "father lost" whose sword he holds, the exultant faces of the heroic community he wishes to rejoin, summoned by nostalgia and "loaded with the memory of days / Buried and mighty." It is in the name of this community that Oisin engages in his endless and futile war with the demon and fills the hall with epic songs "of loves and angers without sleep / And all the exultant labours of the strong." Yet the shadowy and flowing quality of the multitude that fills the void also suggests the complementary image of the protean opponent that, in the later poetry, is associated with the degraded "reality" of "Tom and Dick and all that troop." It is interesting to compare the passage just quoted with another description of vain battle and a meeting by a stream, this time in "The Fisherman" (1916):

> It's long since I began
> To call up to the eyes
> This wise and simple man.
> All day I'd looked in the face
> What I had hoped 'twould be
> To write for my own race
> And the reality;
> The living men that I hate,
> The dead man that I loved,

The craven man in his seat,
The insolent unreproved,

. . . .
The beating down of the wise
And great Art beaten down.

Maybe a twelvemonth since
Suddenly I began,
In scorn of this audience,
Imagining a man,
And his sun-freckled face,
And grey Connemara cloth,
Climbing up to a place
Where stone is dark under froth,
And the down-turn of his wrist
When the flies drop in the stream;
A man who does not exist,
A man who is but a dream;
And cried, "Before I am old
I shall have written him one
Poem maybe as cold
And passionate as the dawn."
[6–40]

There are, this poet says, two sorts of audience. One is the ideal "face," "a man who does not exist" who is associated with the vacancies of the skies and the passionate dawn and, implicitly, with the lost "dead man that I loved";[16] the other, "the reality" of his race (ironically, the object of Oisin's Fenian nationalism), the audience that does exist, craven, insolent, and philistine, but ultimately "dull and unsubduable," that Yeats scorns so bitterly in both the late ballads and, during the years of his early "estrangement" and "responsibilities," in poems like "September 1913" and "At the Abbey Theatre":[17]

Dear Craoibhin Aoibhin, look into our case.
When we are high and airy hundreds say
That if we hold that flight they'll leave the place,
While those same hundreds mock another day
Because we have made our art of common things,
So bitterly, you'd dream they longed to look
All their lives through into some drift of wings.
You've dandled them and fed them from the book
And know them to the bone; impart to us—
We'll keep the secret—a new trick to please.

> Is there a bridle for this Proteus
> That turns and changes like his draughty seas?
> Or is there none, most popular of men,
> But when they mock us, that we mock again?[18]

The haughty tone of this treatment of "the reality" by the man who readily admitted that he "coveted" its honors when they were finally granted him was maintained throughout Yeats's career, from the "new commonness" denounced in "In the Seven Woods" (1902) to the shrieking crowds described in "High Talk" (1938). Its "mockery" is in part an expression of the general indictment of "man's enterprise" made by the "images" that mothers worship in "Among School Children": the poet's relation to his audience is a form of narcissistic self-consciousness. But the passage from *Oisin* suggests that when the poet's self-consciousness takes this form it also expressed the way his enterprise in particular is further complicated by the "vain battle" that the sons of absent fathers are condemned to wage endlessly. In such poems, the speaker portrays himself as someone heroically but fruitlessly allied with "a man who does not exist" against a "reality" that mocks him with its protean evasiveness. The face of the crowd, real or imaginary, was for Yeats always either an idealized vacancy or a sea of faces, never the exultant face by the flowing stream that, as both adversary and friend, would at last clear the enterprise of art from the indictment of the mocking Muse and her degraded, protean lover. In its absence, the only alternative to irony is the reconstitution of a private, lyric "audience," the narcissistic "community of the self" afforded by the "cold and passionate" solipsism of the "upstanding men" apostrophized in "The Tower" who, like the Fisherman,

> climb the streams until
> The fountain leap, and at dawn
> Drop their cast at the side
> Of dripping stone,

or those who, like "my Self" in "A Dialogue of Self and Soul" and Oisin as he waits for the dawn under Manannan's dome, feel themselves merging with a "buried and mighty" multitudinous "we."

In the context of poems like "The Fisherman" and "At the Abbey Theatre," then, the sword that the poet-hero holds as he endures the "leisured gaze" of the shadowy faces is an ironic symbol not only of the vanity of a son's phallic grandiosity but of the oedipal vicissitudes of the

great Art as well: of the unresolvable aspect of the poet's creative purposes implicit in Yeats's early conviction that "a man must know how to
speak in Ireland just as a man in old times had to carry a sword."[19] On
the whole, Oisin's reminiscences in book II suggest a complementary and
overdetermined relationship between the private and public functions of
art which, taken together, comprise a complex of relationships that includes poet, Muse, and audience. This aesthetic complex is Yeats's version of the oedipus complex: the vain attempt of the son to resolve his
narcissistic relationship with the mother by engaging in an unresolvable
conflict with the protean "father found" in the name of the idealized
"father lost":

> "But till the moon has taken all, I wage
> War on the mightiest men under the skies,
> And they have fallen or fled, age after age.
> Light is man's love, and lighter is man's rage;
> His purpose drifts and dies."

The "vain battle" that characterizes Yeats's way of imagining the
episode on the Isle of Victories is not the sort of encounter that is likely to
lead a son, and particularly as perplexed a son as Oisin, out of the Land
of the Young. But Niamh has not yet exhausted the alternatives. When,
after a hundred years, Oisin sees the beech bough on the waves that
makes his "heart grow sore, / Remembering how he had stood by
Finn / Under a beech at Almhuin," Niamh murmurs to him,

> . . . "Love, we go
> To the Island of Forgetfulness, for lo!
> The Islands of Dancing and of Victories
> Are empty of all power."
>
> "And which of these
> Is the Island of Content?"
>
> "None know," she said;
> And on my bosom laid her weeping head.
> [II.245–50]

The account of Oisin's stay on the Island of Forgetfulness in book III
is Yeats's only completely original addition to the story of the poet's
wanderings. It is also the shortest episode in the poem, although like the
others it represents a narrative time of 100 years.[20] It is, as Niamh
implies, the last to be "emptied of all power" by wandering, both pro-
spectively as the final effort of the "woman lost" to prevent her lover's

inevitable betrayal of her world and retrospectively as the stage of reminiscence that frees the "wandering mind" of the poet from the depressive and hypochondriacal obsession with the past that is the result of that
betrayal. The power that is the last to be "emptied" is that of "Forgetfulness" or, as Yeats would put it in "The Circus Animals' Desertion," of
"repose." The temptation it offers is apparently simply a version of the
oblivion of Homer's lotos-eaters, in which the wanderer "forgets the way
home." The shores of the island are described in a way that suggests (and
provokes) an appropriate feeling of waning consciousness:

> Were we days long or hours long in riding, when, rolled in a grisly
>   peace,
> An isle lay level before us, with dripping hazel and oak?
> And we stood on a sea's edge we saw not; for whiter than new-
>   washed fleece
> Fled foam underneath us, and round us, a wandering and milky
>   smoke.
>
> And we rode on the plains of the sea's edge; the sea's edge barren
>   and grey,
> Grey sand on the green of the grasses and over the dripping trees,
> Dripping and doubling landward, as though they would hasten
>   away,
> Like an army of old men longing for rest from the moan of the seas.
>
> . . . .
>
> And the ears of the horse went sinking away in the hollow night,
> For, as drift from a sailor slow drowning the gleams of the world
>   and the sun,
> Ceased on our hands and our faces, on hazel and oak leaf, the light,
> And the stars were blotted above us, and the whole of the world
>   was one.
> [III.9–24]

The "grisly peace" of the island's marches is followed by a scene of
strange beauty. Inland, Oisin and Niamh find a valley filled with "a
monstrous slumbering folk, / Their naked and gleaming bodies poured
out and heaped by the way. / ... / And each of the huge white creatures
was huger than fourscore men." The giant sleepers have feathers on the
tops of their ears and the claws of birds, and their faces are weary and
beautiful. Their chief holds the magical bell branch, "sleep's forebear, far
sung of the Sennachies." Oisin tries to wake him, but when he does the
huge creature shakes his branch over them, and Oisin and Niamh too lie
down in oblivious sleep. They sleep for 100 years; but as the "heel of the

century falls," Oisin half wakes and sees an exhausted starling fall from the sky "like them that forgathered . . . / When the Fenians made foray at morning." The spell is broken; "the strength of the bell-branch is naught," and once more Oisin longs, "if only a twelve-houred day," to see his father's face again.

> O had you seen beautiful Niamh grow white as the waters are
>   white,
> Lord of the croziers, you even had lifted your hands and wept:
> But, the bird in my fingers, I mounted, remembering alone that
>   delight
> Of twilight and slumber were gone, and the hoofs impatiently stept.
> [III.109–12]

The exhaustion of the power of the "bell-branch" leads directly to the familiar moment of betrayal and transformation in *Oisin*. The poet-hero will return to Ireland and decrepitude; Niamh will become the "woman lost," the "white woman" on whom the imagination dwells the most. Apparently the "strength" of the bell branch lies in its power to make its hearers "forget"; in this sense it is simply a representation of an escape from the past, and specifically from the nostalgic memory of the masculine community of the Fenians. A few lines further on, when Oisin gives Patrick a list of the things "a century there I forgot," he says, "I forgot / How the fetlocks drip blood in the battle . . . / And the name of the demon whose hammer made Conchubar's sword-blade of old / . . . / That the spear shaft is made out of ash-wood . . . / How the slow, blue-eyed oxen of Finn low sadly at evening tide" (77–84). Yet the sense in which all this is "forgotten" is ambiguous, for Oisin goes on to dream:

> . . . In dreams, mild man of the croziers, driving the dust with their
>   throngs,
> Moved round me, of seamen or landsmen, all who are winter tales;
> Came by me the kings of the Red Branch, with roaring of laughter
>   and songs,
> Or moved as they moved once, love-making or piercing the tempest
>   with sails.
>
> . . . .
>
> And by me, in soft red raiment, the Fenians moved in loud streams,
> And Grania, walking and smiling, sewed with her needle of bone.
> So lived I and lived not, so wrought I and wrought not, with crea-
>   tures of dreams,
> In a long iron sleep, as a fish in the water goes dumb as a stone.
> [III.85–96]

The distinction between the sort of thing Oisin "forgets"—the name of Conchubar's swordmaker or the oxen of Finn, for instance—and what he "dreams" when he seems to see the "kings of the Red Branch" (of whom Conchubar was one) and the "Fenians" moving about him is by no means clear on the face of it. The difference Yeats had in mind, however, is suggested by the meaning assigned to the "bell-branch" in a poem published about a year later than *Oisin,* "The Dedication to a Book of Stories Selected from the Irish Novelists."[21] The speaker, the editor whose selections were published simultaneously in London and New York, addresses himself to the Republican exiles:

> There was a green branch hung with many a bell
> When her own people ruled this tragic Eire;
> And from its murmuring greenness, calm of Faery,
> A Druid kindness, on all hearers fell.
>
> It charmed away the merchant from his guile,
> It turned the farmer's memory from his cattle,
> And hushed in sleep the roaring ranks of battle:
> And all grew friendly for a little while.
>
> Ah, Exiles wandering over lands and seas,
> And planning, plotting always that some morrow
> May set a stone upon ancestral Sorrow!
> I also bear a bell-branch full of ease.
> [1–12]

One way of characterizing the difference between what is forgotten and what is "dreamed" in book III of *Oisin,* then, is to say that it is the difference between reality and fiction, life and art. There are on one hand Oisin's personal memories and on the other the "winter tales" that move about him in his dreams. That the content of both is the same does not alter the fact that they are being experienced differently; the experience of objects through the medium of fiction is not the same as the immediate experience of objects. One could elaborate the distinction psychologically by saying that fiction implies the experience of objects in terms of regressive, narcissistic structures and that it is this reconstitution of the archaic blurring of self and object that Oisin registers in "So lived I and lived not, so wrought I and wrought not." When he arrives on the island, he enters a state of mind in which "the whole of the world was one"; when he describes the effect of the music of the bell branch, he uses the complementary oral images characteristic of narcissistic fantasy, the swallowed and the swallowing:

> Wrapt in the wave of that music, with weariness more than of
>   earth,
> The moil of my centuries filled me; and gone like a sea-covered
>   stone
> Were the memories of the whole of my sorrow and the memories of
>   the whole of my mirth,
> And a softness came from the starlight and filled me full to the
>   bone.
> [III.69–72]   ·

If the strength of the bell branch seems to beckon Oisin even deeper into the Land of the Young, however, it is equally important, indeed critical to our understanding of Yeats's way of imagining what a poet might remember, to observe that Oisin is also a hero. His "heroic" temper perfers "the reality" associated with the world of the father, with all its irony, passion, and decrepitude, to permanent residence in the solipsistic world of the white woman. It is in the hope of recovering the father's world, "if only a twelve-houred day," that he turns aside from Niamh and returns to Ireland to become not the victim but the creative "bearer" of the bell branch in the public interest. The poet's creativity is the outgrowth of both private and public purposes, a complex determined by both narcissistic weakness and paternal absence. The function of the aesthetic elaboration of the contents of his "wandering" mind is, as the poem as a whole suggests, the neutralization of the narcissistic anxiety expressed by depression and hypochondria. But it also, and just as significantly, satisfies his object-related (if ironically disarmed) oedipal aspirations. The poet's "passion" invites the reader to unite himself regressively with an audience of one that is at once the narcissistic, "remade" self and the public community solicited by the poem-as-object, the brotherhood of artist and audience that has a real as well as a delusory claim to being a communion of many selves rather than a depressed and conflict-ridden "I":[22]

> It were sad to gaze on the blessèd and no man I loved of old there;
> I throw down the chain of small stones! when life in my body has
>   ceased,
> I will go to Caoilte, and Conan, and Bran, Sceolan, Lomair,
> And dwell in the house of the Fenians, be they in flames or at feast.

At the same time, however, it is worth emphasizing again that even the very real measure of autonomy, authority, and honor that creativity could (and did) offer Yeats's poet was highly qualified in its effects. The rewards sought by "the work" were not, as he puts it in the little poem called "The Choice," those that might be offered by "the life." Man's enterprise, as he would realize most poignantly when at sixty he seemed to have completed his own, was for him a mockery; Oisin's journeyings could be imagined as complete only in their final irony and ambiguity. "For years," he wrote in 1934,

> I have been preoccupied with a certain myth that was itself a reply to a myth. I do not mean a fiction, but one of those statements our nature is compelled to make and employ as a truth though there cannot be sufficient evidence. When I was a boy everybody talked about progress, and rebellion against my elders took the form of aversion to that myth. I took satisfaction in certain public disasters, felt a sort of ecstasy in the contemplation of ruin, and then I came upon the story of Oisin in Tir nà nOg [sic] and reshaped it into my *Wanderings of Oisin*. . . . I did not pick these images because of any theory, but because I found them impressive, yet all the while abstractions haunted me. I remember rejecting, because it spoilt the simplicity, an elaborate metaphor of a breaking wave intended to prove that all life rose and fell as in my poem. How hard it was to refrain from pointing out that Oisin after old age, its illumination half accepted, half rejected, would pass in death over another sea to another island.[23]

To have done otherwise would indeed have considerably reduced the heroic "simplicity" of Oisin's final vow to the Fenians "in flames or at feast." Yet it would require a naiveté equal to his own not to feel, as Yeats did and I do, that the story of fathers and sons he has to tell implies more complicated "illuminations." Yeats's version of Oisin's tale "re-shapes" the masculine myth to express the vicissitudes of the archaic and, for him, compelling demands of the narcissistic "phantasmagoria" that he was already beginning to conceive in imagery suggesting the tidal pull of "the phases of the moon." In *Oisin* man's purpose, his love, his rage, "drifts and dies"; in the absence of a reliable oedipal teleology he remains, nostalgically, ironically, anxiously, and ecstatically stranded on the threshold between the apocalyptic inner world of pre-oedipal ambivalence and the "progressive" outer world of men and things.

Yeats's version of his own story, moreover, suggests a similar complex of myth and antimyth, an illumination that in his own old age he was still half unwilling to accept. Implicit in his sense of what "rebellion against his elders" might have meant to an aspiring young epic poet is an intimation of narcissistic excitement and anxiety; hence his otherwise puzzling way of identifying their overthrow with an "ecstasy in the contemplation of ruin" more familiar from his lyrics. It is this that accounts more than anything else for the aesthetic failure of his most "public" works. His version of the story of fathers and sons is in *Oisin,* and would remain in his plays, something that he would later diagnose as "over-complicated," insofar as its ostensible subject was overshadowed by the archaic image of the maternal will, Niamh's face "white as the waters are white." Indeed in this respect if in no other Oisin's story is one Yeats might have told about himself, for in both cases the value of poethood was rendered ambiguous by the transforming "touch" of decrepitude. In 1887, just as he was completing the final book of *The Wanderings of Oisin,* he suffered for the first time the debilitating symptoms of "nervous collapse" that would haunt him for the rest of his life.

The Father Found

Yeats's journey out of the Land of the Young, like Oisin's, was protracted, complex, and belated. His earliest memory of his father dates from the spring of 1873, when J. B. Yeats came to Sligo for the funeral of his second son, Bobbie. It was only then, as he was approaching his eighth birthday, that Willie had the "first clear image" of his father "fixed in his imagination." "He had just arrived," he says in *Reveries,* "from London and was walking up and down the nursery floor. He had a very black beard and hair, and one cheek bulged out with a fig that was there to draw the pain out of a bad tooth. One of the nurses (a nurse had come from London with my brothers and sisters) said to the other that a live frog, she had heard, was the best of all."[24]

If the image is clear enough, the feelings it expresses are less so. Besides whatever unremembered complications may have been added by the circumstances of the black-haired stranger's appearance in the nursery—by the observation, for instance, that the death of sons brings back absent fathers—there is in Yeats's memory of him a charming but slightly blurred mixture of the wonder and alarm a child might have felt and the irony of maturer perceptions. The father he remembers is at once formidable and helpless, fiercely bearded and yet as painfully in need of a nurse's care as a younger brother or sister. In this Yeats is faithful not only to the way an adult might remember being a child but also to how even a child might have perceived something of the fundamental contradiction in his father's character.

Of his two "fathers"—the helpless and the formidable—it is the latter who receives the most attention in the *Autobiography* as a whole and in *Reveries* in particular. "Someone to whom I read the book," Yeats wrote his father after he had finished it in 1914, "said to me the other day 'If Gosse had not taken the title you should call it "Father and Son."'"[25] The observation is the obvious one. With the exception of his earliest memories, in which "no one was so important as my grandfather," the story Yeats tells in *Reveries* is that of a son's growth into and out of the influence of a brilliant and opinionated father who took firm, if somewhat belated, control of his son's destiny:

> ... I was sent to a dame school kept by an old woman who stood us in rows and had a long stick like a billiard cue to get at the back rows. My father was still at Sligo when I came back from my first lesson and asked me what I had been taught. I said I had been taught to sing, and he said, "Sing then" and I sang
>
> Little drops of water,
> Little grains of sand,
> Make the mighty ocean,
> And the pleasant land
>
> high up in my head. So my father wrote to the old woman that I was never to be taught to sing again, and afterwards other teachers were told the same thing.[26]

Among the melancholy, self-absorbed, and fatalistic Pollexfens, John Butler Yeats was an anomaly, a defiantly cheerful extrovert, a freethinker who had scorned convention and worldly success in the name of Art. And indeed he would have distinguished himself even in less conventional company. His charm and brilliance in conversation were such that his friend Edward Dowden thought him "a genius," and John Todhunter called him "the only man I ever really worshipped." "Todhunter," Murphy tells us, "visited JBY in London at his Fitzroy Road home and wrote Dowden: 'The man lives in a whirlwind of ideas. It is like breathing pure oxygen after the CO_2 of Dublin.'"[27] Nor did age, which in the intervening fifteen years had turned his black hair and beard pure white, do anything to stale the man whom Oliver Elton met in the late 1880s. In his preface to a posthumous selection of J. B. Yeats's letters, Elton remembers in particular his "large bright eyes, changeful and ever-watchful," and his "peculiar eloquence":

> The conversation was rapid and cheerful. If it were too rapid or buzzed too loudly, Yeats would hold his peace and wait for a pause; and then he might pour forth, without effort or study and

> without rhetoric, and in is soft flexible voice, a stream of his
> peculiar eloquence. The voice is now silent; but for the same play of
> mind and fancy, the same pure good English and naturally good
> rhythm, we have but to turn to Yeats's letters. They are just like his
> talk, and flow on with hardly an erasure.[28]

There was much in such a father for a son to admire, perhaps even to
worship, and soon after his reappearance at Merville J. B. Yeats's "peculiar eloquence" became a pervasive force in his son's life. The family, it
appeared, was now to be reassembled in London. In the years after 1873
the elder Yeats brought first Willie and later the rest of his children back
to London to live with him in Edith Villas, West Kensington. His wife,
however, did not join them until after the birth and death of her sixth
child, Jane Grace, in 1876. By then the family had moved to Norman
Shaw's Pre-Raphaelite "village," Bedford Park. Willie, who had been
tutored by his father at home, was sent to the Godolphin School in
Hammersmith. There, amid the bullying and toadying of the sons of the
English middle class, Susan Yeats's withdrawn and sensitive son suffered
new humiliations and at the same time became aware of a new inner
resource, the image, and probably the very words, of his father. "I have
climbed to the top of a tree by the edge of the playing field," he recalls in
Reveries,

> and am looking at my school-fellows and am as proud of myself as
> a March cock when it crows to its first sunrise. I am saying to
> myself, "If when I grow up I am as clever among grown-up men as
> I am among these boys, I shall be a famous man." I remind myself
> how they think all the same things and cover the school walls at
> election times with the opinions their fathers find in the newspa-
> pers. I remind myself that I am an artist's son and must take some
> work as the whole end of life and not think as the others do of
> becoming well off and living pleasantly.[29]

At the Godolphin School the work that would make him a famous man
was natural science: Willie was particularly partial to entomology. He
remained there until 1880, when the family left Bedford Park to return to
Ireland. At first they lived in cottages at Howth, and Willie attended the
High School in Dublin, where it was at first still one of his ambitions
"some day to write a book about the changes through a twelvemonth
among the creatures of some hole in the rock, and [I] had some theory of
my own, which I cannot remember, as to the colour of sea-anemones:
and after much hesitation, trouble and bewilderment, was hot for argument in refutation of Adam and Noah and the Seven Days."[30] He also

found, however, that now his interest in science "began to fade." Under the influence of an adolescent sexual awakening that felt like a "bursting shell," he began to imagine his "work" in far more grandiose and far less rational terms: "I still carried my green net but I began to play at being a sage, a magician or a poet."[31]

The content of his new ambition suggested a renewal of the unresolved "spiritual" commotions of a much earlier period; but its form continued to be directed by his father's example. "My father's influence upon my thoughts," Yeats says in *Reveries,*

> was at its height. We went to Dublin by train every morning, break-fasting in his studio. He had taken a large room with a beautiful eighteenth-century mantelpiece in a York Street tenement house, and at breakfast he read passages from the poets, and always from the play or poem at its most passionate moment. He never read me a passage because of its speculative interest, and indeed did not care at all for poetry where there was generalisation or abstraction however impassioned.[32]

At the High School Yeats began to write, first in collaboration with a schoolfellow and then by himself, "poetry in imitation of Shelley and of Edmund Spenser, play after play—for my father exalted dramatic poetry above all other kinds."[33] His choice of career, however, at first followed his father's example even more closely. In 1884, after finishing the High School, he decided not to take the examinations for the university; instead, he entered the Metropolitan School of Art where his "father, who came to the school now and then, was [his] teacher."[34]

His apprenticeship was brief, for it was also at about this time that the interest in magic that had accompanied his first poetry blossomed into the "study of psychical research and mystical philosophy" which, according to *Reveries,* was the occasion for his first break with his father's influence. J. B. Yeats, his son says, "had been a follower of John Stuart Mill and so had never shared Rossetti's conviction that it mattered to nobody whether the sun went round the earth or the earth round the sun. But through this new research, this reaction from popular science, I had begun to feel that I had allies for my secret thought."[35]

In March 1885 his first published poetry, "The Song of the Faeries" and "Voices," appeared in the *Dublin University Review;* in June he helped found the Dublin Hermetic Society; in July, just after his twentieth birthday, he left art school to take up literary work exclusively. As a budding poet and student of the occult he was, however, still not entirely his own man. When his first book, *Mosada: A Dramatic Poem,* appeared a year later, it was graced by a "portrait of the author by J. B. Yeats." "I was alarmed," Yeats wrote in 1904 in a copy belonging to John Quinn, "at the impudence of putting a portrait in my first book, but my father was full of ancient and modern instances."[36] His father's impudence was easily outstripped by his own "secret thought." Only a few months before he had begun the task of reviving the voice of "the greatest poet of the Gael."[37]

Oisin took almost two years to write. By the time Yeats finished it, at Sligo in November 1887, his peripatetic father had moved the family to London again, and it was there that *The Wanderings of Oisin and Other Poems* was published by subscription in January 1889.[38] *Oisin* (or *Usheen,* as he sometimes spelled it), and not *Mosada,* would be the book he would prefer to remember as "my first," and it was as its author that he made his first impression on literary London. Oscar Wilde "had, before our first meeting, reviewed my book and . . . praised [it] without qualification; and what was worth more than any review he had talked about it; and now he asked me to eat my Christmas dinner with him believing, I imagine, that I was alone in London."[39] William Morris read it too and told Yeats, "You write my sort of poetry."[40] By the late 1880s he had "already met most of the poets of [his] generation," and found himself "growing jealous" of them. "We will grow jealous of each other," he remembers saying to Ernest Rhys, "unless we know each other and so feel a share in each other's triumph." In 1891 they founded the Rhymers' Club,

> which for some years was to meet every night . . . in an ancient eating house in the Strand called The Cheshire Cheese. Lionel Johnson, Ernest Dowson, Victor Plarr, Ernest Radford, John Davidson, Richard le Gallienne, T. W. Rolleston, Selwyn Image, Edwin Ellis, and John Todhunter came constantly for a time, Arthur Symons and Herbert Horne, less constantly, while William Watson joined but never came and Francis Thompson came once but never joined; and sometimes if we met in a private house . . . Oscar Wilde came.[41]

In short, the young man Yeats remembers being after 1889 in his *Autobiography* was well launched on the voyage to fame imagined by the boy at the Godolphin School. His story, in fact, is no longer that of "Childhood and Youth" but of *The Trembling of the Veil,* the section of his memoirs that covers the years between the completion of *Oisin* in 1887 and his love affair with Olivia Shakespear in 1896. He has emerged from his father's influence as a man among men, praised by the great and an equal of the near great, a founder of institutions for the benefit of all.

There is much in this version of himself that accurately foreshadows the achievements of the mature poet of, for example, "Among School Children." In *The Trembling of the Veil* the gloomy, self-absorbed, and illiterate child of *Reveries* has become someone who is recognizably "the poet William Yeats," and much of the credit for the transformation is due, as he suggests, to his admiration of and competition with his influential father. Yet the picture of public manhood painted there, as a poem like "Among School Children" also suggests, is not without its ambiguities. *The Trembling of the Veil,* like *Reveries,* is misleadingly, if admirably, discreet. "Yesterday," Yeats wrote his father on December 26, 1914, "I finished [*Reveries*]; I have brought them down to our return to London in 1886 or 1887. After that there would be too many living people to consider and they would have besides to be written in a different way. While I was immature I was a different person and I can stand apart and judge. Later on, I should always, I feel, write of other people. I dare say I shall return to the subject but only in fragments."[42]

Much of one's impression of Yeats as a young poet-about-town in his "return to the subject" in *The Trembling of the Veil* is in fact due to his reluctance to speak of anything but the part of his life that had to do with "other people." He seems to have had at that time virtually no private life at all, and it is easy to get the impression, as Oscar Wilde did, that he was "alone in London." This inaccuracy has been partially corrected by the recent publication of the 1916 memoir on which *The Trembling of the Veil* was based; Yeats still considered it "private ... containing much that is not for publication now if ever" when the first part of *The Trembling* was published in 1921.[43] What did not find its way out of the private and into the public record, it now appears, was in part another chapter of the story of fathers and sons. The manuscript opens with a recollection of London in 1887:

> I began to read Ruskin's *Unto This Last,* and this, when added to
> my interest in psychical research and mysticism, enraged my
> father. . . . One night a quarrel over Ruskin came to such a height
> that in putting me out of the room he broke a glass in a picture
> with the back of my head. Another night when we had been in
> argument over Ruskin or mysticism, I cannot now remember what
> theme, he followed me upstairs to the room I shared with my
> brother. He squared up at me, and wanted to box, and when I said
> I could not fight my own father replied, "I don't see why you
> should not." My brother, who had been in bed for some time,

started up in a violent passion because we had awakened him. My father fled without speaking, and my brother turned to me with, "Mind, not a word till he apologizes." Though my father and I are very talkative, a couple of days passed before I spoke or he apologized.

I imagine he feared for my sanity. Everything had become abstract to me.[44]

The process of breaking from his father's influence was considerably more protracted, truculent, and ambiguous than a reader of *Reveries* might suspect. Nor was its outcome as conclusive as *The Trembling of the Veil* might lead us to believe, for in the 1916 memoir the young poet praised by Wilde and Morris suffers in his own estimation from another example. He had at that time, Yeats says, "a conviction that I was without industry and without will. I saw my father painting from morning to night and day after day; I tried to work, not as long as he, but four or five hours. It is only during my recent years that, though I am working very steadily, more than two hours' original composition [does not] bring me almost at once to nervous breakdown. In almost all the members of my family there is some nervous weakness."[45]

In the 1916 memoir, as in *Oisin,* the price of maturity ("When I was immature I was a different person") is decrepitude. Yeats's first significant confrontation with his own nervous weakness had in fact occurred at virtually the same moment that his poet-hero had fallen to the earth in Patrick's Ireland. In the fall of 1887 at Sligo he began to be afflicted, as he told his friend Katherine Tynan a year later, by depression, insomnia, "nerves," and a variety of "colds and headaches," culminating after several weeks in vocal paralysis. The last book of *Oisin* "was the greatest effort of all my things. When I had finished it I brought it round to my Uncle George Pollexfen and could hardly read, so collapsed I was. My voice was quite broken. It really was a kind of vision. It beset me day and night."[46] By the following April, the symptoms had become familiar enough to be called "my collapses." "I thought," he wrote his friend, "I was in for a considerable collapse but it wore off. I could only speak with difficulty at first. I was the same way, only worse, when finishing Oisin."[47]

Much of Yeats's vulnerability to the attacks that led his father to "fear for his sanity" can be attributed to the "Hysterica passio" or "visionary" excitement that accompanied creativity. In 1901, in an essay called "Magic," he would write that "if you speak over-much of the things of Faery your tongue becomes like a stone, and it seems to me . . . that I have often felt my tongue become just so heavy and clumsy";[48] twenty-five years later, in "A Dialogue of Self and Soul," the Soul, intimating the state of idealized fusion in which consciousness "ascends to heaven," finds that "when I think of that my tongue's a stone." The story of the poet in 1887 is the story of sons and mothers, of narcissistic vulnerability or, in the sexual metaphor of *Oisin* and "The Tower," of the overexciting "woman lost." "Women," Yeats says in his 1916 memoir, "filled me with curiosity and my mind seemed never long to escape from the disturbance of my senses. I was a romantic, my head full of the mysterious women of Rossetti and those hesitating faces in the art of Burne-Jones which seemed always anxious for some Alastor at the end of a long journey."[49]

But the story of Yeats's journey, like Oisin's, was more than the story of his obsession with the "hesitating" face "white as the waters are white" that became Maud Gonne's face in 1889. "The almost unendurable strain on my senses" caused by his "dread of the subject of sex" was, he says, greatly augmented by his attempts to emulate his industrious and self-disciplined father. Throughout the *Autobiography,* as the boy who hoped to become a "famous man" and the Nobel laureate who "coveted honour," he is most recognizable to us and to himself as his father's son. Yet it is in this respect that his way of remembering that "exultant face" is also, like Oisin's, most misleading. Of all the "living people" Yeats felt he had to consider in continuing his memoirs past 1887, the most important was J. B. Yeats himself. The elder Yeats's own account of the period covered by his son's "Four Years: 1887–1891," he confessed to his friend and benefactor John Quinn, "was not pleasant to write nor is it pleasant reading, so it cannot appear in my memoirs."[50] He was consequently, he told his daughter Lily, "rather dreading" the appearance of his son's version.[51] His fears were groundless; Yeats's letter to him in December 1914 had been an assurance of discretion. When "Four Years" was serialized in the *Dial* in the summer of 1921 it contained, and still contains, little to offend; it is mostly about "other people."

What remained untold in the first book of *The Trembling of the Veil* was the last chapter of the story of the decay of J. B. Yeats's fortunes. By the late 1880s his house, like Manannan's, had been falling "stone after stone" for some years; by the time his eldest son decided to take up the brand of art "no centuries could dim," it was in imminent danger of going the seaward way for good. The restless wandering of the Yeats family between Ireland and England was among other things the record of steadily increasing financial pressures. The income from the estates in

Kildare that had come down to them from the Butlers had never been large, and J. B. Yeats's portrait painting brought in little or nothing. But with some help from his wealthy father-in-law, it had been enough to keep the family until, in 1880, the income was substantially reduced by the Land War. One of his reasons for returning to Dublin in that year had been the hope of finding more and larger commissions where he was better known. Despite his efforts, nothing prospered. By 1884 the Yeatses were forced to move from their pleasant cottage by the sea in Howth to cheaper lodgings at Ashfield Terrace, Dublin, "in a villa," Yeats says in *Reveries,* "where the red bricks were made pretentious and vulgar with streaks of slate colour, and there seemed to be enemies everywhere."[52]

The real enemies were elsewhere. In 1886 J. B. Yeats was told that his estates were to be sold to his tenants under the provisions of the Ashbourne Act for a sum that would probably only pay what he owed on the mortgage. No more help could be expected from William Pollexfen, whose Sligo firm had begun to lose money in 1882; by 1887 Merville itself had to be sold.[53] The Yeatses' return to London in the spring of that year was an act of economic desperation, and once there they found themselves in very difficult circumstances. There was sometimes no money to buy food, and in the spring of 1888 they were told by the Land Commission that nothing would be realized from the sale of the Kildare property.[54]

It was at this time that, at the age of twenty-two, Yeats began to make the contributions to his family's support that not only complicated his personal and artistic life to a considerable extent but also left him continually "very hard up" until 1913, when friends were able to get him a Civil List pension of £150. The record of his efforts in the decade covered by *The Trembling of the Veil* is in Wade's *Bibliography:* between 1887 and 1896 Yeats edited six books (mostly collections of Irish poetry, fiction, and fairy tales), contributed poems or essays to as many more, and published, in addition to his creative work, some 115 items (essays and reviews) in periodicals.

What J. B. Yeats most dreaded reading in the first chapter of *The Trembling of the Veil,* however, was not the catalog of his misfortunes but an account of his own part in creating them. Happily for him, it was also the side of the story of fathers and sons that Yeats was least willing to commit to paper. Like Oisin's Manannan, J. B. Yeats had a "demonic" alter ego that is discreetly unmentioned even in the "private" 1916 memoir and emerges only fleetingly and indirectly from the nostalgia of

Reveries. In the latter, for example, Yeats recalls that soon after his father had decided to take him back to London in 1874 he heard a Pollexfen aunt say,

> "You are going to London. Here you are somebody. There you will be nobody at all." I knew at the time that her words were a blow at my father not at me, but it was some years before I knew her reasons. She thought so able a man as my father could have found out some way of painting more popular pictures if he had set his mind to it and that it was wrong of him "to spend every evening at his club." She had mistaken, for what she would have considered a place of wantonness Heatherley's Art School.[55]

The nameless aunt whom Yeats here implicitly accuses of all that was worst in the Pollexfen puritanism was, as he would have admitted himself less publicly, only superficially mistaken. The Pollexfens were certainly rather philistine in their values; but in his father's case their opinion was entirely justified. Like his uncle Robert Corbet before him, J. B. Yeats was at best an impractical man. At worst he seems at times to have been deliberately, even resolutely, unsuccessful. His decision to become an artist, for example, was made in spite of an offer by his father's old friend Isaac Butt "to do something for him" in his legal career "that, because of my resolution to go to England, was vain, but it would have been a substantial help to me."[56] His "resolution" had been partly made for him; a judge had discovered his habit of making malicious caricatures during his idle moments in court. "Afterwards," as he vaguely summed it up in his memoirs, "various things happened," and his satirical sketches became the portfolio of a London art student.[57]

In itself the episode seems, as it probably seemed to J. B. Yeats himself at the time, to express his artistic integrity and disdain for what he called "getting on." Yet the career that began as a joke in many ways continued to be one, and his resolution continued to avoid as unswervingly anything that might have been "of substantial help." His difficulty was not just in painting "more popular pictures"; it was in painting any pictures at all. The case of the landscape begun at Burnham Beeches in the spring of 1874 that "changed with the seasons until it was abandoned after the snow had been painted on its banks" is extreme but typical.[58] "He goes," Lady Gregory said years later, "his own way, spoiling portraits as hopefully as he begins them, and always on the verge of a great future."[59]

Worst of all, his hopefulness fed only on failure. In the face of real opportunity it usually evaporated, leaving behind a paralyzing diffidence and unwillingness to prosecute advantages. There is, for instance, his recollection in his *Early Memories* of how Rossetti, whom he greatly admired, "seldom went to picture exhibitions; by rare chance he did go to the Dudley, and saw there a picture of mine which he liked so much that he sent to me by three messengers, one of whom was his brother, an invitation to come and see him. I did not come. I regret it very much. I think I was afraid of the great man; diffident about myself and my work. To be afraid of anything is to listen to the counsels of your evil angel." The angel was hearkened to not once but many times. He also, he goes on to remember, "threw away" a chance to meet George Meredith and adds, "There was another great poet that I missed. Browning had seen a design I had made for a picture of Job's wife bidding him curse God and die, and he came to see me. Unfortunately I was not in my studio when he called." [60]

How much of himself J. B. Yeats may have put into his admirable design remains to be seen. But there is in the analogy between his plight and Job's undeserved sufferings a hint, as in everything else about him, of caricature: John Butler Yeats as Job too easily becomes Job as Mr. Micawber. Besides his exasperating professional attitude, which alone would have been enough to make a Pollexfen bid him curse God and die, Susan Yeats's husband was notoriously unthrifty, a vice he compounded by his unabashed willingness to be supported in part or in full by family or friends until something turned up. Since nothing, either by accident or contrivance, ever did turn up, this meant that in practice he was never, except perhaps in the earliest years of his marriage, self-supporting. In 1907, seven years after his wife's death, he emigrated to New York City ("Anything," he said, "may turn up here"),[61] where he remained until his death in 1922 a contrite but unrepentant remittance man. He once even went so far as to chide his eldest son for the "fuss" he sometimes made over paying out money for his father's support. "In my family," he wrote complacently in 1904, "we have always all of us been in the same situation in life for many generations living naturally and have entirely occupied ourselves with mutual affections and ideas; for instance we supported Aunt Ellen and enabled her to bring up a large family of little children. Among us we gave her an income for about 30 years. There was no fuss—no one in Sligo, above all none of the Pollexfens knew of it."[62]

In later years he was able to muster a more becoming humility toward a son whom fate had unaccountably denied the benefits of an independent income and a "natural" life. Yet if by 1921 he was willing to admit that he had been "an unconscionable burden," it all, in the stream of his eloquent rationalization, came to the same thing. "I do assure you," he wrote Yeats on June 25, "that I have sleepless nights thinking of it. Yet from the moment that you invited my burthening of you, I have given all my thoughts to the portrait of myself. So all my sleepless nights only ended in my going on with the painting. When you see my magnum opus, I think you will forgive me."[63] The portrait of the artist had been commissioned ten years before and it remained unfinished on the day of his death.[64] As it is reproduced as the frontispiece of his *Letters,* it deserves to be set beside his son's "clear image" of him in *Reveries,* for it too, as Yeats accurately anticipated in his preface to his father's *Early Memories,* is the man he had always known. His father

> worked for several years at a large portrait of himself, commissioned by Mr. John Quinn. I have not seen this portrait, but expect to find that he had worked too long upon it and, as often happened in his middle life when, in a vacillation prolonged through many months it may be, he would scrape out every morning what he had painted the day before, that the form is blurred, the composition confused, and the colour muddy. Yet in his letters he constantly spoke of this picture as his masterpiece, insisted again and again, as I had heard him insist when I was a boy, that he had found what he had been seeking all his life.[65]

That the man with black hair and bulging cheek whom his son first remembers pacing so purposefully in the nursery should ultimately make a mockery of his life and purpose was due, in his own opinion, to the rigors of his early education. J. B. Yeats's boyhood had been spent at Atholl Academy on the Isle of Man under a flogging Scots schoolmaster. This misfortune, he came to think, had so weakened him morally "by its constant discipline and vigilance" that when he went up to Trinity "I did not think, I did not work, I had no ambition, I dreamed."[66] These were the years spent at Robert Corbet's castle, "my Capua," whose chained eagles eventually reappeared in book II of *Oisin;* but it was only after he had taken his degree that, he says, he "began to think" under the influence of John Stuart Mill. But by then it was too late for anything but superficial reform. He found himself "making the mistake, common among polemical minded poeple, of thinking that when I was severe to other people and the world generally, I was severe to myself, although in reality I was acquiring the most disagreeable of qualities, picking up the habits of dictatorial emphasis & dogmatism, which I shall now never get rid of. This was not due to Mill's teaching. . . . Never would he have allowed any authoritative self-conceit to come between him and the truth."[67]

He often thought that the characteristics others found so influential—his opinions, his eloquence, even his optimism—were really the symptoms of inner demoralization and despair. At bottom he found himself to be a man without convictions, a dreamer contented with the manipulation of abstractions, and while he often defended his tendency toward vacillation and self-contradiction in theory ("Man's inconsistency," he wrote in *Early Memories,* "is always a charm and it has often been his safe-guard"),[68] in practice he found it of a piece with the most troublesome and depressing aspects of his character. "It always mortifies me to think how cheerful I am, for I am convinced it is a gift which I share with all villains: it is their unsinkable buoyancy that enables these unfortunates to go from disaster to disaster and remain impenitent," he says in *Early Memories* and then complains of his inability to escape "this entangling web of grey theory in which I have spent my life."[69] "I am not at all the man you think I am," he once wrote to John Quinn, "not at all the happy, indifferent, reckless man with 'healthy' nerves; far otherwise. The fact is we both have nerves, only yours rouse your will to action, and they paralyse my will. Of course, as is evident, you are the better friend to others. Yet my sufferings are real, not that that matters except to my-self."[70]

That J. B. Yeats was not the sort of man John Quinn thought him was perhaps no great matter; that he had not been the sort of father his son (or for that matter the rest of his family) needed was the cause of consid-erable anguish to both. Under other circumstances the sort of man he really was might have made less or a different kind of difference. As it was, his efforts to befriend his "curious" eldest son were doomed to failure or at best to an ambiguous kind of success. Describing his first lesson with his father in 1873 at Sligo, Yeats says in *Reveries,*

> Because I had found it hard to attend to anything less interesting than my own thoughts, I was difficult to teach. Several of my uncles and aunts had tried to teach me to read, and because they could not, and because I was much older than children who read easily, had come to think, as I have learned since, that I had not all my faculties. But for an accident they might have thought it for a long time. My father was staying in the house and never went to church, and that gave me the courage to refuse to set out one Sunday morn-ing. I was often devout, my eyes filling with tears at the thought of God and for my own sins, but I hated church. . . . My father said if I would not go to church he would teach me to read. I think now that he wanted to make me go for my grandmother's sake and could think of no other way. He was an angry and impatient

teacher and flung the reading-book at my head, and next Sunday I
decided to go to church. My father had, however, got interested in
teaching me, and only shifted the lesson to a weekday till he had
conquered my wandering mind.[71]

Something of what the son might have hoped to find in an alliance with
his father is suggested by his initial eagerness to exchange the mute and
despondent Christianity of his mother's family for pagan "courage"
and literacy. His later conviction that their meeting was in some sense an
accident, however, also indicates something of the final ambiguity of the
conquest of his mind's wanderings. The reappearance of his lost father,
of course, was not accidental. J. B. Yeats's letters to his wife in the early
1870s show that he had often been "very anxious" about his strange son,
who was "never out of his thoughts." "I think," he wrote Susan on
November 1, 1872, "Willie was greatly disimproved by Merville. He was
coming on from being so much with his mother and away from his
grandfather and dictatorial Aunts. From his resemblance to Elizabeth, he
derives his nervous sensitiveness. I wish he could be made more ro-
bust . . . [but] *not by going to school.*"[72]

Aunt Elizabeth was like Willie in her tendency toward "woolgather-
ing" and her learning difficulties, though neither suffered, as the Pollexfens thought, from any defect of intellect.[73] The difficulty of teaching
such a child might have made anyone angry and impatient, and in J. B.
Yeats's case it was compounded by his fears about the Pollexfen "nervousness." It seems likely, in fact, that his principal reason for reassem-
bling the family in the mid 1870s was therapeutic; something of both the
quality of his anxiety and the hopeful "robustness" of his approach to
resolving such problems is at any rate still apparent in his naively athletic
confrontations with his son in the late 1880s. But what contributed most
to his inability to "square up" with Willie in any way that made more
than a temporary difference was his response not to the "Merville"
influence but to his own. In insisting that his son not be sent to school in
1873, he was implicitly recalling the consequences of his own early education. "Subconsciously," he wrote in his unpublished memoir, "I resolved that [Willie] should be a distinguished man, and I think he caught
the infection from me, so that my anxieties became his anxieties."[74]

In practice, this meant that he also transferred to his son, as he often
did to "the world in general," the "severity" and "dogmatism" that
expressed his own worst fears about himself. Yeats says in *Reveries* that,
up to the time he entered the Godolphin School in Hammersmith, "the
only lessons I had ever learned were those my father taught me, for he

terrified me by descriptions of my moral degradation and he humiliated me by my likeness to disagreeable people."[75] Later, at the High School in Dublin, he was still learning his lessons "in the terror that alone could check my wandering mind."[76] But there was also something in J. B. Yeats's tyrannical ways that his son, and indeed all of his children, recognized for what it was. For all his outward show of quarrelsomeness, severity, and even violence, "Papa" was not a man his family took very seriously. By the mid and late 1880s there is even a note of contempt in the way his sons could face him down in a midnight quarrel, and in 1888 his daughter Lolly wrote in her diary on September 9, "I can hear a murmur of talk from the dining room where Papa and Willie are arguing something or other. Sometimes they raise their voices so high that a stranger might fancy that they were both in a rage, not at all, it is only their way of arguing because they are natives of the Emerald Isle."[77]

His was, as J. B. Yeats would put it when he was in a mood to make a virtue of his defects, a fundamentally "benign" nature, and from time to time he saw it, like everything else about himself, in his son. "This," he wrote him from New York in 1909, "...you get from me; I say this remembering my father's family. They all of them in every fibre of their being were 'the Good People,' in a sense the fairies are not. For that reason people loved them but did not fear them, so they passed making no mark."[78] "Good," he would have added in another mood, in his case meant good for nothing, and the "subconscious" complications of his resolve that Willie, at least, would make his mark were compounded by a corresponding uncertainty about how one best became "distinguished." At the Godolphin School in the 1870s the path had seemed clear: J. B. Yeats had thought, "He will be a man of science; it is a great thing to be a man of science."[79] But a career in the arts was not something he was willing to encourage openly. Indeed, his chief anxiety during his son's years at the High School and art school was that, instead of becoming "distinguished," he was becoming like his father. "This," he wrote in his unpublished memoir, is "a practical world in which the impractical man comes to tribulation of every sort for himself and anyone that might be dependent on him." Thus "a poor man's son should avoid poetry." "Nevertheless," he went on in his impractical way, "I encouraged him. It was a secret between us. I was not anxious to proclaim to the world that I, a poor man, was bringing up my eldest son to be a poet."[80]

Much of the ambiguous "weakness" of Yeats's coming of age as a man and poet in the 1880s and 1890s, then, can be attributed not, as *Reveries* might suggest, to the influence of a father who was too admirable and too severe, but to the "secret" they shared. Like Oisin, Yeats had two fathers: one the "lost" father, the nostalgic vestige, perhaps, of the way a man had once impressed a boy of eight, the exultant conqueror of his mind's wanderings, admirable, brilliant, industrious, true to himself and scornful of the virtues that merely "earn the sun"; the other the "found" father, weak, tyrannical, improvident, demoralized, evasive, cowardly, and unsuccessful. One is the image of the unresolved yearning of a son who preferred to remember his father as a child had once imagined him; the other, of the bitterness of a child forced to imagine a man who did not exist. The disparity between the two is measured not only by the explicit ironies of Yeats's treatment of "man's purpose" in poems like "The Fisherman" and the late ballads but also in the implicit, unintended ironies of his autobiographical writings. There the father one seems to see is not the father one is seeing: the pedagogue of *Reveries* and the artist of the 1916 memoir represent not authority and industry but anxiety and panic. It is hardly surprising that the man Yeats became had difficulty accepting the limitations or appreciating the value of what a man could be or could accomplish, or that, like his father before him, he was often conscious "of something helpless and perhaps even untrustworthy in myself; I could not hold my opinions among people who would make light of them if I felt for those people any sympathy. I was always accusing myself of disloyalty to some absent friend. I had, it seemed, an incredible timidity."[81]

In all this Willie was, in a way J. B. Yeats had never intended, his father's son, and the compensatory achievement of the young man announced by *Oisin* as a poet to be reckoned with is even more formidable than it first appears. But the complications of the story of the self-invented man have not yet been exhausted. In declaring himself a poet, Yeats was faced not only with the problem of becoming "a man who does not exist" but also with the pain of becoming the man his mother would have least wished him to be. The hidden narrative of "Four Years: 1887–1891" is an account of both J. B. Yeats's personal weaknesses and the climax of his unhappy marriage: in the fall of 1887, just before his son's first "nervous collapse," his wife suffered the first of two "strokes" that left her first a semi-invalid and, by the end of her life, "in possession of only half her mind."[82]

Four

FATHERS AND MOTHERS

Cuchulain and Aoife

The Wanderings of Oisin introduced the public to a poet of impressive, if not entirely explicit, pretensions. The persona of its narrator was the legendary "poet of the Gael," the revitalized and revitalizing voice of Ireland's heroic culture. In this capacity Yeats declared himself, and for some time continued to think himself, a writer of narrative verse. "I have in fact begun," he wrote to Robert Bridges as late as 1901, "what I have always meant to be the chief work of my life—the giving life not to a single story but to a whole world of little stories, some not indeed very little, to a romantic region, a sort of enchanted wood. The old Irish poets wove life into life, thereby giving to the wildest and strangest romance the solidity and vitality [of] the *Comédie Humaine*...."[1] *Oisin* was followed in 1892 by the poem now called "Cuchulain's Fight with the Sea" (originally "The Death of Cuchulain"), *Baile and Aillinn* (1902), *The Old Age of Queen Maeve* (1903), "The Grey Rock" (1913), and "The Two Kings" (1913).[2]

Yet despite its persistence, the "bardic" Yeats is, and probably always was, the least public of his voices. His Irish public first knew him best as

139

the controversial producer-manager of the Abbey Theatre and the eloquent spokesman of the Irish Dramatic Movement, and it is this Yeats who, in the long run, came closest to being the Balzac of Ireland's "romantic region." Insofar as Yeats was a man of the people (and it was never very far), he was a man of the theater.[3] If, as he suggested in his Nobel Prize lecture to the Swedish Royal Academy in 1923, his public success could only be accounted for in terms of his public ambitions, those ambitions had always been connected with the drama:

> Your Royal Highness, ladies and gentlemen, I have chosen as my theme the Irish Dramatic Movement, because when I remember the great honour that you have conferred upon me, I cannot forget many known and unknown persons. Perhaps the English committees would never have sent you my name if I had written no plays, no dramatic criticism, if my lyric poetry had not a quality of speech practised upon the stage, perhaps even—though this could be no portion of their deliberate thought—if it were not in some degree the symbol of a movement. I wish to tell the Royal Academy of Sweden of the labours, triumphs, and troubles of my fellow-workers.

To reach and to revive the culture of a people that "read little," he went on to recall, "from the very start we felt that we must have a theatre of our own."[4]

The work of organizing the Irish National Theatre is well documented elsewhere.[5] It began, with Lady Gregory's help, in 1898, and when the company opened the Abbey Theatre on December 27, 1904, one of the first plays to be performed was Yeats's *On Baile's Strand*. The subject of the play was a story Yeats had told a dozen years before in "The Death of Cuchulain": Cuchulain, the greatest hero of the Red Branch cycle, unwittingly fights and kills his own son and in his remorse is deluded into taking a suicidal revenge on the waves of the sea.[6] In 1906 he retold it again, radically altering the first part of the 1904 play to produce the version that, with a few changes, is the one now found in the *Collected Plays*. In the years that followed, Cuchulain went on to become the dominant persona of Yeats's dramatic career, the central figure of a cycle of five plays in three distinct dramatic styles. The stately blank verse of *On Baile's Strand* was followed in 1908 by *The Golden Helmet*, a "heroic farce" in prose that he recast in hexameter couplets and renamed *The Green Helmet* in 1910; in 1916 by the first of his "plays for dancers," *At the Hawk's Well*; and finally by two more plays in the same style, *The Only Jealousy of Emer* (1919; in 1929, in a prose version, *Fighting the Waves*) and *The Death of Cuchulain* (1939).

Although *On Baile's Strand* was the first to be written, it is in the narrative sequence of the cycle (that followed by, e.g., the *Variorum Plays*) the third of its episodes, preceded by *At the Hawk's Well* and *The Green Helmet* and followed by *The Only Jealousy of Emer* and *The Death of Cuchulain.* Its chronological centrality is reinforced by its interpretive centrality. The cycle as Yeats planned it was from the outset conceived of as a gloss on *On Baile's Strand.* "It must always," he wrote in a note to the 1906 version,

> be a little over-complicated when played by itself. It is one of a
> cycle of plays dealing with Cuchulain, with his friends and enemies.
> One of these plays will have Aoife as its central character, and the
> principal motive of another will be the power of the witches over
> Cuchulain's life. The present play is a kind of cross-road where too
> many interests meet and jostle for the hearer to take them in at a
> first hearing unless he listen carefully, or know something of the
> story of the other plays of the cycle.[7]

In the end, the work of unraveling what remained so intractably "over-complicated" about the story of Cuchulain and his son even in its third telling was the work of a dramatic lifetime that involved problems not only of exposition but also of style. It is worth noticing at the outset, however, that Yeats's description of the dramatic problem set by *On Baile's Strand* is much like what psychoanalysis would call a "complex" of manifest and latent psychological contents. What we are told is that the play's plot—in its simplest form a story of father and son—is determined to a significant extent by the "interests" of persons or events that lie outside its action. These interests are represented by Aoife, the "fierce woman of the camp" who was Cuchulain's mistress and is the mother of his son, and by "the witches" who have "power over his life." What is "manifest" and "latent" in *On Baile's Strand,* in other words, corresponds in its arrangement of dramatis personae to the overdetermined complex of relationships I have called the Yeatsian version of the oedipus complex. The latent story involves mistresses and lovers, sons and mothers, and the perilous control exercised by "the witches" over man's purpose; the manifest story involves the conflicts of fathers and sons who, like Laius and Oedipus, meet and destroy each other where not two, but three "ways" meet.[8]

Before going into what is "complex" about the 1906 version of *On Baile's Strand,* however, let us consider its manifest plot and try to understand the way in which Yeats found it "over-complicated." Leaving aside for the moment its opening and closing scenes, the play as we now have it

is primarily concerned with two interrelated events: first the binding of
Cuchulain by the High King Conchubar and second the meeting between
Cuchulain and the Young Man. The former, which is the longest section
of the play (250 lines), is for the most part an extended dialogue in which
Conchubar, made uneasy by the threat of war with Scotland, tries to
convince Cuchulain to bind himself by oath to defend his country against
all comers. Scotland is now ruled by Cuchulain's old mistress, Aoife, and
Conchubar has heard that one of her "young men" has recently come
ashore in Ireland. Cuchulain, who, though growing old, still prefers the
wild, unfettered ways of his youth, at first refuses:

Cuchulain.   . . . I'll not be bound.
              I'll dance or hunt, or quarrel or make love,
              Wherever and whenever I've a mind to.
              If time had not put water in your blood,
              You never would have thought it.

Conchubar.   I would leave
              A strong and settled country to my children.
              [210–15][9]

But finally even the young kings who follow Cuchulain agree that he
should do the bidding of the high king. "There is not one but dreads this
turbulence," says Conchubar, "now that they're settled men." The oath
is reluctantly taken; at that moment, there is a cry at the door and the
Young Man enters with the challenge that begins the second part of the
play:

Young   I have come alone into the midst of you
Man.   To weigh this sword against Cuchulain's sword.

Conchubar. And are you noble? for if of common seed,
              You cannot weigh your sword against his sword
              But in mixed battle.

Young   I am under bonds
Man.   To tell my name to no man; but it's noble.
              [459–64]

Cuchulain, however, is so taken with the Young Man's spirit and
appearance—"His head," he says, "is like a woman's head / I had a fancy
for" (554–55)—that he wants to make a friend of him in defiance of his
oath. Conchubar, enraged, offers to fight the Young Man himself, but
Cuchulain "seizes him": "You shall not stir, High King. I'll hold you

there" (602). But the other kings tell him he is "bewitched" and remind him he has laid his hands on the high king himself. Cuchulain hesitates and then, in a sudden burst of rage, says,

> Yes, witchcraft! witchcraft! Witches of the air!
> [*To Young Man.*] Why did you? Who was it set you to this work?
> Out, out! I say, for now it's sword on sword!
> [610–12]

The battle on Baile's Strand in which the Young Man is killed takes place offstage. When Cuchulain reenters in triumph, he finds a Fool and a Blind Man, quarreling. The Blind Man, who has spent time in Aoife's country when "he had his eyes," tells him that the Young Man is her son; then, when Cuchulain asks him about the father, the Fool says that the Blind Man

> . . . said a little while ago that he heard Aoife boast that she'd never but the one lover, and he the only man that had overcome her in battle.
> [739–41]

Cuchulain realizes that he has killed his own son and in his grief blames Conchubar and his "old rod of kingship." He rushes offstage to avenge himself. But at the last minute, he turns his sword from the high king to the waves of the sea. "He sees King Conchubar's crown on every one of them," the Blind Man says, and the Fool, who has followed Cuchulain as far as the door, describes the final scene:

> There, he is down! He is up again. He is going out in the deep water. There is a big wave. It has gone over him. I cannot see him now. He has killed kings and giants, but the waves have mastered him, the waves have mastered him!
> [791–95]

Apparently *On Baile's Strand* is about the oedipal "tragedy." Both events in the play are conflicts between fathers and sons: Conchubar (who the stage directions say is a man much older than Cuchulain)[10] and Cuchulain, Cuchulain and the Young Man. Moreover, the context of both conflicts is the integration of the individual into the community, whether of Cuchulain's adolescent "turbulence" into the "settled country" of responsible family men ruled by Conchubar or of the young mother's boy into his father's heroic brotherhood. The play as we have it is in its least complex sense a representation of the conflict between the two, and the tragedy of Cuchulain is in both cases the defeat of the former by the latter: Cuchulain kills his son, and Conchubar escapes Cuchulain's revenge. It is, as Cuchulain says in his debate with Conchubar, the defeat of fire by water, of the hard by the soft, of the sun by the sea:

> We in our young days
> Have seen the heavens burn like a burning cloud
> Brooding upon the world, and being more
> Than men can be now that cloud's lifted up,
> We should be the more truthful. Conchubar,
> I do not like your children—they have no pith,
> No marrow in their bones, and will lie soft
> Where you and I lie hard.
> [251–58]

Yet to describe the action of the play only in terms of this very masculine struggle between young and old "kings" is to ignore, as Yeats acknowledged in his 1906 note, the way in which it is "overcomplicated" by other interests. The most obvious of these is the story of Cuchulain and Aoife. In the early lines of the play, for instance, we are prepared for the entrance of Conchubar and Cuchulain by a "secret" about the Young Man told to the Fool by the Blind Man as they are waiting for their dinner:

> That young man is Aoife's son. I am sure it is Aoife's son, it flows in upon me that it is Aoife's son. You have often heard me talking of Aoife, the great woman-fighter Cuchulain got the mastery over in the North? . . . There was a boy in her house that had her own red colour on him, and everybody said he was to be brought up to kill Cuchulain, that she hated Cuchulain. She used to put a helmet on a pillar-stone and call it Cuchulain and set him casting at it.
> [128–43]

In fact, as the play proceeds from this revelation it becomes increasingly clear that the "latent" content of the nominally oedipal drama of *On Baile's Strand* is the conflict not of fathers and sons but of fathers and mothers. It is Aoife's relationship with Cuchulain, not the antagonism between one generation of men and another, that is the real threat to the stability of the masculine community. She sets the unwitting father and son into murderous collision; by threatening Conchubar with war, she provides the occasion for the oath that forbids their reconciliation. The hostility between the worlds of father and mother implicit in the confrontation of Finn and Niamh in book I of *Oisin* has broken out into

open conflict, and once again it is the son who suffers by it. The Young
Man's "heroic" mission is to kill his father; but his oedipal enterprise is
explicitly in the service not of his own "interests" but of those of his
mother's jealousy and hatred. It is Aoife who sets him casting at the pillar
stone. How this came to be the case—and it seems that something of the
same motivation may also underlie the maternal kidnapping in *Oisin*—is
not yet clear. Cuchulain is the only one who addresses himself specifically
to the problem, and his answer is not very helpful:

Conchubar. [Aoife] now hates you and will leave no subtlety
        Unknotted that might run into a noose
        About your throat, no army in idleness
        That might bring ruin on this land you serve.

Cuchulain. No wonder in that, no wonder at all in that.
        I have never known love but as a kiss
        In the mid-battle, and a difficult truce
        Of oil and water, candles and dark night,
        Hillside and hollow, the hot-footed sun
        And the cold, sliding, slippery-footed moon—
        A brief forgiveness between opposites
        That have been hatreds for three times the age
        Of this long-'stablished ground.
        [327–39]

Cuchulain's account of heroic love is identical with the intuitions of
duality—the "whispering in the dark between Daimon and sweetheart"—
that pervades the development of Yeats's metaphysics of *Anima Hominis*
from *Estrangement* to *A Vision*. Here too it has an axiomatic force, at
least for Cuchulain: he has "never known love" of any other sort. Yet
there is also an intimation that what he has never known is also what he
has never chosen to know. In the passage immediately preceding the one
quoted above, Conchubar taxes Cuchulain for his childlessness ("You
despise our queens") and reminds him that

               I have heard you boast,
When the ale was in your blood, that there was one
In Scotland, where you had learnt the trade of war,
That had a stone-pale cheek and red-brown hair;
And that although you had loved other women,
You'd sooner that fierce woman of the camp
Bore you a son than any queen among them.

Cuchulain. You call her a "fierce woman of the camp,"
           For, having lived among the spinning-wheels,
           You'd have no woman near that would not say,
           "Ah! how wise!" "What will you have for supper?"
           "What shall I wear that I may please you, sir?"
           And keep that humming through the day and night
           For ever. A fierce woman of the camp!
           But I am getting angry about nothing.
           You have never seen her. Ah! Conchubar, had you seen her
           With that high, laughing, turbulent head of hers
           Thrown backward, and the bowstring at her ear,
           Or sitting at the fire with those grave eyes
           Full of good counsel as it were with wine,
           Or when love ran through all the lineaments
           Of her wild body—although she had no child,
           None other had all beauty, queen or lover,
           Or was so fitted to give birth to kings.
           [300–323]

Cuchulain, in short, is partial to a certain sort of woman, and in his partiality he chooses in particular the woman who is, among other things, the most aggressive in her behavior toward men, the "great woman-fighter" who must be "mastered," kissed in mid battle. Beneath his ironical condemnation of the life of the "spinning-wheels" Cuchulain betrays an antipathy not just for softness and passivity but for any sort of love that is not related to antagonism: that is, for anything but ambivalence. Given this partiality for mingled love and hate, it is not surprising that the consequence of his "mastery" of Aoife should be the birth of a son who is his father's nemesis, a personification as much of a mother's revenge as of his own oedipal wishes.

There is, however, another factor involved in the drama of father and mother besides the underlying conditions determined by their choice of each other, one already familiar from book II of *Oisin:* the absence of the father. Like the sad-eyed lady in Manannan's deserted hall, Aoife has been abandoned by her "exultant" lover. The difference is that here she responds not with depressed resignation ("Neither the living, nor the . . . dead, nor the high gods . . . may fight / My enemy and hope") but with vengeful hatred. The precondition of the Young Man's heroic mission—and, it may be added, its inevitable failure to serve his purposes rather than his mother's—is the fact that he neither knows his father nor is allowed to identify himself in any way that will allow his father to know him ("I am under bonds / To tell my name to no man").

In the 1906 version of the play the crucial role played by Cuchulain's abandonment of Aoife is implicit and can only be deduced from the scenario: the vengeful mother sends her son against his absent father. But in the earlier (1904) version, and particularly in the even earlier "Death of Cuchulain" (1892), the real conjugal bitterness underlying Cuchulain's rather complacent and self-centered way of accepting "a brief forgiveness between opposites" is more explicit. In the 1904 text, for example, the secret of the Young Man's origins is not withheld until the final scene but revealed to the Fool by the Blind Man ("Barach" and "Fintain" in this version) after only a hundred lines:

Fintain.   He is Cuchullain's son.

Barach.   And his mother has sent him hither to fight his father.

Fintain.   It is all quite plain. Cuchullain went into Aoife's country when he was a young man that he might learn skill in arms, and there he became Aoife's lover.

Barach.   And now she hates him because he went away, and has sent her son to kill the father. I knew she was a goddess.

Fintain.   And she never told him who his father was, that he might do it. I have thought it all out, fool. . . .
[104–15]

The motif of conjugal conflict is most predominant, however, in the earliest (and by far the least "over-complicated") of the versions, "Cuchulain's Fight with the Sea." Here the whole action is motivated by the mother's (in this text Cuchulain's wife Emer's rather than Aoife's) jealous hatred of her wandering husband.[11] The poem begins with a scene in which we are told the part of the story of father and son that is left out of *On Baile's Strand:* Emer, who has set a watch on the road to warn her of Cuchulain's return from the wars, is told that he has come with a concubine, "one sweet-throated like a bird." She summons her son:

> "It is not meet
> To idle life away, a common herd."
>
> "I have long waited, mother, for that word:
> But wherefore now?"
>
> "There is a man to die;
> You have the heaviest arm under the sky."
>
> "Whether under its daylight or its stars
> My father stands amid his battle-cars."

"But you have grown to be the taller man."

"Yet somewhere under the starlight or the sun
My father stands."

                              "Aged, worn out with wars
On foot, on horseback or in battle-cars."

"I only ask what way my journey lies,
For He who made you bitter made you wise."

"The Red Branch camp in a great company
Between the wood's rim and the horses of the sea.
Go there, and light a camp-fire at wood's rim;
But tell your name and lineage to him
Whose blade compels, and wait till they have found
Some feasting man that the same oath has bound."

Among those feasting men Cuchulain dwelt,
And his young sweetheart close beside him knelt,
Stared on the mournful wonder of his eyes,
Even as Spring upon the ancient skies,
And pondered on the glory of his days. . . .
[20–43]

If the earlier versions of the story dramatized in *On Baile's Strand*
place the tragic consequences of the conflict of father and son squarely in
the context of conjugal rather than oedipal rivalry, it is also interesting to
note that the earliest of them is in several respects reminiscent of the
"heroic" passage of arms described in book II of *The Wanderings of
Oisin*. Once again it is the abandoned woman who enlists the aid of the
son against the absent oppressor who, once again, is represented in two
complementary aspects: as Emer describes him ("Aged, worn out with
wars") and as his son finds him in the Red Branch camp (his eyes like
"ancient skies" in which are seen the "glory of his days"). The first is
much like the ironically diminished "dusky demon" Oisin encounters in
"vain battle," the unconfrontable "father found"; the second is
metaphorically related to the description of Manannan's dome, at once
vacant as the heavens and filled with memories "buried and mighty," and
thus to the idealized lost father who appears in his benign aspect in "The
Fisherman." The difference between the scenarios that involve these
dramatis personae in *Oisin* and in *On Baile's Strand* is in effect the
difference between the "poetic" and the "heroic" interpretations of the
conflict between the son and his absent father. In one case the "father
found" is "the reality" that for Yeats became the equivalent of his own

protean poetic audience; in the other, he is the ideal, the embodiment of the "return" of the transcendently powerful oedipal presence Yeats might hopefully and anxiously imagine but had never known. To the extent that *On Baile's Strand* expresses anything about what a son might wish for in his father, it expresses the wish to die gloriously at his hands, and Yeats recalls in *Reveries* that as a boy he had indeed dreamed "for years" of "being killed upon a seashore."[12]

On the whole, then, it seems reasonable to assume that Yeats's continuing fascination with the events that had occurred on Baile's Strand was in part an expression of the poet's unfulfilled need for the traumatic conflict that would free him from the Land of the Young.[13] It is equally important to notice, however, that, as Yeats himself points out, the story of fathers and sons in the play is constantly in danger of being submerged by outside interests and that in fact these interests, in the madness (and in the 1892 version of the story the death)[14] of the father, dominate events. The Young Man of *On Baile's Strand* is not, like Hamlet and Oedipus, the central figure of the play; he remains peripheral, explicitly (if not, in the 1906 version, overexplicitly) in the service of his mother's revenge, an unidentified person "of Aoife's country."[15] Unlike Oisin, the Young Man does not "turn aside" from his mother. He has no story of his own; he is an extension of her purposes, the idealized image of maternal affection, submissive, self-effacing, his aggression and grandiosity the expression not of his oedipal fantasies but of hers in him: "You have grown to be the taller man," Emer says, and he answers, "Yet somewhere...my father stands."

The Young Man of the 1906 version is in this respect the precursor of Yeats's much more famous (and uncharacteristically sentimental) apostrophe to the Republican martyrs in "Easter 1916." The "terrible beauty" of the sacrifice that elevates them above the "casual comedy" is, as the poet imagines it, only superficially and ironically related to the defeat of the absent English oppressor. What moves him most, instead, is the extent to which their devotion to the mysterious purpose that seems to "make a stone of the heart" resembles another relationship:

> Too long a sacrifice
> Can make a stone of the heart.
> O when may it suffice?
> That is Heaven's part, our part
> To murmur name upon name,
> As a mother names her child
> When sleep at last has come

On limbs that had run wild.
What is it but nightfall?
No, no, not night but death;
Was it needless death after all?
For England may keep faith
For all that is done and said.
We know their dream; enough
To know they dreamed and are dead;
And what if excess of love
Bewildered them till they died?
I write it out in a verse—
MacDonagh and MacBride
And Connolly and Pearse
Now and in time to be,
Wherever green is worn,
Are changed, changed utterly:
A terrible beauty is born.
[57–80]

Yeats, murmuring the names of the sixteen dead men who had "run wild," confirms lyrically what is less obvious in his dramatic heroes: that the feeling validating even the most public enterprises of Ireland's sons is a mother's feeling, and that only death will suffice to bring it forth.

The Red Man and the Mountain Witch

One of the major complications of the story of fathers and sons told in *On Baile's Strand,* then, is the extent to which its "interests" are modified by the story of fathers and mothers. As in the case of *The Stories of Red Hanrahan,* the "complicating" of the text is the history of its revision: as the play approached its final form in 1906, the scenario of "Cuchulain's Fight with the Sea" became more "latent," that is, the more obscured by the drama of oedipal rivalries. The problem addressed by revision, particularly in the dramatic versions of the story, was that of supplying an appropriate motive for Cuchulain's rather abrupt decision to kill the Young Man. The scene is given its briefest (and in many ways most effective) treatment in "Cuchulain's Fight with the Sea." Cuchulain and his son have paused in their battle, and Cuchulain says that

"Your head seemed like a woman's head
That I loved once."

> Again the fighting sped,
> But now the war-rage in Cuchulain woke,
> And through the new blade's guard the old blade broke,
> And pierced him.
> [63–67]

The awakening of Cuchulain's "war-rage"—he is, like many heroes in Western literature from Achilles to Lancelot, a berserk—is of course critical to the story's outcome, which up to this point has apparently been leading toward recognition and reconciliation. The scene is thus central to its tragic coherence, and in the play Yeats is unwilling to let it pass without elaboration. In doing so, however, he also brings in the second of the major "over-complications" of the story, "the power of the witches over Cuchulain's life." The scene is basically the same in both 1904 and 1906 versions. Conchubar, who has forbidden any friendship between Cuchulain and the Young Man, interferes at the moment that they are about to exchange gifts and offers to take the quarrel on himself. Cuchulain seizes Conchubar, and in the struggle all the kings take up the cry of "witchcraft":

First
Old King.   Some witch has worked upon your mind, Cuchulain.
             The head of that young man seemed like a woman's
             You'd had a fancy for. Then of a sudden
             You laid your hands on the High King himself!

Cuchulain.   And laid my hands on the High King himself?

Conchubar.   Some witch is floating in the air above us.

Cuchulain.   Yes, witchcraft! witchcraft! Witches of the air!
             [*To Young Man.*] Why did you? Who was it set you to this work?
             Out, out! I say, for now it's sword on sword!

Young   But . . . but I did not.
Man.
[604–13]

The climax of the story of fathers and sons is, I think, one of the play's weakest moments, and actors playing Cuchulain appear to have had difficulty with it from the beginning. "I have . . . to make the refusal of the son's affection tragic," Yeats wrote in answer to Frank Fay's queries during the early rehearsals of the 1904 production,

> by suggesting in Cuchullain's [*sic*] character a shadow of something a little proud, barren and restless, as if out of sheer strength of heart

or from accident he had put affection away. . . . He is a little
hard . . .—perhaps this young man's affection is what he had most
need of. Without this thought the play had not had any deep
tragedy. I write of him with difficulty, for when one creates a character one does it out of instinct and may be wrong when one
analyses the instinct afterwards.[16]

In the end Yeats seems to have become convinced that instinct in itself
was not enough to explain to an audience why the man who had moments before calmly dismissed the idea of witchcraft ("No
witchcraft . . . / The winds are innocent," 554–61) is suddenly enraged by
the thought of it. The answer suggested by the text is that the reversal of
his opinion occurs when he realizes that he has "laid [his] hands on the
High King himself," and it was apparently with this in mind that Yeats
drastically rewrote the first half of the play in 1905.

The 1904 version of the play is much more explicitly about the relationship of Aoife and Cuchulain; but it also differs from the later text in
containing no reference whatever to either the oath that binds Cuchulain
to Conchubar or the war that makes it necessary. All of the "oedipal"
trappings of the first part of the play, in other words—the extended
dialogue between Conchubar and Cuchulain, the latter's capitulation, the
elaborate oath ceremony that ends with the entrance of the Young
Man—are late additions to the scenario, and all were apparently added
to make better dramatic sense out of the sudden fury that pits Cuchulain
first against the Young Man, then against Conchubar, and finally against
the sea. The result, however, is not the deepened sense of tragedy Yeats
hoped for but, as he put it himself, a significant complication of the play's
effect. The 1906 version gives at best only a nominal motivation for the
sudden extremity of madness and rage into which Cuchulain is thrown.
The implied analysis remains an afterthought, unequal to the power of
Yeats's "instinctive" certainties: it is simply not enough (or complexly
too much) to know that in befriending the Young Man Cuchulain has
violated his oath to Conchubar, or that it is this oath that forces him to
kill the Young Man whom he has clearly, if preconsciously, recognized as
his son. This is not to say that the oath has nothing to do with the matter;
it is, on the contrary, remarkably expressive. What matters about it,
however, is not its form (who is being bound to whom) but its content
(what is being bound).

The content of the oath, as one might expect, is directly related to the
circumstances that call it forth. But these circumstances are not, as an
outline of the plot might lead us to expect, an oedipal threat—

Conchubar's need to quell Cuchulain's turbulence and aggression in the interests of social order—but a narcissistic threat. The problem, as Conchubar says, is that in this particular case Cuchulain's motives have become ambiguous; he is not to be trusted where the woman he "once had a fancy for" is concerned. Conchubar opposes Cuchulain not simply for his "turbulence"—it is after all the same force that, as Cuchulain points out, has served the country well until now against "Maeve of Cruachan and the northern pirates, / The hundred kings of Sorcha, and the kings / Out of the Garden in the East of the World" (222–24)—but for the threat it offers when it is coupled with the ambivalent interests of his prior love. Cuchulain must take the oath, Conchubar explains, to scotch the conspiracy between his nostalgia for the woman who had "all beauty" and the reality of Aoife's destructive hatred:

> Listen to me.
> Aoife makes war on us, and every day
> Our enemies grow greater and beat the walls
> More bitterly, and you within the walls
> Are every day more turbulent; and yet,
> When I would speak about these things, your fancy
> Runs as it were a swallow on the wind.
> [339–45]

It is Cuchulain's "fancy" that "runs on the wind"—ultimately the "fancy" that the Young Man's head resembles Aoife's—and not his masculine aggressiveness that Conchubar fears most, and it is this "apocalyptic" quality in him that the high king seeks to bind with an oath. Conchubar opens the ceremony with a rite of purification, sung by three women, against the "power of the witches." It "has come down from the old law-makers," he says,

> To blow the witches out. Considering
> That the wild will of man could be oath-bound,
> But that a woman's could not, they bid us sing
> Against the will of woman at its wildest
> In the Shape-Changers that run upon the wind.
> [387–92]

The rite itself, which the stage directions say should be sung during the ceremony of the oath "in a very low voice . . . so that the others all but drown out their words," is one of the points where, as Yeats suggests in his 1906 note, one must indeed "listen carefully" if one is to understand the latent interests of the action:

May this fire have driven out

. . . .

The women none can kiss and thrive,
For they are but whirling wind,
Out of memory and mind.

. . . .

But the man is thrice forlorn,
Emptied, ruined, wracked, and lost,
That they follow, for at most
They will give him kiss for kiss
While they murmur, "After this
Hatred may be sweet to the taste."
Those wild hands that have embraced
All his body can but shove
At the burning wheel of love
Till the side of hate comes up.
Therefore in this ancient cup
May the sword-blades drink their fill
Of the home-brew there, until
They will have for masters none
But the threshold and hearthstone.
[393–432][17]

The motivation for the conflicts that nominally express "man's pur-pose" in the play—Cuchulain/Conchubar and Cuchulain/Young Man—is not the father's fear of the man in his son but the anxieties aroused by the "woman's will" that works through him. The murderous ambivalence of the vengeful wife in turn arouses the even deeper terrors associated with "a fancy on the wind," something "out of memory and mind": the apoca-lyptic fears of autoerotic fragmentation ("emptied, ruined, wracked, and lost") to which the narcissistic personality is particularly vulnerable. This, and not Cuchulain's formal profession of allegiance to Conchubar, is what accounts for the violent rage that so closely follows his impulsive wooing of the fierce Young Man whose head is "like a woman's." Cuchulain responds to the Young Man as if he were Aoife, and in attri-buting this response to "the witches of the air" he implies that the antagonisms of fathers and mothers are themselves an expression of con-flicts that are much older, so old they seem "out of memory and mind." As a husband, he sees in his son both his wife's seductive beauty and her castrating hatred; as a man who was once a son himself, his response resonates with an archaic "turbulence within the walls" that threatens his very identity.[18]

This account of Cuchulain's "instinctive" refusal of the young man's affection also suggests how even the most admirable and terrifying fathers can, at certain critical moments, be tragically "absent" from the lives of their sons. What Cuchulain responds to in the Young Man is not "man's purpose" but the image of the mother and "the power of the witches"; what the Young Man sees in the eyes of the father he faces on Baile's Strand is not the flicker of recognition that, for better or worse, would acknowledge their companionship in rivalry but the blank, glorious vacancy that betrays the intensity of his "heroic" self-absorption. By failing to recognize the Young Man as his son, Cuchulain becomes unrecognizable as a father; both are in effect bound to tell their names to no man, and as "Cuchulain's Fight with the Sea" indicates, this oath, the one sons make to mothers, is the oath that matters. Oisin, the story of the poet, shows us how some sons are doomed to wander forever in search of fathers who do not exist; On Baile's Strand, the story of the hero, shows us that the sons who find them are doomed to be annihilated by an impersonal burst of narcissistic rage. Insofar as On Baile's Strand expresses anything about man's purpose beyond its inevitable defeat by something "out of memory," it suggests the lengths to which a son must be willing to go to restore a "lost" father to his paternal and conjugal rights. Absent fathers, as Yeats's own experience had shown him at least once, return to reveal themselves only to dead sons.

"The power of the witches over Cuchulain's life," then, corresponds to the "heroic" intensity of his own unresolved narcissistic conflicts and vulnerabilities. We may begin to suspect, moreover, that his literal absence from his family, and indeed his choice of sexual partners, is similarly determined. He loves Aoife the most partly because she is the least maternal of his women—so much so that he seems never to have considered her capable of having a child by him—and partly because her own fierce ambivalence toward men guarantees him a safe exile from the anxiety-provoking demands of family life. The scenario of the play is in this sense an expression of the way in which the psychogenetic circumstances of the narcissistic personality are part of a recurrent overdetermination of conflicts from generation to generation: the demand of the narcissistically vulnerable son on the narcissistic father is for precisely that assurance of masculine integrity and authority that he, for all the "glory of his days," is at bottom least prepared to give. For Cuchulain himself is the son of an absent father: as he and the Young Man challenge each other, he boasts of his superhuman strength, saying it has descended to him from the gods:

> I am their plough, their harrow, their very strength;
> For he that's in the sun begot this body
> Upon a mortal woman, and I have heard tell
> It seemed as if he had outrun the moon
> That he must follow always through waste heaven,
> He loved so happily. He'll be but slow
> To break a tree that was so sweetly planted.
> [492–98]

Cuchulain's story of his "begetting" by Lugh, the god of the sun, confirms the direct connection between the heroic powers of the son over other men and a father who is both highly idealized—in this case, as in *Oisin,* a deity—and, even more significantly, absent.[19] Indeed it is difficult not to conclude from Cuchulain's description of his relationship with his father that what sets him apart from other men ("I'll not be bound") is above all the fact that his strength has never been subjected to an oedipal defeat. Thus Cuchulain in his wooing of the Young Man is inevitably reminded—in a way that betrays his clear, if preconscious, grasp of the issues at stake—of the time his father had come to try him, as we might expect, in the cold and passionate dawn:

> He came to try me, rising up at dawn
> Out of the cold dark of the rich sea.
> He challenged me to battle, but before
> My sword had touched his sword, told me his name,
> Gave me this cloak, and vanished. . . .
>
> . . . .
> Nine queens out of the Country-under-Wave
> Had woven it with the fleeces of the sea
> And they were long embroidering at it.—Boy,
> If I had fought my father, he'd have killed me,
> As certainly as if I had a son
> And fought with him, I should be deadly to him;
> For the old fiery fountains are far off,
> And every day there is less heat o' the blood.
> [543–47; 590–97]

The most significant fact about this "oedipal" confrontation, once again, is its peculiar evasiveness: the trial is rhetorical; the father's presence, though quite distinct in its threat to the son, is marginal and elusive in its implication in relation to the mother. There is, moreover, mingled in the son's triumphant acquisition of heroic manhood in the form of the talismanic cloak an ironic intimation of psychogenetic failure: the undefeated son of the undefeatable father will never be able to identify himself fully with his father's "heat o' the blood." The heroic invulnerability that sets Cuchulain apart from other men defines both his strength and his weakness: he is on one hand free of the burden of oedipal guilt that underlies the institutions of Conchubar's community of "settled men" and on the other dangerously susceptible to the "power of the witches" exerted through his narcissistic anxieties.[20] It is this peculiar constellation of strengths and weaknesses that accounts for the essentially adolescent quality of the heroic community as it is represented in *On Baile's Strand* and in the nostalgia of *Oisin,* and it is this constellation that became the subject of Yeats's second Cuchulain play, *The Green Helmet,* a reworking of the "trial" episode that was, as Yeats significantly emphasized in its subtitle, "An Heroic Farce."[21]

The action of *The Green Helmet* takes place on the eve of Cuchulain's return from Aoife's country. He himself is now the "Young Man,"[22] and he arrives home to find that things have not gone well in his absence with his old companions, Laegaire and Conall. Two years before, they tell him, when "you were gone but a little while," a strange man in "a red foxy cloak, / With half-shut foxy eyes and a great laughing mouth," had come to them as they were making merry at a midnight feast and offered to show them a "game,"

> ...the best that ever had been;
> And when we asked what game, he answered, "Why, whip off my
>   head!
> Then one of you two stoop down, and I'll whip off his," he said.
> "A head for a head," he said, "that is the game that I play."
> [75–78]

Conall, angered by the Red Man's mockery, had cut off his head; upon which he had picked it up and "splashed himself into the sea." A year later, he had returned with it on his shoulders to claim the forfeit for the following year, and Conall and Laegaire are at this moment waiting for him to arrive to make it good.

When the Red Man arrives, however, he assures them all that it was but "a drinking joke and a gibe and a juggler's feat." He has come instead, he says, with a gift, the Green Helmet, "for the best of you all to lift / And wear on his own head, and choose for yourselves the best" (127–32). It quickly becomes apparent that his gift is worse than his forfeit, for the house is immediately thrown into confusion by the conflicting claims of the heroes, their wives, and their servants, as to who is "the best of all." Cuchulain alone is unaffected by the dispute; but in spite of his best efforts it erupts into a murderous brawl, in the midst of which the Red Man reappears and sternly demands "the debt that's owing. Let some man kneel down there / That I may cut his head off, or all shall go to wrack" (260–61). Ignoring the pleas of his wife, Emer, Cuchulain offers his head, upon which the Red Man, instead of cutting it off, places the Green Helmet on it and concludes,

> I have not come for your hurt, I'm the Rector of this land,
> And with my spitting cat-heads, my frenzied moon-bred band,
> Age after age I sift it, and choose for its championship
> The man who hits my fancy.
>   And I choose the laughing lip
> That shall not turn from laughing, whatever rise or fall;
> The heart that grows no bitterer although betrayed by all;
> The hand that loves to scatter; the life like a gambler's throw,
> And these things I make prosper, till a day come that I know,
> When heart and mind shall darken that the weak may end the
>   strong,
> And the long-remembering harpers have matter for their song.
> [275–84]

The similarities between the plot of *The Green Helmet* and the story Cuchulain tells the Young Man about his meeting with Lugh in *On Baile's Strand* are striking enough to suggest that the Red Man who awards the talismanic prize to "the best of all" is once again the absent father.[23] The play, Yeats says in a note in the 1908 edition of his *Collected Works,* was "meant as an introduction to *On Baile's Strand*";[24] this, taken together with the fact that in the original version the helmet was "golden" rather than green, makes it seem all the more probable that *The Green Helmet* is in fact a dramatization of Cuchulain's encounter with the sun god who also rises "out of the rich sea." This observation, however, only makes the differences between the two versions of the event all the more striking. Aside from numerous differences in detail, there is a very noticeable difference in tone. Cuchulain's story in *On Baile's Strand* is told with majestic simplicity and nostalgic awe; *The Green Helmet* is argumentative, chaotic, comic, and above all ironic. Its deus ex machina is, for all his apparent seriousness at the end, fundamentally a "great laughing mouth," a joker and a trickster. At first there seems to be no obvious way of accounting for the transformation of Lugh into the Red Man, except as an arbitrary decision on Yeats's part. Yet it remains puzzling that he should have chosen to revise so radically the "oedipal" pathos of the event that is presented in *On Baile's Strand* in the rhetoric of high tragedy.

A resolution to the difficulty begins to suggest itself when we imagine, as Yeats suggests we should, that the two plays have been performed in sequence. The difference between Lugh and the Red Man is now the difference between Cuchulain's story in *On Baile's Strand* and what we remember about *The Green Helmet* as we hear him tell it, and as such it expresses not arbitrary anachronism but the sort of wishful distortion of the past that often occurs in recollection. Lugh is the father Cuchulain wants to remember meeting, and the Red Man is the man he actually—if fictively—met, the nostalgically idealized "father lost" and the ironically protean "father found" we have already encountered in book II of *Oisin*. Taken together, the two versions of the father—"the reality" and what "does not exist"—comprise the characteristic complex of paternal images associated with the "absent" oedipal father, and both, consequently, are equally appropriate to Yeats's "instinctive" certainties about the circumstances that would confirm his hero's privileged (pre-oedipal) grandiosity and fatal (narcissistic) vulnerability. The paradox of the heroic personality as Yeats imagines it is expressed, in *On Baile's Strand,* by Cuchulain's masculine invincibility and his susceptibility to the will of the "witches" and is summed up in *The Green Helmet* by the Red Man's final speech. Cuchulain, he says, is "the best of all" not because he is the strongest (though he may be this too) but because his undefeated narcissism makes him the least likely to be tempted by the Green Helmet. He is the champion precisely because he does not care to be: his interests are not motivated by the oedipal rivalry and guilt that define the purposes and brotherhood of other men. In the security of his untested grandiosity he is, in this respect, indifferent and therefore invulnerable; his eyes, like those of the Chinamen in "Lapis Lazuli," are gay, "whatever rise or fall . . . although betrayed by all." Yet at the same time, the sort of "prosperity" his fate brings him will also bring him to an ironic end, the final betrayal by the divine "moon-bred" jester that, as we shall see in *The Death of Cuchulain,* is an expression not of man's purpose but of the murderous maternal ambivalence that here, as in "Easter 1916," sacrifices sons to the terrible beauty of art:

> And these things I make prosper, till a day come that I know,
> When heart and mind shall darken that the weak may end the
>   strong,
> And the long-remembering harpers have matter for their song.

Once the complementary relationship of Lugh and the Red Man has been established, a number of differences in detail between the two plays also fall into place. The "game" proposed by the Red Man, for example, corresponds to Oisin's "vain battle": like the dusky demon, the Red Man is powerful because he is capable of surviving an infinite number of defeats. His power is in this respect once again his unconfrontability; he is, like the hero to whom he gives his helmet, invulnerable because he is indifferent to the "rise and fall" of things and the loss of organs and limbs that, to less privileged men, is like the loss of life itself. Like the demon, moreover, he is associated primarily (rather than secondarily, as in *On Baile's Strand*) with the mutable, protean power of the sea that is "goaded" by the moon, and the fact that the comic brawls he incites and presides over are in part a satire on "the reality" of Yeats's contemporary audience once again suggests an implicit relationship between the story of a son's vain battle with the "father found" and his feelings about the "many-headed" mob at the Abbey.[25] Thus as they wait alone for the arrival of the Red Man at the beginning of the play, Conall remarks to Laegaire that it is unlikely Cuchulain will ever come home because

> he has all that he could need
> In that high windy Scotland—good luck in all that he does.
> Here neighbour wars on neighbour, and why there is no man
>   knows,
> And if a man is lucky all wish his luck away,
> And take his good name from him between a day and a day.
> [14–18]

If the elaboration of the encounter between Cuchulain and Lugh in *The Green Helmet* indicates that Cuchulain, like Oisin, has two fathers, the real and the ideal, ironic and heroic, found and lost, the plot of *On Baile's Strand* suggests that after his son's death many of the attributes of the ironic father have been transferred to Conchubar. In Cuchulain's last speech, for instance, his darkening mind wanders among the multitudinous faces of memories "buried and mighty" in a desperate search for the one confrontable face that would absolve him of the terrifying consequences of his narcissistic rage at the witches. He has just learned from the Fool that he has killed his own son:

> 'Twas they that did it, the pale windy people.
> Where? where? where? My sword against the thunder!
> But no, for they have always been my friends;
> And though they love to blow a smoking coal

Till it's all flame, the wars they blow aflame
Are full of glory, and heart-uplifting pride,
And not like this. The wars they love awaken
Old fingers and the sleepy strings of harps.
Who did it then? Are you afraid? Speak out!
For I have put you under my protection,
And will reward you well. Dubthach the Chafer?
He'd an old grudge. No, for he is with Maeve.
Laegaire did it! Why do you not speak?
What is this house? [*Pause.*] Now I remember all.
'Twas you who did it—you who sat up there
With your old rod of kingship, like a magpie
Nursing a stolen spoon. No, not a magpie,
A maggot that is eating up the earth!
Yes, but a magpie, for he's flown away.
Where did he fly to?

Blind Man.   He is outside the door.

Cuchulain. Outside the door?

Blind Man.   Between the door and the sea.

Cuchulain. Conchubar, Conchubar! the sword into your heart!
              [*He rushes out. . . .*]
              [749–70]

The speech records the onset of one of the periods of "darkened mind" predicted by the Red Man; Cuchulain rushes out to kill Conchubar by the sea but in his fury mistakes one for the other and is "mastered" by the waves. The consequences of his attack on Conchubar's "old rod" are in this respect another version of the "vain battle" between the son and the "father found." Cuchulain's madness, like Oisin's "exultant labour" on the Isle of Many Fears, is an ironic illusion cast by his protean opponent, and in "Cuchulain's Fight with the Sea" it is Conchubar, "the subtlest of all men," who after the Young Man's death,

Ranking his Druids round him ten by ten,
Spake thus: "Cuchulain will dwell there and brood
For three days more in dreadful quietude,
And then arise, and raving slay us all.
Chaunt in his ear delusions magical,
That he may fight the horses of the sea."
[76–81]

However, Cuchulain's story is the story not, like Oisin's, of ironic survival but of the crisis that ends in death or, at a later point in Yeats's development of the cycle, in the period of deathlike psychotic withdrawal that is the subject of *The Only Jealousy of Emer*.[26] If the waves that master him suggest at first the transcendent elusiveness of the absent oedipal opponent, in the end it is clear that they are a way of representing the moment in which, as Yeats puts it in "The Second Coming," "the ceremony of innocence is drowned." The ironic illusion that in *Oisin* both declares man's defeat and affirms his nostalgic longing is now a psychotic delusion created, as Cuchulain impulsively admits and anxiousy denies, by the "pale windy people" who remind us of Aoife's country and the place "out of mind" ruled by "the witches." The climax of the story of the hero as Yeats imagines it is the moment in which Cuchulain's rigidly "invulnerable" narcissism is at last overwhelmed by the rage that makes "things fall apart"; the method in his madness is, as his final speech indicates, to reconstitute his deeply shattered sense of grandiose integrity. The self that the hero remakes is a self that restores his lost feelings of "glory and heart-uplifting pride" in a paranoid delusion that only outwardly resembles oedipal rage: "He sees," the Fool says, looking at the waves, "King Conchubar's crown on every one of them."[27]

The function of the "darkened mind" that brings first the withdrawal and then the dissolution of the self in what Yeats would later call "our mother the sea" is, as I mentioned earlier, analogous to the function of the creative mind in Yeats's "decrepit" poet. The difference between the poet and the hero is that, to use terms that first seemed appropriate in our discussion of Red Hanrahan, one is only "touched" while the other is "taken"; or, to put it in more psychological terms, that one is able to make a controlled use of "reminiscence" as a source of narcissistic supplies while the other does so at the risk of being withdrawn into a permanent residence in the Land of the Young.[28] Insofar as the story of Cuchulain is the story of the poet, consequently, it is not about a character but about the dramatist who imagines him. As such it is partly the record of Yeats's continuing obsession with a certain kind of "apocalyptic" subject matter; but it is also, as the 1904 and 1906 versions indicate, the story of an attempt to construct a viable scenario for "man's enterprise." The measure of his success in doing so is in effect the dramatic success of the revised text, and we know that Yeats, at least, remained dissatisfied with its "over-complicated" effect.

In 1906 the solution to the difficulty seemed relatively straightforward:

what was needed was a "cycle" of plays giving a programmatic exposition of the various "interests" that uncomfortably jostled each other in *On Baile's Strand*. In practice, however, the development of the cycle proved to be more than a matter of content; it was also, as I have suggested, a matter of style. *The Green Helmet* is both an elaboration of the story of Cuchulain and Lugh and a "farce," an essay in comic business and dialogue, and in the latter respect it expresses not only the ironies implicit in the encounters of fathers and sons Yeats could imagine but also the corresponding ambiguity in the evolution of his own encounter with the Irish public. "I find," he wrote to his father in early 1909, "that my talent as a stage manager is in the invention of comic business, in fact I am coming to the conclusion that I am really essentially a writer of comedy, but very personal comedy. Wilde wrote in his last book 'I have made drama as personal as a lyric,' and I think, whether he has done so or not, that this is the only possible task now."[29]

What made it seem particularly impossible to maintain the serious public manner of high tragedy at the time was, in Yeats's opinion, the taste of the Abbey audience. If by 1908 the Abbey had in fact become something very like the theater of the people he had dreamed of founding, it had done so by evolving, as he disdainfully put it, into a forum for "peasant comedy." "We did not," he would recall ten years later, "set out to create this sort of theatre, and its success has been for me a discouragement and a defeat."[30] His triumph as a public man was marred by the unworthiness of his opponent, the Irish "Proteus" whom the ironies of *The Green Helmet* were intended to both entertain and attack. The story of the poet-as-dramatist unfolded by the vicissitudes of style in the Cuchulain cycle is in this respect itself a version of the story of fathers and sons, an expression of the unresolvable "public" aspect of his way of imagining man's purposes. His battle, like Oisin's was "vain," and like Oisin his response to the mockery of his enterprise was to abandon the field of conflict. In 1914 he began a third play about Cuchulain in which both matter and manner had become entirely "personal," lyrical, and literally private. Two years later, he was able to announce that in *At the Hawk's Well* he had "invented a form of drama, distinguished, indirect, and symbolic, and having no need of the mob . . . an aristocratic form."[31] The shift away from the "mob"—always, as his nostalgic remarks to the Swedish Royal Academy seven years later indicate, an ambivalent one—was intended to be irrevocable and complete: the play was "performed for the first time . . . in a friend's drawing-room, and only those who cared for poetry were invited."[32]

The form of drama that Yeats had "invented" with the help of the Japanese Noh tradition was the first of his "plays for dancers." Those who gathered in Lady Cunard's drawing room that March found that the elaborate scenery and properties of the proscenium-arch stage had been replaced by a few screens and squares of cloth and a small group of masked or heavily made-up actors and musicians. The play was introduced and concluded by choral poems accompanied by simple instruments; the actors' speech and gestures were deliberate and stylized; and the play's emotional climax was expressed not by action or dialogue but by the choreographed movements of a dancer. What would please the few who "cared for poetry" most was, Yeats felt, a drama that sought not to imitate what he called "the disordered passion of nature" but to remake it into something that had the formality, simplicity, and intimacy that he associated with the lyric. The result would be, as he put it in his essay on "Certain Noble Plays of Japan," "a group of figures, images, symbols" that would "enable us to pass for a few moments into a deep of the mind that had hitherto been too subtle for our habitation."[33] His purpose thus was not to arouse feelings associated with "natural" objects but to enhance the depth of the self's relationship to itself, and it is interesting to observe that in attempting to do so the poet-as-dramatist became exclusively concerned with the causes and consequences of Cuchulain's "heroic" narcissism. The "overcomplicated" oedipal matter of On Baile's Strand has disappeared, along with its "disordered" histrionic manner; we are left in these final plays with events that either precede (in At the Hawk's Well) or supersede (in The Only Jealousy of Emer and The Death of Cuchulain) the conflicts of fathers and sons.[34]

The subject of At the Hawk's Well is the event that gives "the witches" their power over Cuchulain's life. Its concerns, consequently, are similar to those of "Red Hanrahan" and implicitly "The Tower" and "Among School Children," and it opens with a choral lyric reminiscent of other pale young men and other imaginary desolations, of sons, and of mothers:

> I call to the eye of the mind
> A well long choked up and dry
> And boughs long stripped by the wind,
> And I call to the mind's eye
> Pallor of an ivory face,
> Its lofty dissolute air,
> A man climbing up to a place
> The salt sea wind has swept bare.

What were his life soon done!
Would he lose by that or win?
A mother that saw her son
Doubled over a speckled shin,
Cross-grained with ninety years,
Would cry, "How little worth
Were all my hopes and fears
    And the hard pain of his birth!"
[1–16]

The scene is "the Hawk's Well," called, like the landscape of "The Tower," "to the mind's eye" and represented by a square of blue cloth on the floor, a dry cup in the stone beside which a young girl, the Guardian of the Well, is sitting motionless and silent, covered by her cloak:

Upon the old grey stone at its side,
Worn out from raking its dry bed,
Worn out from gathering up the leaves.
Her heavy eyes
Know nothing, or but look upon stone.
[26–30]

As the play begins, two masked figures join the Guardian by the well, both in search of the "miraculous water" of eternal life that flows there in "A secret moment that the holy shades / That dance upon the desolate mountain know, / . . . and when it comes / The water has scarce plashed before it is gone" (117–20). The first is an Old Man, who comes to renew a vigil he has kept for fifty years; the second is Cuchulain, newly arrived in the place and, we soon realize, on his way to meet his "fierce woman of the camp" in dubious battle. The Old Man jealously tries to discourage Cuchulain from trying his luck in the "accursed place." He is, he says,

One whom the dancers cheat. I came like you
When young in body and in mind, and blown
By what seemed to me a lucky sail.
. . . .
                              . . . I waited
While the years passed and withered me away.
. . . .
And yet the dancers have deceived me. Thrice
I have awakened from a sudden sleep
To find the stones were wet.
[128–39]

But worse than this, the Old Man explains, is the threat of the "Woman of the Sidhe" who comes to "possess" the Guardian of the Well at the moment the water flows. "Who knows whom she will murder or betray / Before she wakes in ignorance of it all, / And gathers up the leaves?" (191–93). The moment is at hand, for the Guardian is already in a trance, and Cuchulain says that he has been attacked on the mountain by a "great grey hawk" that, the Old Man explains, is "the Woman of the Sidhe herself." Again, his description of her has a cumulatively familiar ring. She is

> The mountain witch, the unappeasable shadow.
> She is always flitting upon this mountain-side,
> To allure or to destroy. When she has shown
> Herself to the fierce women of the hills
> Under that shape they offer sacrifice
> And arm for battle. There falls a curse
> On all who have gazed in her unmoistened eyes;
> . . . .
> . . . That curse may be
> Never to win a woman's love and keep it;
> Or always to mix hatred in the love;
> Or it may be that she will kill your children,
> That you will find them, their throats torn and bloody,
> Or you will be so maddened that you will kill them
> With your own hand.
> [162–79]

Cuchulain, however, is resolved to stay and promises to share the water with the Old Man. The entranced Guardian rises and begins to dance, "moving like a hawk." The Old Man, who "cannot bear her eyes, they are not of this world, / Nor moist, nor faltering," covers his head and falls asleep as before; Cuchulain, however, defies her: "I am not afraid of you, bird, woman, or witch." He tells her,

> Do what you will, I shall not leave this place
> Till I have grown immortal like yourself.
> [211–12]

The dance goes on; Cuchulain rises from the side of the well, entranced, for "the madness has laid hold upon him now, / For he grows pale and staggers to his feet" (216–17). "As if in a dream" he is led offstage by the dancer just as the water "plashes" in the well. The Old Man wakes to find the stones "dark" yet the well empty; he has once again been "deluded."

Cuchulain returns from his vain pursuit of the Guardian among the rocks, and they hear war cries in the distance. "She has roused the fierce women of the hills," says the Old Man,

> Aoife, and all her troop, to take your life,
> And never till you are lying in the earth
> Can you know rest.
> [242–45]

Cuchulain goes out to "face them," "no longer in a dream," and the play ends with a second choral lyric that begins,

> Come to me, human faces,
> Familiar memories;
> I have found hateful eyes
> Among the desolate places,
> Unfaltering, unmoistened eyes.
> [250–54]

In *At the Hawk's Well* as in "Red Hanrahan," then, the genetic event in the hero's story is a meeting with a Woman of the Sidhe, the difference being that the poet, like the Old Man, must at the last moment turn aside from her and is therefore only "touched" with decrepitude and depression. Paradoxically, it is the "exultant" hero who has looked most deeply into her eyes and been absorbed most deeply into the "curse" of her will, "to allure or to destroy." It is explicitly (rather than interpretatively) the working out of her curse that leads to the meeting of Aoife and Cuchulain, to their son's tragic death, and to the heroic madness of the father; Cuchulain's masculine purposes are from this moment swallowed up in the feminine will that in its extreme is the murderous rage that destroys both fathers and sons. The curse of her "unmoistened eye," moreover, is implicitly associated with the curse of the unempathic mother whose "brightening glance" is so ecstatically solicited in the final stanza of "Among School Children," and her delusive and maddening shadow with the depressive shadow cast on man's enterprise in the opening lyric,

> . . . "How little worth
> Were all my hopes and fears
> And the hard pain of his birth!"[35]

The extent to which the "witches" are given control over what Yeats would later have called Cuchulain's *"Body of Fate,"* then, suggests that his conception of the "lyric" drama has much in common with the vicissitudes of *Anima Hominis* that, in *A Vision,* are described in terms of the commedia dell'arte. In effect it is a drama of the "antiself," of the peril-ous alternation between extremes of somebodiness and nobodiness that expresses the extent to which a son's "natural ego or *Will*" can be isolated by maternal indifference and preempted by maternal fantasy. His world is, literally and figuratively, "Daimonic" and stage-managed; his gran-diosity is a *"Mask,"* his *"Body of Fate"* a scenario, his *"Creative Mind"* the artifice of an actor. The voice of Cuchulain an audience hears is not, like the voice of the lyric poet or the poet-hero, that of someone imagining himself but of someone being imagined, and we can now see that what "someone else" might imagine is not just the "image" a mother might wor-ship but a drama of apotheosis and rage, of the idealizing love that makes men feel invulnerable and immortal and the murderous hatred that maddens and destroys them. The landscape called to the mind's eye here is one in which the fountains of life are not only capricious and grudging but also hostile and, as Cuchulain puts it, implacably "far off." The "abounding jet" and the "little runnel" have been replaced by the dry well; the landscape of the heroic mission is that of total oral deprivation.[36]

The extremity of what Yeats would refer to in *The Only Jealousy of Emer* as Cuchulain's "drouth" accounts for both the extremity of his compensatory demands on life and honor ("I'll not be bound"; "I shall not leave this place / Till I have grown immortal like yourself") and his brittle susceptibility to the overwhelming rage at "all things" that periodically darkens his mind. This increase in the power of archaic forces "out of memory" is accompanied by a corresponding decrease in the dramatic importance of oedipal conflict. It is true that the meeting of Cuchulain (here, as at the beginning of *The Green Helmet,* called simply the "Young Man") and the Old Man by the dry well suggests, among other things, the meeting of father and son and is reminiscent of other more hopeful, if less heroic, encounters: Oisin and the demon beside the "little runnel" and the poet and the fisherman by the flowing stream. But here the oedipal content of their rivalry is not even ironically recognized, and its associations only serve to emphasize the extent to which the version of the hero's story that takes place in the "deep of the mind" has become a story not of sexual aspirations but of the overwhelming pre-genital thirst for the "waters of life" that ebb and flow with the moon. The successful resolution of the story of fathers and sons—suggested here by Cuchulain's offer to share the "miraculous water" with the Old Man—is meaningless in the presence of the unempathic well "long choked and dry"; the brotherhood of man and the viability of the "public" self, itself ironically "but a dream," can only be imagined by a "stone dark under froth," at that magical, unforeseen, and unforeseeable moment when maternal supply yields to filial demand and the water "plashes" in the dry well.

As it is, Cuchulain must remain wholly estranged from the demands of his "inner" self, obeying only the will of the maternal "other" and keeping, in the face of the apocalyptic force of his repressed rage, only the most tenuous hold on the *"Mask"* that assures his integrity and self-esteem. Unlike the poet, he is incapable of turning aside in his own interests; for the hero there is no alternative to the stirring of the beast but madness, and his madness and its peculiar cure is the subject of Yeats's next Cuchulain play, *The Only Jealousy of Emer.*

Bricriu and Emer

The Only Jealousy of Emer was first published in *Poetry* in January 1919. In its original form, it was intended to reproduce the "lyric" style of *At the Hawk's Well* exactly, even to the point of makeup and props;[37] after ten years, it reappeared in a "simplified" version for the public stage, *Fighting the Waves.*[38] It needed simplifying. *The Only Jealousy of Emer* is a confusing play, and this in the end may be the clearest thing about it. The clearest and, I think, the most important thing for the subject of the play is the way people and events *are* confused by the

> . . . bonds no man could unbind,
> Being imagined within
> The labyrinth of the mind.
> [22–24]

The First Musician's song warns us that this play concerns an inner world, and as the action proceeds it becomes plain that these figures and voices obey a logic that, like the "primary process" Freud discovered in dreams, is a logic of condensation and displacement.[39] Here, "within," images merge, separate, and merge again: two men with the same face are with a woman; now there are two women; now one of the men has a different face, and there is one woman again; now a third woman comes and takes one of the men away; now the other man has his old face, and the second woman comes back. Are they all the same man and woman? Are

they all, as the musician suggests, aspects of the same labyrinthine mind? The
question is not whether I am about to make the play seem more confusing than it is, but whether I will be able to make it seem confused enough.

The Only Jealousy of Emer begins where On Baile's Strand ends.
Cuchulain's lifeless body has been taken from the waves and laid in a
fisherman's cottage:

> On one side of the stage [is] the curtained bed or litter on which lies
> a man in his grave-clothes. He wears an heroic mask. Another man
> with exactly similar clothes and mask crouches near the front.[40]

Emer, Cuchulain's estranged wife, is sitting by the bed; presently Eithne
Inguba, his mistress, enters. Emer tells her the story of On Baile's Strand
and explains that Cuchulain is not dead but in the deathlike trance of the
"changeling." The two women decide to call back the man they love:

Eithne
Inguba.   Cry out his name.
            All that are taken from our sight, they say,
            Loiter amid the scenery of their lives
            For certain hours or days, and should he hear
            He might, being angry, drive the changeling out.

Emer.   It is hard to make them hear amid their darkness,
            And it is long since I could call him home;
            I am but his wife, but if you call aloud
            With the sweet voice that is so dear to him
            He cannot help but listen.

Eithne
Inguba.   He loves me best,
            Being his newest love, but in the end
            Will love the woman best who loved him first
            And loved him through the years when love seemed lost.

Emer.   I have that hope, the hope that some day somewhere
            We'll sit together at the hearth again.

Eithne
Inguba.   Women like me, the violent hour passed over,
            Are flung into some corner like old nut-shells.
            Cuchulain, listen.
            [90–107]

Eithne Inguba cries out passionately to the silent Figure of Cuchulain
and kisses its lips; but when it finally stirs and speaks it is wearing not the

"heroic" mask of Cuchulain but the mask of a "distorted face" and has "a withered right arm." Eithne Inguba flees in terror, but Emer stays to question him. He is, he says "Bricriu, / Maker of discord among gods and men," and when Emer asks him why he has come, he replies,

> I show my face, and everything he loves
> Must fly away.

Emer.   You people of the wind
> Are full of lying speech and mockery:
> I have not fled your face.

Figure of
Cuchulain.   You are not loved.

Emer.   And therefore have no dread to meet your eyes
> And to demand him of you.

Figure of
Cuchulain.   For that I have come.
> You have but to pay the price and he is free.
>   [151–57]

The price Bricriu demands is that Emer "but renounce the chance" of some day becoming "the apple of [Cuchulain's] eye again." When she at first refuses to abandon her only hope of happiness, he shows her the crouching Ghost of Cuchulain. As they watch, Fand, the Woman of the Sidhe, enters and wakes the Ghost with a dance and tempts it to kiss her mouth and lose all memory of its mortal life. She is, the Ghost remembers, the same woman he had met "long ago" at the Hawk's Well: "You, / That now seem friendly, fled away, / Half woman and half bird of prey" (243–45). She is, however, "all woman now," and the Ghost, reluctant at first to abandon his memories of Emer, finally follows her offstage. Bricriu, now calling himself "Fand's enemy come to thwart her will" (289), tells Emer that there is still time to save the Ghost from being taken, and at the last moment she cries out, "I renounce Cuchulain's love for ever." The Figure of Cuchulain falls back on the bed and rises again wearing the heroic mask, and Eithne Inguba reenters triumphantly to claim him: "It is I that won him from the sea, / That brought him back to life" (301–2).

As the reappearance of the Woman of the Sidhe indicates, *The Only Jealousy of Emer* is a continuation of the story about the *Daimonic* "power of the witches over Cuchulain's life" that begins in *At the Hawk's Well.* It is consequently also a reinterpretation of the events of

On Baile's Strand and *The Green Helmet:* the protean oedipal opponent (the waves, the Red Man from the sea) is now associated with a power that is explicitly feminine and implicitly narcissistic, the sea—"our mother the sea," as Yeats calls it in a note to *Fighting the Waves*[41]—that swallows up the heroic father after he has killed his son. The first thing to be done for Cuchulain, Emer says, is to "hide the sea," which the musician's song tells us is "beyond the open door . . . / The shining, bitter sea, is crying out."

> I'll cover up his face to hide the sea;
> And throw new logs upon the hearth and stir
> The half-burnt logs until they break in flame.
> Old Manannan's unbridled horses come
> Out of the sea, and on their backs his horsemen;
> But all the enchantments of the dreaming foam
> Dread the hearth-fire.
> [108–14]

Even Emer, however, misconceives the therapeutic problem at first. She thinks that Cuchulain has been replaced by some masculine rival and hopes that Eithne Inguba can bring back his jealous Ghost by making love to his "changeling." But Eithne's kiss summons Bricriu instead, and he tells Emer that (as the association between this hearth-fire and the oath that drives out the witches in *On Baile's Strand* suggests) what must be overcome is not one of Manannan's horsemen but Fand, the Woman of the Sidhe:

> She has hurried from the Country-under-Wave
> And dreamed herself into that shape that he
> May glitter in her basket; for the Sidhe
> Are dexterous fishers and they fish for men
> With dreams on the hook.
> [202–6]

In fact the main conflict in the play is between Bricriu and the "woman's will" personified by Fand. It is Bricriu, "maker of discord among gods and men," and not Emer who finally brings the hero back; it is he who, as he says at the crisis of the action, is "Fand's enemy, come to thwart her will, / And you stand gaping there. . . . / Renounce him, and her power is at an end."[42] Both his peculiar attributes and his power to bargain for Cuchulain's return are related to the fact that he is Cuchulain's "changeling," a word used by the Irish to describe psychotic states in which a personality appears to have been "taken" by some external force and replaced either by an inanimate object (as in catatonia) or by another personality. "It may be," Emer says,

> An image has been put into his place,
> A sea-born log bewitched into his likeness,
> Or some stark horseman grown too old to ride
> Among the troops of Manannan, Son of the Sea,
> Now that his joints are stiff.
> [85–90]

Bricriu is one of the latter; or, in more psychological terms, he is Yeats's way of imagining the schizoid self that appears when the tenuous integrity of the heroic "*Mask*" has been destroyed by narcissistic rage. "Fand's enemy" is in this respect a version of the "great beast" of *Anima Mundi* whose vicissitudes determine the apocalyptic aesthetic of the Yeatsian lyric. The image summoned by the heroic father's mistress, however, is unlike the images summoned by the poet's Muse in implying a persona imposed from without rather than a "self" remade from within: like the exultant face that the actor reassumes at the end of the play, it is one of the "masks" of *Anima Hominis*. The story of Cuchulain the father, as indicated by the story of Cuchulain the Young Man that Yeats tells in *At the Hawk's Well,* is the "public" drama of possession, the story of the "taken" somebody whose face is a mask and whose life is a play. The numinous inner "stirring" that a poet-son might entertain, gratify, and even solicit manifests itself in the hero-father he imagines only as an "other" somebody "bewitched into his likeness," the pitiful, withered "little beast" reflected in the distorting mirror of maternal aversion: "I show my face, and everything he loves / Must fly away."

"Everything," of course, includes not only his earliest but also his latest loves. *The Only Jealousy of Emer* is a story about husbands and wives, and so far speculation about the infantile origin of Cuchulain's psychotic "absence" has explained nothing about Emer's ability to end it. The therapeutic power of her "only jealousy" is the most puzzling thing about the play: Why should Fand's power over Cuchulain end when Emer renounces him? We are not told directly in this or any of the other plays in the cycle, and an answer to the question begins to suggest itself only when we recall that in Yeats's earliest version of the story, "Cuchulain's Fight with the Sea," the benign and loving wife who now saves him "from the sea" is the malignant and vindictive wife who drives him into it.[43] The elaboration of Cuchulain's story, in other words, has been a process of displacement: in the intervening versions Emer's rage has been transferred first to Aoife (*On Baile's Strand*) and then to Fand (*At the Hawk's Well*). Like the 1905 version of "Red Hanrahan," the strange "symbolic" transaction of *The Only Jealousy of Emer* is a way of "half remembering" other texts: Emer can cure Cuchulain's illness because, in another aspect, she is its cause. When she explicitly renounces his love, consequently, she implicitly renounces her rage at the man who abandoned her; her only hope is, as the title suggests, her "only jealousy." Bricriu's "distorted" face and "withered" form are in this respect the attributes of the absent father—the "husband found" by the wife who is not loved—that correspond to the ironically "laughing mouth" and protean evasiveness of her son's "father found"; indeed we may begin to suspect that, as the last section of this chapter will show more clearly, the story of the real and ideal fathers is among other things the story of the real and ideal husbands.

Yet if the resolution of Cuchulain's "heroic" psychosis suggests that here, as in *On Baile's Strand*, the implicit scenario is the story of a wife's rage, the peculiar bargain that Bricriu strikes with her also indicates that her power to save him "from the sea" is the power of the archaic maternal "will." In the "deep of the mind" represented in *The Only Jealousy of Emer* there is no longer any distinction between the images of adoration and loathing that express the "power of the witches" over fathers and the schizoid "masks" of the husband that it is Emer's privilege to summon and dismiss. Fand's power and Emer's are coterminous because, in the symbolic language of the "lyric" drama, their claims on Cuchulain's Ghost are psychically analogous. "In the end," Eithne Inguba says, "he will love the woman best who loved him first." In effect, what Bricriu demands in exchange for an "absent" husband's return is that a wife relinquish the unconditional conjugal "hope" that is like a mother's hope: the selfless devotion to a heroic image that is also the self-absorbing hatred of a "little beast." What Fand's enemy opposes is the all-consuming, unempathic ambivalence toward man's enterprise that is "woman's will," the power that at certain critical moments reduces, or threatens to reduce, both fathers and sons to ghosts, swallowed up in an overwhelming wave of "spiritual" love and hate.[44]

Cuchulain's "fancy" has been "taken" by a son whose head was bewitched into a likeness of a woman's; it will be returned only when Emer renounces the claim that makes that likeness her own. The consummation of her bargain with Bricriu is the hero-father's equivalent of the depressed and ambivalent betrayal of mothers by poet-sons. The beloved heroic mask will be reassumed by Cuchulain's wave-mastered

figure when the "spiritual" priority of the conjugal bond has been replaced by the sort of uncommitted love Cuchulain extols in *On Baile's
Strand.* As Yeats imagines it, the husband who returns from the deep of
the mind is at best a "husband lost," the aspect of the prepsychotically
"absent" father that corresponds to the son's nostalgically idealized
"man who does not exist." The resumption of the *Daimonic* drama of
Anima Hominis and the hollow face of the antiself requires a rejection of
all loves except the sexual that, like Eithne Inguba's, are founded on
"spiritual hate" and loved only for a "violent hour." As Emer cries out,
"I renounce Cuchulain's love for ever," the Figure of Cuchulain "sinks
back on the bed, half-drawing the curtain." Eithne Inguba reenters and
kneels beside him:

> Come to me, my beloved, it is I.
> I, Eithne Inguba. Look! He is there.
> He has come back and moved upon the bed.
> And it is I that won him from the sea,
> That brought him back to life.

Emer.   Cuchulain wakes.
> [*The figure turns round. It once more wears the heroic mask.*]

Cuchulain. Your arms, your arms! O Eithne Inguba,
> I have been in some strange place and am afraid.
> [298–304]

In *The Only Jealousy of Emer,* then, we are given what amounts to the
final episode in the story of the poet that began with the story of the
"woman lost" in "The Tower." The sum of his imaginary biography is in
one sense a "complex"—an expression of the emotional economy of a
single personality—and in another a "family"—an account of the
psychogenetic circumstances that produced that personality. The unavoidable complexity of its formulation is somewhat reduced if we think of
what is being expressed as a circular process in which the "resolution" of
one set of conflicting forces recreates the circumstances that produce the
conflict. The ambivalent relationship of sons and mothers expressed in
the mistress/Muse conflict is both resolved and reproduced in the estrangement of fathers and mothers, which in turn reproduces (via paternal absence and maternal rage) the circumstances of that ambivalence in
the relationship of mothers and sons; and thus in both its poetic and
dramatic forms (the "private" *Anima Mundi* and the "public" *Anima
Hominis*) the measures taken to assure the repression of feelings that

threaten narcissistic weakness also assure the return or "second coming" of the repressed in the form of either creative "decrepitude" or heroic psychosis.

Ultimately, as we have already seen, this circularity is the essence of Yeats's historical and psychological intuitions. In these plays, however, it is primarily present as the complex state of idealization and aggression that we register in the response we call "irony." As a rule, this irony interprets what the protean demon of *Oisin* calls "man's purpose": here the most obvious example is the treatment of Cuchulain's encounter with the Red Man, which is both "heroic" and a "farce." It is also present, however, in the general subjection of man's "heroic" temper to "woman's will" in the dance plays, and in *On Baile's Strand* it presides not only over the dramatic failure of the play's "over-complicated" oedipal scenario but also over the relation of that scenario to the play's comic subplot, which involves the nefarious activities of the Blind Man and the Fool:

> And when the Fool and the Blind Man stole the bread
> Cuchulain fought the ungovernable sea;
> Heart-mysteries there. . . .

Since it is the Blind Man who returns in *The Death of Cuchulain* to make a final end of him, it is important to preface a discussion of the last play with a brief digression that concludes our analysis of the first.

The ironical artifice of *On Baile's Strand* is of a relatively simple sort. As in the case of *Oisin,* the main events of the action are presented in a kind of frame narrative, in this case provided by the repartee of the Blind Man and the Fool that opens and closes the play. Briefly, the situation is this: the two beggars have together (employing the Blind Man's brain and the Fool's brawn) contrived to steal a hen, and as the play opens they are waiting for it to cook. Later, as Cuchulain and the Young Man go offstage to fight, they come onstage to do the same: the Fool is in a rage because the Blind Man has secretly eaten the whole fowl himself. Both remain onstage to reveal the Young Man's identity to the victorious Cuchulain and then, as we have seen, to describe the progress of his madness to the audience. The Fool is fascinated, but the Blind Man's thoughts are elsewhere, and the play ends with this exchange:

Fool.   The waves have mastered him.

Blind Man. Come here, I say.

Fool.   What is it?

Blind Man. There will be nobody in the houses. Come this way; come quickly!
The ovens will be full. We will put our hands into the ovens.
[*They go out.*]
[799–804]

One of the most obvious ways our response to the tragic events of *On Baile's Strand* is complicated, then, is by the reaction of the two lower characters in the frame plot, and their message is that heroism and tragedy are all very well, but when all is said and done one must eat. Cuchulain's "oedipal" magnificence, in other words, is being presented in a context that suggests, like the dry and rocky landscape of the Hawk's Well, the "little runnel" of *Oisin,* and for that matter all the ironies associated with the aspirations of Yeats's "old scarecrows," that such genital aspirations must always be brought to nothing by the overwhelming sense of oral deprivation by which the "witches" master man's purpose. The narcissistic rage that is the latent content of both the poet's creative depression and the hero's madness is among other things oral rage, the sword a symbol for the tongue as well as the phallus or, in its creative manifestation (as in *Oisin*), for language itself.[45] In the latter, the tongue-as-sword expresses the progressive need to put oral aggression in the service of oedipal aspiration; but it is also (as the sword-as-tongue) what ironically disarms those aspirations by making them vulnerable to the narcissistic weakness of the affectively starved pre-oedipal infant.[46]

The conflict between the Blind Man and the Fool is thus, as Yeats himself noted in 1934, the "shadow" of the conflict of Conchubar and Cuchulain.[47] As Conchubar cheats Cuchulain of his son, so the Blind Man cheats the Fool (who, like Cuchulain, is subject to the persecution of the witches of the sea)[48] of his dinner. The implication of this ironic interpretation of the oedipal conflict in the main plot is that Cuchulain's relation to his son is essentially a relation to an oral object, and it is precisely this sort of relation—the fantasy of eating or being eaten, and its attendant anxieties—that characterizes the narcissistic personality's perception of the objects that excite its affection. The resonance between the death of the Young Man and the fate of the hen is an ironically disarmed version of the cannibalistic fantasies that define the complementary "structures" of secondary narcissism, and this sort of fantasy is precisely what Cuchulain's Ghost will rediscover in the depths of psychotic withdrawal (itself an expression of the infantile fear of being swallowed by the maternal "sea").[49] With a kiss, the Woman of the Sidhe says, she can bring him "oblivion / Even to quench Cuchulain's drouth, / Even to still that heart"; and as he follows her offstage he cries, "Your mouth, your mouth!" (265–85). This is also the mixture of "spiritual" desire and fear that, one may surmise, is expressed in many of the lyrics: love and hate, enfolding roses and ravening beasts, and, less obviously, in the ironic restriction of genital strivings by the "woman lost":

> Wine comes in at the mouth
> And love comes in at the eye;
> That's all we shall know for truth
> Before we grow old and die.
> I lift the glass to my mouth,
> I look at you, and I sigh.[50]
> ["A Drinking Song"]

In *The Death of Cuchulain,* which was published posthumously by the Cuala Press in the *Last Poems and Plays* (1939), Yeats's implicit sense of the narcissistic ironies that are "all we shall know for truth" are bitterly dramatized in the second demise of his dissolute and "exultantly" phallic hero. The last episode in the story of the poet-as-dramatist is, moreover, an explicit expression of his ambivalence toward his audience. Although it was written some twenty years after *The Only Jealousy of Emer,* it is clearly in the "private" style of the dance plays, with minimal, stylized props and a choreographed climax; the first person to appear on the stage is an "Old Man" who says he is the play's "producer" and eagerly proceeds, like the poet of "At the Abbey Theatre," to engage the "draughty sea" of faces before him:

> I am sure that as I am producing a play for people I like, it is not probable, in this vile age, that they will be more in number than those who listened to the first performance of Milton's *Comus.* On the present occasion they must know the old epics and Mr. Yeats's plays about them; such people, however poor, have libraries of their own. If there are more than a hundred I won't be able to escape people who are educating themselves out of the Book Societies and the like, sciolists all, pickpockets and opinionated bitches.
> [n–x]

The subject of *The Death of Cuchulain,* like that of *On Baile's Strand,* is the destructive attack of one of Cuchulain's old mistresses upon the land he guards, and once again it becomes the occasion for the ironic death predicted by the Red Man in *The Green Helmet.* In the opening scene, Cuchulain is told of an invasion by Queen Maeve and her "Connacht ruffians"; in the closing scene he is discovered wounded and bound upright to a pillar stone, where he is killed by the Blind Man because Maeve has offered him twelve pennies for Cuchulain's "head in a bag." In the intervening scenes he has in effect reviewed the history of his "heroic" love affairs in encounters with Eithne Inguba and Aoife, now an "erect white-haired woman."

Both now seek his death. First, Eithne Inguba—revealing the "spiritual hatred" implicit in her "sexual love"—attempts to trick Cuchulain into thinking that Emer wants him to face Maeve heroically, "no matter what the odds." A moment later she claims that she has done so only because "Maeve put me in a trance" and says that she has seen the crow-headed figure of the "Morrigu, war goddess," by which she understands that Cuchulain is about to die. In her regret and grief she threatens to denounce herself to Cuchulain's servants after he is gone, but he forestalls her by commanding one of them to drug her and give her to another man "should I not return." The stage is darkened and cleared, and Cuchulain reenters, weak and delirious from "six mortal wounds." He tries to bind himself to a pillar with his belt. Aoife enters to help him, saying that of all Maeve's "terrified army" she alone dares approach to make an end of him. Cuchulain recognizes her and admits that she has "a right" to kill him to avenge the death of her son. He allows her to bind his hands with one of her veils, but she is prevented from killing him by the approach of the Blind Man. "I will keep out of his sight," she says, "for I have things / That I must ask questions on before I kill you" (150–51). After Cuchulain has been killed by the Blind Man, however, it is the Morrigu that enters, describes his last battle with Maeve's lovers and sons, and introduces a valedictory dance performed by Emer before a black parallelogram representing her husband's head:

> The dead can hear me, and to the dead I speak.
> This head is great Cuchulain's, those other six
> Gave him six mortal wounds. This man came first;
> Youth lingered though the years ran on, that season
> A woman loves the best. Maeve's latest lover,
> This man, had given him the second wound,
> He had possessed her once; these were her sons,
> Two valiant men that gave the third and fourth:
> These other men were of no account,
> They saw that he was weakening and crept in;
> One gave him the sixth wound and one the fifth;
> Conall avenged him. I arranged the dance.
> [184–95]

As a whole, the scenario of *The Death of Cuchulain* is subject to—and, I think, dramatically weakened by—the same sort of "complication" as *On Baile's Strand.* The Morrigu, who seems to be having the last word in the matter, suggests that the story of Cuchulain's "six mortal wounds" is the story of husbands, lovers, and sons, and one could plausibly extend this interpretation to include the Blind Man, who was, as we have seen, connected in Yeats's mind with King Conchubar.[51] This, however, is at worst a contrived and at best an ironic interpretation of his demise, for the scene she describes is clearly the moment when, as the Red Man puts it in *The Green Helmet,* "the weak will end the strong": "These other men were men of no account, / They saw that he was weakening and crept in." The importance of all Cuchulain's male adversaries, moreover, is belied by the fact that, while they are necessary, they are not sufficient to kill him; with the exception of the Blind Man they are not even significant enough to appear onstage.

What does appear onstage is, as in the other dance plays, a dramatic encounter between the hero and "woman's will." Cuchulain's significant opponents are all women, he is mourned by a woman, and the play is presided over by a female war goddess. The proliferation of female figures suggests, like *The Only Jealousy of Emer,* that the real stuff of the Yeatsian drama is the murderous ambivalence women feel toward the men they love best, a drama of adoration and loathing that is summed up visually in the pillar stone to which Aoife binds Cuchulain and the severed head before which Emer dances.[52] The hero's phallic symbols are his own neither in the giving nor the taking away; instead, they are, as the Old Man reminds the audience at the beginning, abstractions that acquire meaning only as they are interpreted for us in the medium of feminine fantasy. "I had thought," he says, "to have those heads carved, but no, if the dancer [playing Emer] can dance properly no wood-carving can look as well as a parallelogram of painted wood" (kk–nn). As such, the shapes we see on the stage suggest, like the other "images" apostophized in "Among School Children," not the affirmation but the betrayal of a man's real "shape" and the mockery of his labor and his enterprise. "There floats out there," Cuchulain says as the Blind Man is groping for his throat,

> The shape that I shall take when I am dead,
> My soul's first shape, a soft feathery shape,
> And is not that a strange shape for the soul
> Of a great fighting-man?[53]
> [177–81]

But the dramatic complications of *The Death of Cuchulain* do not end with the usurpation of "man's purpose" by woman's will. In the traditional account of the event, Cuchulain dies alone, upright against the pillar to which he has bound himself with his belt after receiving his six wounds, and it is only after the birds have begun to settle on his corpse that anyone in Maeve's army has the courage to approach and behead him.[54] To this simple scenario of heroic defiance Yeats has added not only the episode of Aoife and her veils but also the entrance of the Blind Man with his bag; despite her acknowledged "right," it is not Aoife but the Blind Man who takes the head. Yeats's insistence on this point, moreover, leads to a puzzling bit of stage business: Aoife's exit at the last moment is, as Ure points out, "contrived, awkward, and feebly explained."[55] Apparently Yeats is trying to relate the events of the play to the story of fathers and sons in *On Baile's Strand* by reintroducing Conchubar's ironic "shadow." The irony, however, cuts two ways: in contriving to have the strongest ended by the weakest, Yeats is also reviving the kind of awkward jumbling of "interests" that, I think, is his chief weakness as a "public" dramatist.

Whatever general conclusions one might be inclined to draw from the climax of the last scene of Yeats's last play, it is clear that the final confrontation between the hero and his nemesis has little to do with the conflicts of the generations of men. The subject here is a terror of a far more archaic sort, more so even than a hero's fear of being "bound" and unmanned by vindictive women. The Blind Man, it is true, is in Maeve's service. But in cutting off Cuchulain's head with the knife he keeps sharp "because it cuts my food" (172) and stuffing it in his bag, he is above all acting in the interests of his own greed. In brief, the fear of being unmanned by women that haunts Cuchulain's heroic career is itself haunted by fantasies of oral aggression. The "remade" self apostrophized by the lyric poet is, as we have seen, characteristically imagined in images of swallowing and being swallowed, and at the moment of Cuchulain's death the manner of his death suggests that the dissolution and spiritual rebirth of his "shape" is something that the dramatic poet too imagines as an act of cannibalism, the incorporation of the self by the indiscriminate greed of its "shadow," the blind devourer who lies behind the mask of the heroic fool. The dea ex machina of *The Death of Cuchulain* is in one sense a way of representing how the working through of "woman's will" ends in cutting down a country's manhood in senseless battle; but her bird's head betrays the fact that her murderousness is also in the service of more primitive impulses. As the final version of the tutelary deity of man's purpose, the Rose of Battle, the Secret Rose, the Dark Rosaleen of Irish patriotism, she is the carrion crow, eater of corpses, and it is she, and no one else, who "has arranged the dance."[56]

> Are those things that men adore and loathe
> Their sole reality?
> What stood in the Post Office
> With Pearse and Connolly?
> What comes out of the mountain
> When men first shed their blood?
> Who thought Cuchulain till it seemed
> He stood where they had stood?
>
> No body like his body
> Has modern woman borne,
> But an old man looking on life
> Imagines it in scorn.
> A statue's there to mark the place,
> By Oliver Sheppard done.
> So ends the tale that the harlot
> Sang to the beggar-man.
> [*Music from pipe and drum.*]
> [212–27]

Yeats and Pollexfen

In retrospect, it is difficult to imagine two people less suited for a life together than John Butler Yeats and Susan Mary Pollexfen. Yet the match must have seemed suitable enough when it was made. On one side, the attractions and advantages were obvious: in 1863 Susan Pollexfen was "the most beautiful girl in Sligo,"[57] and her father's commercial success promised an uninterrupted supply of the stuff of which the "natural" life is made.[58] On the other, the eldest daughter of an ambitious, newly rich family had the satisfaction of knowing that her fiancé was attractive, charming, and well connected and had respectable, and perhaps brilliant, prospects in the law.

But it soon became clear that whatever they had seen in each other was not what it seemed. The quiet and docile daughter made an austere, melancholy, and hypochondriacal wife; the charming law student and Butler heir was an unreliable and improvident husband. Either one would have been difficult for anyone to live with, and an open, if not openly acknowledged, breach soon formed between them. "I think," J. B. Yeats wrote his wife shortly after she had left London to live with her father in 1871, "that living here . . . is doing me a great deal of good. I shall have more 'morale'—get over many weaknesses and foibles. I shall be more worth your liking when we next live together. The wearing anxiety of the last few years has told on us both, injuring our characters as our physical strength."[59]

They did not live together again for five years. When Susan finally returned to London things were much the same, or worse. Her "nervous weakness" had not been improved by the loss of her sixth child, Jane Grace; she hated the city, and in the months that followed her arrival at Bedford Park in 1876 she became more and more irritable and depressed. She was only contented when she was by the sea, and in the late 1870s she and the children were given holidays in Devon.[60] In 1879 her youngest son, Jack, then eight, had to be sent to live with his grandparents at Merville, where he remained until 1887;[61] by 1880 the state of her health had become alarming enough to hasten J. B. Yeats's decision to return to Dublin.[62] The cottages in Howth overlooking the sea, where her eldest son would remember her talking happily with a fisherman's wife and "telling stories Homer might have told," were taken as long as the money lasted, "for my mother's sake." "I remember all this very clearly," Yeats says in *Reveries,* "and little after it until her mind had gone in a stroke of paralysis and she had found, liberated at last from financial worry, perfect happiness feeding the birds from a London window."[63]

The liberation of his mother's mind was a considerably more painful, protracted, and ambiguous process than Yeats was willing or perhaps able to remember. The happy years at Howth were followed by three years in cheaper lodgings at Ashfield Terrace in Dublin and in 1887 by J. B. Yeats's decison to try his luck again in London.[64] There, while her husband desperately looked for work as a black-and-white illustrator and her family experimented with what her son bravely called "cheap dining" in his letters to his friend Katharine Tynan ("For a man, if he does not mean to bow the knee to Baal, must know all such things"),[65] Susan Yeats suffered through the "torrid June of Jubilee" and the noise of the American Exhibition near their lodgings in Eardley Crescent.[66]

Willie, who immediately found that life in "hateful London" made him "horribly irritable and out of sorts," escaped to Sligo in the middle of August to work on *Oisin.* He was still there that fall when he received word of his mother's first stroke.[67] The news arrived only shortly before his own "nervous collapse"; his poem, which had "gone ahead famously" at first, was now "very obdurate," having had to be "all rewritten once—the third part, I mean." "I hear," he added in a letter to Katharine Tynan, "they wish me not to come home just yet. Lilly [*sic*], you see, is not well yet of her bad suppressed rheumatism attack and Mamma is not well either. However, I dare say a week longer here is all I shall stay. But it is very hard for me to fix a day for certain, 'Oisin' being unfinished."[68]

Finishing the story of the poet he was soon calling "that savage greybeard, Oisin" subjected him to the ominous symptoms of "nerves"—depression and vocal paralysis—that made the third part of the poem "the greatest effort of all my things."[69] His mother and his sister Lily had gone to convalesce at the remote home of a Pollexfen aunt near Huddersfield, in Yorkshire. There, in snowbound loneliness, Susan Yeats suffered another stroke and fell down a flight of stairs.[70] They could not return to London until the middle of April and arrived just a few days before Willie, who had returned from Sligo some months earlier, had his second collapse. "I was the same way," he told Katharine Tynan, "only worse, when finishing 'Oisin.'"[71]

J. B. Yeats had managed to move the family back to the more pleasant surroundings of Bedford Park a few weeks earlier; Oliver Elton, who visited them there in the later 1880s, remembers Susan as a "silent, flitting figure."[72] "At first," Murphy says in his *Yeats Family and the Pollexfens of Sligo,*

> she was able to be among people and would not allow herself to be described as an invalid. But more and more she kept to her room.
> In her last years she was "in possession of only half her mind." She died on 3 January 1900, after an illness of more than twelve years. The weekly newspaper of St. Michael and All Angels, Bedford Park, lists the date of her death but offers no obituary. She was almost a non-person for the last decade of her life.[73]

It may never be clear whether Susan Yeat's final illness was, as Yeats implies in *Reveries,* wholly or even partly physical in its origins. The published record is ambiguous. On one hand Yeats's biographers agree that his mother's "strokes" were "paralytic"; on the other they say that their chief symptom was their effect on her "mind" or "faculties."[74] Murphy, who is more willing (or able) to be frank about the Pollexfens in other respects, is suggestive but inconclusive. The family's return to London, he says, "cracked Susan's spirit," and he introduces his account of her illness with Lily Yeats's remark in the section of her scrapbook called "Mama's Health" that her mother's "nervous system was easily upset."[75]

Susan Yeats may or may not have begun to go mad in 1887. On the whole it seems likely that the deterioration of her "faculties" over the next twelve years was at least abetted by her existing tendency toward depression, withdrawal, and hypochondria. Nor is it unlikely that, whatever the real nature of her illness, those who knew her best must have feared the worst: that in the autumn of 1887 and the winter of 1888 she had taken the first steps on the journey to the inner island of "perfect happiness" that had already claimed her brother William, the designer of the Sligo quays. The coincidence of her strokes and her son's collapses and, in all probability, her daughter's mysteriously "suppressed" rheumatism, is in this respect a chapter in the story of children and mothers, and all that is least mentionable, most archaic, and yet most poignantly "part of the mind" of the poet,

> O had you seen beautiful Niamh grow white as the waters are
> white,
> Lord of the croziers, you even had lifted your hands and wept.[76]

But Yeats's story, like Oisin's, is more the story of sons and mothers, more even in this case than the story of fathers and sons. Susan Yeats's illness was also the conclusion of another, older story: the "silent, flitting figure" that haunted the house in Bedford Park between 1888 and 1900 whispered the tale of a husband and wife who, like Cuchulain and Aoife, were doomed to destroy each other. J. B. Yeats had known it almost from the beginning. Marriage, he warned John Todhunter in the early 1870s, was "a fatal mistake," something repented "hereafter in sackcloth and ashes," and forty years later he told John Quinn, "Marriage means that two people are bringing into the common stock all their weaknesses, and there are two comparisons possible. Marriage is sometimes like two drunken men seeing each other home. Neither can reproach the other or refuse sympathy or help. The other comparison is this: Marriage is like two mortal enemies (the sexes are enemies) meeting on the scaffold and reconciled by the imminence of the great enemy of both."[77]

Of all the numerous weaknesses that John and Susan Yeats held in common during the twenty-five years of increasingly abrasive married life that preceded the "liberation" of her mind, the most puzzling and, in view of their "mortal" enmity, the most significant was their weakness for each other. J. B. Yeats himself was puzzled by it; the *Early Memories: Some Chapters of Autobiography* published shortly after his death by his daughter Lollie's Cuala Press return to the subject again and again. He recalls there that his fascination with the Pollexfens began when he met Susan's older brothers, Charles, the eldest, and George, at Atholl Academy. He remembers in particular "my dear friend, George Pollexfen, whose sister I afterwards married. . . . George was the most melancholy of men. He was melancholy as a boy and as a man. I think it was his melancholy that attracted me, who am a cheerful & perennially hopeful man."[78]

It is by no means clear from J. B. Yeats's remarks exactly what the attraction of the Pollexfen melancholy was, though some of his observations are suggestive. It may be, for instance, that his friend George's depressed personality helped assuage what he elsewhere calls his "insatiable" longing for his mother during the grim years at Atholl.[79] George Pollexfen's version of "puritanism," he says, "only enhanced his tenderness, which was like that of a nurse by the bedside of a sick man, and veritably there were times when thinking about this benighted and lost human nature he was like a tender mother with a fractious child."[80]

There is in even J. B. Yeats's earliest response to the Pollexfens, then, an ominous intimation of what he would find attractive in the woman he chose to be the "tender mother" of his own children. By the end of his life, it was painfully clear to him that their tenderness, like their puritanism, expressed their solicitude not for others but for themselves. "The master-principle in that family was what I may describe as self-loyalty," he says in *Early Memories*.

> At Sligo, I was the social man where it was the individual man that counted. It is a curious fact that entering this sombre house of stern preoccupation with business I for the first time in my life felt myself to be a free man, and that I was invited by the example of everyone around me to be my very self, thereby receiving the most important lesson in my life. The malady of puritanism is self-exaggeration, "self-saturation" is the medical term.
> . . . But the good side is that the puritan belongs to himself, whereas the votary of the religion of social enjoyment belongs to his neighbours and to society. . . . The Pollexfen charm was in their entire sincerity.[81]

There is much in J. B. Yeats's description of his wife's family that, in language at times consciously "medical," attests to the pathological extremity of their narcissistic intensity. "The question arises," he says elsewhere of his "dear friend" George, "did he himself love anybody? . . . I am not sure."[82] It was a question he could have asked about the sister he married; she too "pretended to nothing she did not feel."[83] But his sympathy and insight betrays something about his own case that is less obvious. The Pollexfen "sincerity" was also their "charm," and the dialectic between "individual" and "social" that J. B. Yeats uses to account for it suggests that, like the "I" and "we" of his son's poems, what appears opposite is really complementary.[84] To feel that one must belong either wholly to oneself or wholly to others is to confess, in both cases, a radical uncertainty about what it means to feel whole; to be prone, like the Pollexfens, to chronic gloom or, like the Yeatses, to chronic optimism about "human nature" is to betray a common inability to accept its real capabilities and limitations.

It is reasonable to surmise, and particularly so in view of their fatal attraction for each other, that if the puritan Pollexfen was afflicted by pathological depression, the "pagan" Yeats suffered equally, but far less obviously, from a "benign" mania. The personalities of both John Butler and Susan Pollexfen Yeats were manifestations, as their son's would be after them, of a preoccupation with "archaic" issues of wholeness and self-esteem. Their preoccupation with each other, consequently, was probably—certainly, in J. B. Yeats's case—an attempt to resolve anxieties related to their common sense of narcissistic defect. A Yeats might hope to find in the society of a Pollexfen the freedom to be himself; a Pollexfen might see in a Yeats the promise of freedom from herself. It is hard to find another explanation for what seems so contradictory in both of them, and yet so much the same: that, in Susan Yeats's case, her husband could declare that she was at once wholly indifferent to others and, in her "inner mind," "all occupied" with them; or that, in his own, he was at once so "social" and so entirely unable to follow any inclination but his own.

In the end, the conspiracy between his manic indifference and her puritanical self-absorption may have produced the symptoms of paralyzed withdrawal that liberated her mind at last from "financial worry." "I knew and never doubted," J. B. Yeats told John Quinn after her death, "that, more than most wives, she was 'wrapt up' in her unworthy husband";[85] and in a letter to Lily in 1912 he added, "Had I had money your mother would never have been ill and would be alive now—that is the thought always with me—*and I would have done anything to get it for her*—but had not the art."[86] His "unworthiness" was no doubt partly to blame, and his guilty feelings about the kind of "art" he did have culminated in 1888 in the conviction that his career as a painter must end because he was going blind.[87] But in considering the causes and effects of Susan Yeats's illness, it is important to observe an "overcomplication" of the story of husband and wife that gives it something of the heroic scale of generations suggested by Cuchulain in *On Baile's Strand,*

> opposites
> That have been hatreds for three times the age
> Of this long 'stablished ground.

Susan Yeats's father, William Pollexfen, was born in Devonshire in 1811. An older branch of his family occupied (and, Murphy says, still occupies) Kitley Manor, near Yealmpton.[88] He made his start in life by running away to sea. In the 1830s his travels took him to Sligo, where he met and married Elizabeth Middleton, the daughter of a widowed cousin. By the late 1850s he had begun to do very well there as a merchant and mill owner; but his dearest hope was to establish a new dynasty of Pollexfens. On the wall of his bedroom, in the great gray house he bought for himself and his family in Sligo, hung a picture of Kitley Manor.[89] The silent and fierce old man his grandson knew was dreaming of the commercial and social glories of his house, and his sons and daughters had been sacrificed to his dream. William Pollexfen's children, as Murphy puts it, "were expected if they were boys to make their way in the world of business and if they were girls to marry well."[90] "Your mother married me," John Butler Yeats once told his son, "because I was always there and the family helped."[91]

Like many daughters before her, Susan Yeats was married to satisfy ambitions that were not her own. More than most, however, she was "wrapt up" in them. "I think," her son says in *Reveries,* "her sense of personality, her desire for any life of her own, had disappeared in her care for us and in much anxiety about money."[92] It was much more than a question of a steady income. Without money, houses, and lands she was stripped of the only assurances of integrity and self-esteem the Pollexfen "canons" allowed,[93] and the extent to which her very life and self had been absorbed in her father's dream was measured by the rigidity of her response to anything that threatened it. Neither she nor her family were ever able to adjust to J. B. Yeats's new career: the Pollexfens still called him a "barrister" as late as 1873,[94] and his mother, Yeats tells us laconically in *Reveries,* "did not care for pictures, and never went to an exhibition even to see a picture of his, nor to his studio to see the day's work."[95] In London she clung desperately to the memory of Sligo and taught her children the longing that her son says was like "some old race instinct like that of a savage." "It was always assumed between her and us that Sligo was more beautiful than other places. I can see now that she had great depth of feeling, that she was her father's daughter."[96]

As her father's daughter, the final blow dealt her in 1887 was the loss of a far dearer illusion than the Butler inheritance. By the mid and late 1880s it was becoming increasingly clear that her husband was not the only man in her life who "had not the art" of getting money. William Pollexfen's charismatic dream of dynasty, it now appeared, had been founded not on what everyone had assumed were his own commercial abilities but on those of his partner, William Middleton. It was a revelation that any of the children or grandchildren who had abused his "customary" authority so freely might have anticipated: Middleton's death in 1882 sent the family firm into a decline that, shortly before Susan Yeats's first stroke, forced her father to cut off his support for the family and, perhaps worst of all, to sell Merville, the great house that had been her refuge. Even Jack, who had become his grandparents' favorite during his years there, had to be sent back to London.[97]

In reality, Murphy says, none of the Pollexfens "were good at business." Their affairs would not improve again until after old William's death in 1892, when the family firm came under the control of his son-in-law, Arthur Jackson.[98] Husband and father, so superficially unlike each other, were far more alike than either would have cared to know. Like all of Yeats's lost, idealized "old fathers," both were men whom it is difficult to contemplate without irony, men whose powers were, in a far less productive sense than his own, largely rhetorical, whose lives were lived mostly in their own imaginations and in the imaginations of others, of sons, and daughters, and grandsons:

> You most of all, silent and fierce old man,
> Because the daily spectacle that stirred
> My fancy, and set my boyish lips to say,
> "Only the wasteful virtues earn the sun";
> Pardon that for a barren passion's sake,
> Although I have come close on forty-nine,
> I have no child, I have nothing but a book,
> Nothing but that to prove your blood and mine.
> ["Pardon, Old Fathers," 15–22]

Susan Pollexfen Yeats had reason to feel doubly bereft that hot noisy London summer. Her husband and her father had betrayed the dream that was her only life and self; she was stranded far from the houses and lands to which, with the loss of Merville, she could never return. The barren passions of men had left her nothing to call her own: even her sons, in whom she might have lived to worship her illusions again, were proving their blood in other ways. Willie's *Mosada* had come out a year before, and by the time she returned from Yorkshire in 1888 Jack had begun to publish drawings in the *Vegetarian*.[99] Both had become artist's sons who would, as Willie had promised himself among the English children at Goldolphin, "take some work as the whole end of life and not think as others do of becoming well off and living pleasantly."[100]

Like Oisin, the young poet who left London to finish his magnum opus in Sligo abandoned a sad-eyed lady on an island of "dark towers." Her captivity could never have been more pathetic, or its meaning more difficult to ignore, than during that summer; the timing of her stroke suggests a Niamh-like instinct for leading her son astray, a final attempt, perhaps, to sabotage his journey out of the Land of the Young. The price of becoming his father's son was a share in his father's guilt and indeed in his own version of his father's symptoms: Yeats's paralyzed collapses on the threshold of poethood were undoubtedly, among other things, a form of self-punishment. As such, however, they imply not only the grief of the betrayed "woman lost" but also her vengeance. Upon Yeats's memories of a young poet's struggle to become himself in *The Trembling of the Veil* there falls, for him if not for us, the shadow of a "silent, flitting figure" that, like Cuchulain's "grey hawk," embodies the murderous maternal rage that finds its objects indiscriminately in fathers, husbands, and sons. "There falls a curse / On all who have gazed in her unmoistened eyes."

> That curse may be
> Never to win a woman's love, and keep it;
> Or always to mix hatred in the love;
> Or it may be that she will kill your children,
> That you will find them, their throats torn and bloody,
> Or you will be so maddened that you will kill them
> With your own hand.[101]

In turning aside from his mother's dream to become "the poet William Yeats," Susan Yeats's eldest son was in effect refusing to play the "heroic" role that, in the years after *Oisin,* became the obsessive subject of his most public fantasies. But her "curse" was not without its effect on his private life, and particularly on the relationship that, as J. B. Yeats must have known since the day he had first seen his "curious" son in the Merville nursery, was both complicated and overcomplicated. His wife's real and imagined grievances against him as a husband inevitably conspired with his profoundly ambiguous sense of himself as a man and his son's equally ambiguous sense of him as a father. In time the boy who had been so effectively terrorized in the image of his father's weaknesses became a terror in his turn and in doing so evoked, like Cuchulain's Young Man, another image. "Like Lollie," J. B. Yeats complained to his brother Isaac in 1915, "he is not always easy to live with, having her tendency to melancholy, and like her when the fit is on him he does not in the least mind how he wounds your feelings. In this way they are both like their poor mother."[102]

The similarity became more pronounced after her death in 1900. By 1904 the traumatic father of *Reveries* was reduced to being his increasingly successful son's querulous sycophant. "I asked Willie last night," J. B. Yeats wrote to Lily the day after he had been treated to "the best seat in the house" for a "splendid" performance of *Where There is Nothing,* "if I could see George Pollexfen. In his fussy way he said I could not. I wish Willie had Jack's tender gracious manner, and did not sometimes treat me as if I were a black beetle."[103] In the end his son's attitude toward him may have had a share in keeping him in hopeful exile in New York City from 1907 until his death in 1922. In 1906 they had quarreled seriously over Yeats's attempts to control the conduct of Lollie's Cuala Press; J. B. Yeats accused his son of having "cast away his humanity" and affection and indulging in "doctrinaire demi-godship."[104] Late in 1907 he accompanied Lily to America for an exhibition of her Dun Emer embroideries, never, despite the urgings of his family and friends, to return.[105] It is clear, at any rate, that in the latter years of his father's life Yeats had affection for his father and from time to time even admiration, but very little respect. After over thirty years of supporting him wholly or in part while he waited "for something to turn up," Yeats had come to see him much as his melancholy mother had, plagued by a chronic "infirmity of will which has prevented him from finishing his pictures and ruined his career. He even," Yeats concluded in a letter to his father's other principal benefactor, John Quinn, in 1921, "hates the sign of will in others. It used to cause quarrels between me and him, for the qualities which I thought necessary to success in art or in life seemed to him 'egotism' or 'selfishness' or 'brutality.' I had to escape this family drifting, innocent and helpless . . . I find even from letters written in the last few months that he has not quite forgiven me."[106]

The final and most formidable complication of the story of the boy who became a poet, then, is the extent to which it was, or at times became, not his own story but a scenario dedicated to another purpose.

As J. B. Yeats and many others have observed, there could be something in Yeats's artificial, fussy, and often ludicrous affectations that, "when the fit was on him," seemed to exceed anything either his family's weaknesses or his own demanded of self-invention. In him the "sign of will" was, among other things, a sign of a will not his own, the strange visitation of the "heroic" antiself. "When I come home after meeting men who are strange to me," he writes in the opening paragraphs of his description of *Anima Hominis* in *Per Amica Silentia Lunae*,

> and sometimes even after talking to women, I go over all I have said in gloom and disappointment. Perhaps I have overstated everything from a desire to vex or startle, from hostility that is but fear; or all my natural thoughts have been drowned by an undisciplined sympathy. My fellow-diners have hardly seemed of mixed humanity, and how should I keep my head among images of good and evil, crude allegories?
>
> But when I shut the door and light the candle, I invite a marmorean Muse, an art where no thought or emotion has come to mind because another man has thought or felt something different . . . and I begin to dream of eyelids that do not quiver before the bayonet: all my thoughts have ease and joy, I am all virtue and confidence. When I come to put in rhyme what I have found, it will be a hard toil, but for a moment I believe I have found myself and not my antiself. It is only the shrinking from toil, perhaps, that convinces me that I have been no more myself than is the cat the medicinal grass it is eating in the garden.[107]

The function of such fantasies is of course manifold. In part, they represent the son's attempt to escape the side of himself he identifies with his father's weaknesses: to invent, in place of "drifting" undisciplined sympathy and dogmatic overstatement, a version of masculine authority worth admiring, "equal to good and grievous chance." Beyond this, they suggest (as indeed J. B. Yeats's weaknesses in turn suggest) a preoccupation with the satisfaction of more archaic demands for integrity and self-esteem in childish dreams of superhuman "virtue and confidence." Yet here as elsewhere the essence of the "soul of man" as Yeats understood it is its defective relationship not with itself or others but with the "other" self that is everything it is not, the image that, in "marmorean" or bronze repose, expresses a mother's profound indifference to what he is. Indeed, insofar as her image of him was the unconscious focus not only of her idealizing worship but also of her vengeful rage at man's treacherous enterprises, it expresses something more ominous than indifference. At its extreme the heroic world where personality is persona is, as Yeats imagines it, a psychotic scenario of murderous maternal ambivalence; to enter it is to immolate oneself in the remorseless, "unmoistened eye" of the dancer who allures and destroys.

But whatever the essence of the matter in this respect, it is evident—and was certainly evident to Yeats—that the poet was not the hero. His lot, like Oisin's and Red Hanrahan's, was to turn aside, to choose the difficult freedom of the "decrepit" self over the dubious glories of the antiself. For him the "heroic" fantasy was not something that life served but something that, in the "hard toil" of creation, served life.

> I said: "A line will take us hours maybe;
> Yet if it does not seem a moment's thought,
> Our stitching and unstitching has been naught.
> Better to go down on your marrow-bones
> And scrub a kitchen pavement, or break stones
> Like an old pauper, in all kinds of weather;
> For to articulate sweet sounds together
> Is to work harder than all these, and yet
> Be thought an idler by the noisy set
> Of bankers, schoolmasters, and clergymen
> The martyrs call the world."
> ["Adam's Curse," 4–14]

Above all, it is the laboriousness of his invention, and not the apparent "ease and joy" of what he invented, that sets Yeats apart from both those less and those more afflicted than he. He was never a prodigy; if in the end it became clear that he had genius—that unanalyzable, fortuitous quality that great poets have and lesser poets lack—it was by no means obvious from the beginning, nor did its extent begin to become clear until he had "come close on forty-nine." Indeed, if the poet *Oisin* introduced in 1889 can be said to have had a genius for anything besides self-invention, it was a corresponding genius for the brutal, hard, and egotistical application of himself to learning the craft of verse that for most of us bears fruit at last only in the 1914 volume called *Responsibilities*. It is this toil from which he "shrinks" and in which, in shrinking, he recognizes what is most profoundly himself, that distinguishes the poet we are uncertain about liking—whose heroism smacks of brutality and whose wisdom is allied to madness—from the poet we like to like, the man whose labor to be beautiful was something at once heroic and wise.

Five

CONCLUSION

Yeats and Psychology

On the whole neither Yeats's biographers (critical and otherwise) nor the few students of his poetry inclined to approach it from a psychological point of view have had much to add to his own interpretation of his story in *Reveries over Childhood and Youth*. It is a commonplace in Yeats studies to define the years that constitute his "prelude to poetry" exclusively in terms of the relationship—and usually in terms of the intellectual relationship—of fathers and sons.[1] The tradition of interpretation established by *Reveries* is carried on in Hone's *W. B. Yeats, 1865–1939* (1943) and in Jeffares's *W. B. Yeats: Man and Poet* (1949) and is usefully summed up by Ellmann in *Yeats: The Man and the Masks* (1948):

> The sociable father, so adept in conversation, so confident of his opinions, so hopeful of the future, had a great influence over a boy so lacking in these qualities. John Butler Yeats realized that his son was very malleable and decided to shape him. He took over his education and, finding him at nine years of age unable to read and a difficult pupil, boxed his ears, like his father before him. Then in

194

> subsequent lessons he adopted the more effective method of ter-
> rorizing him by references to his "moral degradation" and his
> "likeness to disagreeable people." The Puritan conscience incul-
> cated into Yeats by the Pollexfens responded; he was filled with
> remorse over his sins, and, in a state of terror, he learned to read.
> But his timidity was not helped, his mind retained its restlessness
> and may even have increased it as a result of his inner rebellion.
> Certainly he never learned how to study successfully.
>
> To rescue his self-esteem the boy cast about him for defenses; the
> chief defense had to be against his father, and he found it in the
> religious feelings which his mother accepted. . . . These are the first
> signs of the rebellion against his father's scepticism which was to
> carry him in such strange directions.[2]

The version of Yeats's boyhood and youth given here is the generally
accepted one: a timid and sensitive son (whose "wandering mind" already shows signs of poetical temperament) tyrannized by his admirable
and aggressive father, but internally rebelling against him. Insofar as
description is also interpretation, it is a description that lends itself most
readily to more or less explicitly oedipal hypotheses. Ellmann, for instance, cites the psychoanalytic mechanism of "defense" and prefaces his
discussion by generalizing suggestively about the "tension between father
and son" that, he says, is "a common enough phenomenon, but during
the second half of the nineteenth century . . . particularly noticeable."

> The father is killed, attacked, lost, or hunted. . . . "Who doesn't
> desire his father's death?" cries Ivan Karamazov, and, from the
> Urals to Donegal, the theme recurs, in Turgenev, in Samuel Butler,
> in Gosse. It is especially prominent in Ireland. George Moore, in
> his *Confessions of a Young Man,* blatantly proclaims his sense of
> liberation and relief when his father died. Synge makes an at-
> tempted parricide the theme of his *Playboy of the Western World;*
> James Joyce describes in *Ulysses* how Stephen Dedalus, disowning
> his own parent, searches for another father. . . . Yeats, after first
> handling the subject in an unpublished play written in 1884, returns
> to it in 1892 in a poem, "The Death of Cuchulain," turns the same
> story into a play in 1903, makes two translations of *Oedipus Rex,*
> the first in 1912, the second in 1927, and writes another play
> involving parricide, *Purgatory,* shortly before his death.[3]

If the invitation to this sort of intuitive psychologizing offered by
Yeats's *Reveries* is strong enough to affect his more literary-minded
commentators, it is not surprising to find that the oedipal theme is also
what is "most noticeable" to those whose discussions are more sys-

tematically psychoanalytic. These have been, in comparison with other approaches in the Yeatsian critical canon, few and far between and have not dealt in any detail with his lyric output.[4] The most important— indeed the only studies of any length—are Seiden's long article in the *American Imago* in 1948 ("Patterns of Belief: Myth in the Poetry of William Butler Yeats")[5] and Brenda Webster's recent book, *Yeats: A Psychoanalytic Study* (1973).

Seiden, who bases his analysis primarily on the evidence of *The Wanderings of Oisin* and *A Vision,* adopts a deductive procedure similar to Ellmann's. His starting point, however, is not the Irish literature of the late nineteenth and early twentieth centuries but the pagan Irish mythology and ritual of Yeats's Ossianic sources. His approach, he says, is that of "psychoanalytic anthropology," and his aim to define the "psycho-esthetic center" of the overall myth-making process of which Yeats is a part. Starting with a review of the hypothesis of the Primal Horde as found in "Freud, Jones, Rank, Abraham and Geza Roheim," he proceeds to the conclusion that *Oisin* expresses a son's longing for incestuous union with his wife-mother (Oisin and Niamh) and "ritual parricide" (Oisin and the demon). "This," he says, "the primary Oedipal level, is the psycho-esthetic center of the poem."[6] It is this complex of unconscious motives that for Seiden accounts on one hand for Yeats's "nympholeptic" personality (his pursuit of unattainable sexual objects) and on the other for the underlying circularity (via the self-duplicating cycle of repression and revolt described in Freud's myth of the Primal Horde) of his psycho-historical intuitions in *A Vision.*

Both Seiden's approach and his conclusions are of course limited by his interest in Yeats as an "anthropological" phenomenon. He has little to say about the man who sat down to breakfast and nothing to say about the genetic relationship (if any) between the oedipal myth that is the "psycho-esthetic center" of the work and the story of the poet. In this respect he is less comprehensive than Ellmann's intuitions lead us to hope he might be. Webster's *Psychoanalytic Study* is more ambitious. "While concentrating on the inner dynamics of his works," she says, "and showing how details, symbols and characters fit various emotional patterns, I shall try to correlate such patterns with suggestive facts about Yeats's life."[7] In achieving the first of her aims she is more subtle and psychoanalytically comprehensive than Seiden: she finds in addition to his oedipal scenario the pre-oedipal themes of oral deprivation and rage.[8] The scope of her observations, however, is limited. What she somewhat misleadingly refers to in prospect as "his works" is in fact almost exclusively the narrative and dramatic; the lyrics are seldom mentioned. Moreover, while her discussion of them is often perceptive, it is indeed all too "various" and fragmentary in its references to the "emotional patterns" hypothesized by psychoanalysis. One gets little sense of the psychogenetic continuity between what she finds that is "oral" and "oedipal" in the Yeatsian mythology; her procedure is one of random observation from which the "complex" that is Yeats resolutely refuses to emerge as a whole. Her way of referring to the "suggestive facts of Yeats's life" is similarly elliptical. While she makes interesting use of Murphy's recently published material on Yeats's "despondent" mother, she does little to modify our conception of John Butler Yeats as a too powerful and threatening father. Indeed, insofar as Webster tells a version of the poet's story at all, one gathers that it is quite similar to Ellmann's: the son, terrorized by the father, masks his rebelliousness with a passive "dreaming" timidity in which he defensively (and, for Webster, ambivalently) identifies himself with his mother.[9]

It seems fair to say, then, that insofar as anyone has offered a psychological account of what Webster calls Yeats's "creative energy," that account has been of oedipal trauma: the story of the poet is the story of fathers and sons.[10] In the preceding chapters my argument has been less that this view is incorrect than that it is greatly, and misleadingly, oversimplified. Indeed it seems to me that what is most striking about the way Yeats's story is usually told, even to someone unprepared to agree with either my argument or psychoanalytic arguments in general, is this oversimplification of the facts. The conflict of fathers and sons as Yeats tells it is significantly modified by other stories, all of which must be told if its outcome is to be understood.

In Yeats's own case and in the case of his earlier biographers, oversimplification was, I assume, the effect of discretion. The amount the Yeatses have been unwilling to make public about themselves is matched only by the amount they have been willing to record in private. In his preface to *The Man and the Masks* Ellmann mentions some 50,000 pages of manuscript then in the hands of Mrs. Yeats, including her husband's "autobiographical notes, drafts of poems, letters, diaries, and other papers";[11] there are besides, Murphy says in his study of *The Yeats Family and the Pollexfens of Sligo,* the unpublished manuscripts of other members of the family, including letters, John Butler Yeats's three-volume unpublished memoir, and Lily and Lollie Yeats's scrapbooks and diaries.[12] All, or certainly a large part, of these manuscripts were available to Hone, Jeffares, Ellmann, and Virginia Moore; yet none of these scholars, in the generation that has passed since Yeats's death, has been able or willing to add much to the strictly censored version of Yeats's family's life and character already available in the *Autobiography*.

In more recent years, however, the publication of some of J. B. Yeats's letters in Reid's study of John Quinn, *The Man from New York* (1968), Murphy's monograph on *The Yeats Family and the Pollexfens of Sligo* (1971), and the manuscript of Yeats's *Memoirs* edited by Denis Donoghue (1972) suggests that perhaps the family policy towards the materials from which the comprehensive biography of Yeats may some day be written has undergone a change. Whether there will be a corresponding change in the interpretation of those materials, however, remains to be seen. Murphy, for instance, asserts at the beginning of his otherwise revealing study of the "profound influence" of the Pollexfens on J. B. Yeats's children that "Susan Pollexfen Yeats herself...contributed little to [their] character." This rather astounding conclusion (as it seems to me) is explained by Murphy's adherence to a naive genetic or, in his own metaphor, hydraulic theory of personality: the Yeats and Pollexfen families were, he goes on to say, "the twin streams that fed the river of their genius."[13]

Webster's failure to accomodate her version of the accepted picture of "oedipal" conflict to the fresh information Murphy gives us is, in view of her explicitly psychoanalytic approach, more interesting. In part it may reflect the development of psychoanalytic theory itself or, perhaps, of the rate at which its developments have been assimilated by other disciplines. The psychology of narcissism and its relation to the psychoses has been hypothesized in some detail for some time;[14] the psychology of the "narcissistic" personality and its disorders—as distinct from the psychotic—however, has only begun to receive a detailed and comprehensive elucidation, and there is still substantial disagreement about both their nosology and their metapsychology.[15] Moreover, insofar as Freud's first formulation of the complex that is now virtually synonymous with psychoanalysis was, among other things, an exercise in the interpretation of literature, it is not surprising that it has taken some time for his *amateurs* in that field to begin to modify either his approach or his conclusions within a psychoanalytic framework. An important beginning, however, has now been made in Philip Slater's *The Glory of Hera* (1971), in which he concludes that the mythology in which Freud found his Oedipus and the Athenian society that produced it were in fact expressions of predominately narcissistic rather than oedipal anxieties.[16]

One other recent study of Yeats should be mentioned here, Harold

Bloom's *Yeats* (1970). What is worth noting in particular is the part of Bloom's work on Yeats that is "a prolegomenon to a larger study of poetic influence," the even more recent *Anxiety of Influence* (1973) and *Map or Misreading* (1975).[17] What I have to say on the subject concerns Yeats alone. One is justified in suspecting, however, that if Bloom is mistaken in particular, and especially in his first particulars, he may also be mistaken in general; my remarks are in effect a brief prolegomenon to a larger critique of his conclusions.

A psychoanalytic critique of Bloom's thesis in *Yeats* is justified—indeed invited—by the fact that it is openly, if not always explicitly, Freudian in its orientation. Freud is invoked in the first paragraph of the introductory chapter, and he reappears almost immediately to preside over Bloom's initial formulation of "the theory of poetic influence I pursue."

> Poetic influence, as I conceive it, is a variety of melancholy or an anxiety-principle. It concerns the poet's sense of his precursors, and of his own achievement in relation to theirs. Have they left him room enough, or has their priority cost him his art? More crucially, where did they go wrong, so as to make it possible for him to go right? In this revisionary sense, in which the poet creates his own precursors by necessarily misinterpreting them, poetic influence forms and malforms new poets, and aids their art at the cost of increasing, finally, their acute sense of isolation. . . . Freud thought all men unconsciously wished to beget themselves, to be their own fathers in place of their phallic fathers, and so "rescue" their mothers from erotic degradation. It may not be true of all men, but it seems to be definitive of poets *as poets*. The poet, if he could, would be his own precursor, and so rescue the Muse from her degradation.[18]

Leaving aside whatever may be either puzzling or simply irritating about Bloom's way of putting it—he is at times his own best example of someone determined to revise his precursors into triviality and leave as little room as possible (witness his title) for his followers—the hypothesis is both novel and interesting. It is also, as far as it applies to Yeats, clearly in the tradition of interpretation that assigns the poet's "creative energies" an oedipal origin and orientation. I would argue, consequently, that it is thus equally unable to account for what seems so contradictory in what is being described: Yeats's need not only to overcome but to *create* the powerful oedipal antagonist against which he "forms and malforms" himself. What Bloom accurately and acutely observes about Yeats (and perhaps about poets in general) is something that an oedipal teleology cannot explain unless it is modified to include a pervasive sense of narcissistic defectiveness and a correspondingly overdetermined sense of paternal weakness. The poet's—Yeats's—need to "create" his precursors is an expression of his even more fundamental need to create himself; Bloom is nearer the heart of the matter when he emphasizes what I take to be the radically narcissistic orientation of the poet's desire to "be his own precursor." "Poetic influence," he adds, "is analogous to Romantic love," because "both processes are illuminated by Patmore's egregious remark: 'What a Lover sees in the Beloved is the projected shadow of his own potential beauty in the eyes of God.'"[19]

My discussion of Yeats and psychology would be incomplete without a brief reference to a book that is not about Yeats at all but which shares my psychological concerns and, to some extent, my difficulties. Richard J. Onorato's *Character of the Poet: Wordsworth in "The Prelude"* (1971) is the best psychoanalytic study of a poet I have seen; its balance between theoretical scrupulousness and humane attention to the experience of poetry is in many ways the model for the sort of book I have tried to write about Yeats. Onorato's concern is "the subject of Wordsworth himself," and particularly Wordsworth's extended and complex effort to become, or to invent, himself as the Poet in *The Prelude*.[20] Self-invention is the narcissistic (and perhaps in literature the preeminently romantic) subject; Onorato's problem, like mine, was to find an appropriate psychological language for it. What was available was the language of the self's relation to its objects, the language of the oedipus complex; what Wordsworth's peculiar egoism demanded was a language for the self's relation to itself.

Onorato's solution in *The Character of the Poet* is to use what amounts at times to a language of his own. The result is generally successful, but necessarily paradoxical. Wordsworth's obsessive search for the presence of his dead mother through the "vales" of memory is, in the idiom of the oedipus complex, a search for a traumatically lost object. Yet it is equally clear, as Onorato never lets us forget, that the lost "object" of *The Prelude* is always perceived as an aspect of the transcendently completed Self that Wordsworth was preparing himself to become. Onorato is surely right, for example, when he says that Wordsworth's insistence on the "Godliness of the Poet" in Nature was a son's attempt to appropriate for himself God the Father's creative relationship with Nature the Mother. But he knows that Wordsworth means something else too, and it is hard to read passages like the following without thinking that the psychology of narcissism could have made his way of talking about Wordsworth's most "egregious" claims for poetry a good deal less ambiguous. "In its vigor," Onorato says, Wordsworth's

> poetic self-consciousness opposes itself to the imagined union with God in the oblivion of the "one interior life," and seems instead to imagine no limit for itself. It is a temptation to the poetic spirit to find in itself and in its proper activity the very Godliness it seems to risk losing by the assertion of Self. God, Wordsworth says in the passage on the "one interior life," has centrality and wholeness of being within his nature. (One thinks here of Aristotle's self-contemplative God as engaged in the sole activity of the "commerce of his Nature with itself.") But Wordsworth seems consciously to seek his own centrality and Godliness in his poetic account of his growth. If he can fix "the wavering balance" of his mind and show himself how his story leads to his ideal of himself as the Poet, he will have a Godly understanding of his own being.[21]

Art and Madness

In everything I have said so far, it has been my hope that the thesis I have advanced—that of the narcissistic origins of the poet's creativity—will help to explain for others, as it has for me, much that seems in need of explanation about Yeats. I hope, too, that it will be received and amended in the spirit in which it is offered: "all we can know for truth" is never all the truth but only what seems, after a little insight and much labor, like more of it. To demand more than this from what we can know is, I think, vain; yet it would be equally vain to pretend that such demands are not or will not be made. What is really being asked of a mode of knowing is all too often, especially for those of us whose labors it consumes, a mode of feeling: we want to "know" not only what is true but also what is beautiful, what is good, or perhaps, in this post-Freudian age, what is "healthy."

It is probably inevitable, consequently, that any hypothesis, and particularly one about an aesthetic phenomenon, should also be treated as a statement of value; moreover, to the extent that the terminology of that hypothesis is a clinical as well as a theoretical terminology, it inevitably lends itself to clinical questions. To complicate things still further, the two issues often have a way of getting mixed: art may be blamed for being "neurotic" or praised for being "therapeutic." The controversy is at least as old as Plato and is, I think, largely independent of the language in which any particular age chooses to carry it on; whatever truths that may emerge from it are consequently relative rather than absolute. We know what we like and dislike and choose our doctrine accordingly. Nevertheless, the question of why we like what we do remains an interesting one, and the clinical questions, when they are not disguised demands for value judgment, are worth considering from a theoretical point of view. To what extent, one may reasonably ask, was Yeats's creativity pathological? Should his creativity be regarded as symptomatic or therapeutic?

To answer the clinical questions first: both the biographical evidence and Yeats's own intuitions about his creativity indicate an unmistakable association between it and mental pathology. Yeats's Red Hanrahan is "touched"; Yeats himself feels within him the "root of madness" whose conquest is "style." It is equally clear, however, that the symptoms of his pathology were not always—or even often—the sort that usually get called "neurotic" or "psychotic." Yeats was not mad, nor is his poet one of the "taken"; his affectations could (and did) seem to some odd and eccentric, but he never displayed the sort of obviously hysterical or compulsive behavior commonly associated with mental illness; he was a visionary but was not subject to psychotic delusions. On the contrary, his root of madness, with the exception of the acute phases of his "collapses," had the peculiarly diffuse quality characteristic of the narcissistic disorders. If what we know about him suggests anything, it is that there was very little about the "self-invented man" that cannot be described as symptomatic in this sense: his aristocratic fussiness, his personal vanity, his brittle pride, his high susceptibility to shame, his admiration of the "heroic," his nympholepsy, his fascination with ritual, magic, and the "symbolic" meaning of things, his vague depressions, intense exaltations, uncontrollable outbursts of rage and, finally, his creativity itself.[22]

It seems to me, then, that to the extent that Yeats was in fact subject to a form of mental disturbance that caused him a good deal of pain and uneasiness, his creativity was, if not its symptom, certainly as much its manifestation as any other aspect of his personality. It was in this limited sense pathological; but it does not follow that it was also, as Plato might have it, pathogenic. On the contrary, like the symptoms of much more obvious and acute kinds of inner distress, it was among other things a resolution of painful unconscious conflict. In this and only in this sense it can also be said to have been "therapeutic," although as we have observed in the case of *Oisin* it was not always successful: poetry could lead to nervous breakdown as well as the other way round. On the whole I think it would be fair to say that the net effect of creativity in terms of real therapeutic gain was nil. Poetry was one of a number of things, all more or less applicable and all more or less successful, that Yeats did with his pain. I would consequently disagree with those critics, psychoanalytic and otherwise, who imply or conclude, as Webster does, that Yeats's creativity (or indeed creativity in general) was at any time more than an ephemeral and temporary "triumph" in the psychological sense, though certainly it produced many enduring triumphs of art.[23] Yeats's "best late works," Webster concludes in her *Psychoanalytic Study,*

> like no others, come to terms with his fears of dissolution and death. Whereas in earlier works he had used a talismanic object more or less crudely to ward off castration anxiety, in "A Dialogue of Self and Soul" and the Byzantium poems he uses the same device brilliantly to come to terms with aging and death. In "Sailing to Byzantium" he assimilates to himself the object's permanent and beautiful form and so triumphs over death. But in "A Dialogue of Self and Soul" and "Byzantium" there is a further triumph: with the support of his talisman he is able to swing away from its static perfection and accept imaginatively what previously had terrified him—the amorphous dangers of life itself.[24]

Such statements are most distinguished, as Bloom sensibly reminds us, by the "idolatrous" tone of voice common to a great deal of Yeats criticism.[25] They amount to a critical version of the pathetic fallacy, and in a psychoanalytic context they imply significant therapeutic gains which there is little reason to suppose ever occurred. What Webster is apparently describing is the transition from the "dreamy" style of Yeats's early work (for her a counterproductive "flight to fairyland") to the "hard" and "realistic" style of his later period (which for Webster expresses his acquisition of "active mastery").[26] There are obvious objections to this line of reasoning (In what sense is "Byzantium" more real than the "Celtic Twilight"? How does one distinguish between more and less active and masterful forms of creativity?); I think, too, that it is both naive and misleading to imply that stylistic changes indicate changes in fundamental psychological structures. And even if one feels comfortable in doing so, there is little reason to assume such changes in this case. If, as Seiden observes, it seems in some sense to be "immediate reality" to which Yeats turns in his old age, it is still "ugliness" that he sees. "The world that he is at last bold enough to face has no beauty; it is, rather, a place of cant, hypocrisy, philistine vulgarity. Yeats turns to it. He seems almost to rejoice in it. But he also rejects it. And always behind sordid contemporary life there are his mythopoeic visions."[27]

Yet if Webster's clinical conclusions are misleading in one sense, they are illuminating in another. The poem is not the poet; but the fact that it seems to be reflects something about our way of experiencing poetry. The success of Yeats's artifice in this respect corresponds to his ability to induce in us that state of mind that Keats took in part as the subject of his "Ode to a Nightingale":

> Was it a vision, or a waking dream?
> Fled is that music:—Do I wake or sleep?

The "vision" has many names and many occasions; I speak here only of poetry, and in particular of Yeats's poetry. It is the experience in which we briefly recover the archaic way of perceiving objects that, as Yeats puts it in his "General Introduction to My Work," makes them seem part of our "creative power." At its extreme, the aesthetic experience does away with the distinction between subject and object, fiction and reality; we feel as if we have become what we behold, a part of a transcendent unity that is both omniscient and perfect. And this, I think, is what we value most about the experience: even the most secularizing commentators, when deeply moved by a poem, strain the limits of paradox to keep it intact. At such moments the language of analysis becomes the language of fiction: Yeats, years dead, emerges from final paragraphs like a phoenix to transcend and master (or to fail to transcend and master) feelings of despair and confusion that are, after all, really our own.

This is not to say that such feelings are not authentic, only that they are authentic in a different way. In brief, I think that objects (poems, for instance) are experienced aesthetically when they are experienced narcissistically. When we find a poem beautiful we recover, as at so few other times, a sense of integrity and goodness that seems absolute and unconditional: "Everything we look upon is blest." The quality of the feeling, however, belies its occasions; it does not follow that there is an absolute and unconditional standard of beauty in poetry or in anything else. What poem seems most beautiful to what person at what time—of the day, of a life—depends on a complex interaction of factors that are hard to specify and sometimes impossible to reproduce. The most we can say is that some poems seem more beautiful to more people more of the time than others do: they meet a *relative* standard of beauty imposed by a self-selected "personality"—the community of Western, educated, middle-class readers to whom books like this are addressed.

Some of Yeats's poems have met our standard better than others, and in the course of my discussion of them I have tried to suggest why. Art, unlike most other things in life, invites us to experience the terrors and delights of the narcissistic "vision"; its aesthetic value consequently depends on the extent to which we are both willing and able to accept the invitation. In Yeats's case, we are most able to do so when the "remade" integrity of the self implies a community of selves: it is easier to like poems that, like "Among School Children" and "A Dialogue of Self and Soul," end with a "we" that includes us rather than the "I" that often (but not always) shuts us out of poems like "The Tower."[28] Whether being able we are also willing to be visionaries is another and, I think, more important question. In general, it appears to depend on our response to the more or less uneasy balance between the obsessive content of his poems and their elaborated form: "All depends on the completeness of the holding down, on the stirring of the beast underneath." If the elaboration is not complete enough, we are too disturbed to respond; most of us like "Sailing to Byzantium" better than "Byzantium," for example, and prefer "The Wild Swans at Coole" to "Nineteen Hundred and Nineteen." If, on the other hand, the elaboration is too complete, the poetry seems vague, sentimental, and self-absorbed. "The Second Coming" is a great, and greatly disturbing, poem; in "The Secret Rose," an identical and equally disturbing vision of the "hour of hours" is almost lost in the anesthetic cadence of lines like

> Enfold me . . . where those
> Who sought thee in the Holy Sepulchre,
> Or the wine-vat, dwell beyond the stir
> And tumult of defeated dreams; and deep
> Among pale eyelids, heavy with the sleep
> Men have named beauty. . . .
> [2–7]

Yeats's least successful verse carries under- and over-elaboration to extremes. A late poem like "Whence Had they Come" (1935) openly demands that we sanctify the images of terrifying cruelty; an early one like "I walked among the Seven Woods of Coole" (1900) reads like an exercise in self-mystification:

> Whence had they come,
> The hand and lash that beat down frigid Rome?

What sacred drama through her body heaved
When world-transforming Charlemagne was conceived?
["Whence Had They Come," 9–12]

Is Eden out of time and out of space?
And do you gather about us when pale light
Shining on water and fallen among leaves,
And winds blowing from flowers, and whirr of feathers
And the green quiet, have uplifted the heart?
["I walked," 36–40]

Both poems date from Yeats's periods of "nervous collapse," and the language of both is, I suspect, the language of increased, not decreased, "nervous weakness."[29] Their failure reminds us once again of what is less obviously at issue in our response to poems that we are more able and willing to call beautiful: a kind of pleasure that both mobilizes and renders vulnerable our most fundamental sense of what is good, whole, and beautiful about ourselves, of *our* creative power. It is in this context that what is particularly elating and disturbing about Yeats's art must be interpreted. The praise (and more recently the blame) Yeats has received has a psychological basis that reflects in each case the rigidity or flexibility of our own (or our age's or our society's) defenses against narcissistic excitement. It also suggests why in some cases we are so unwilling to give up the idea that his poetry at its best is somehow "transcendent" and why, if we are forced to do so—to admit, with Auden, that "poetry makes nothing happen"—we too feel a deeply ironic sense of loss. This is in itself the measure of what remained to a large extent perpetually unresolved for Yeats and remains to some extent perpetually unresolved for anyone. The fancy, as Keats concludes, cheats us only when it no longer cheats us well enough; ultimately it is our belief, and not our disbelief, that we are most unwilling to suspend.

NOTES

One Mistress or Muse

1. T. S. Eliot, "The Poetry of W. B. Yeats," in J. Hall and M. Steinmann, eds., *The Permanence of Yeats*, p. 331.

2. Lennox Robinson, "The Man and Dramatist," in Stephen Gwynn, ed., *Scattering Branches*, p. 58.

3. For Yeats's use of the Wisdom tradition, see Allen R. Grossman's *Poetic Knowledge in the Early Yeats;* for his use of *A Vision*, see, among others, Helen Hennessey Vendler, *Yeats's "Vision" and Later Plays;* and Thomas R. Whitaker, *Swan and Shadow.*

4. Louis MacNeice, "Yeats's Epitaph," in Jon Stallworthy, ed., *Last Poems*, p. 44.

5. Eliot, in Hall and Steinmann, p. 333.

6. The texts of Yeats's poems cited and the line numbers indicated in parentheses are those standardized by Peter Allt and Russell K. Alspach in *The Variorum Edition of the Poems of W. B. Yeats.*

7. See ibid., p. 778; and Allan Wade, *A Bibliography of the Writings of W. B. Yeats,* p. 87.

8. The most recent and comprehensive literary study of this theme in Yeats is in Robert Langbaum's *The Mysteries of Identity*, pp. 147–247. "The old sincerity," Langbaum says, "reveals the unreconstructed self; the new sincerity the recon-

structed self. The distinction between these two orders of identity determines everything Yeats has to say on the subject" (p. 152; see also p. 247).

9. W. B. Yeats, *Essays and Introductions,* pp. 509–10.

10. William Magee, *A Memoir of AE,* p. 111.

11. W. B. Yeats, *The Letters of W. B. Yeats,* p. 589.

12. The various sections of what is now called the *Autobiography* (or, in some editions, the *Autobiographies*) did not appear together in one volume until 1938; see Wade, pp. 197–98.

13. See William Michael Murphy, *The Yeats Family and the Pollexfens of Sligo,* pp. 34–35; also W. B. Yeats, *Memoirs.*

14. "The Circus Animals' Desertion" was completed in September 1938 and published in January 1939; see Curtis Bradford, *Yeats at Work,* p. 164.

15. See, e.g., Keats's "La Belle Dame sans Merci" and the Moneta passage in canto 1 of *The Fall of Hyperion: A Dream,* esp. lines 256–71; or the "veiled maid" dream in Shelley's *Alastor,* lines 151–211.

16. Gwynn also suggests something to this effect in his introductory essay in *Scattering Branches,* pp. 7–8.

17. See W. B. Yeats, "Dust Hath Closed Helen's Eye," in *Mythologies,* pp. 22–30; and "The Philosophy of Shelley's Poetry," in *Essays and Introductions,* p. 87; both essays are dated 1900.

18. Joseph Hone, *W. B. Yeats, 1865–1939,* pp. 331–32.

19. See Yeats, *Letters,* p. 709.

20. Harold Bloom, *Yeats,* p. 350.

21. See Whitaker, p. 197; and Bloom, *Yeats,* p. 351.

22. Wade, pp. 149–51; the dedication to *Early Poems and Stories* is dated May 1925, and the volume was published on September 22.

23. Yeats, *Mythologies,* pp. 221–22,

24. See "Kidnappers," ibid., pp. 70–76.

25. There are a dozen altogether, although "Hanrahan's Curse on Old Age" is for some reason omitted from the *Variorum Poems* and can now be found only in *Mythologies,* p. 243. Besides those mentioned, poems attributed to Hanrahan either in earlier versions of the stories or as separate titles are "Maid Quiet" (in "The Twisting of the Rope," *National Observer,* December 1892); "The Song of the Wandering Aengus" (in "Red Hanrahan's Vision," *Stories,* 1905); "A Poet to his Beloved" and "He Tells of Perfect Beauty" (originally stanzas I and II of "O'Sullivan Rua to Mary Lavell," printed in the *Senate,* March 1896); "The Lover Speaks to the Hearers of His Songs in Coming Days" (in "Red Hanrahan's Vision," *New Review,* April 1896); "He Remembers Forgotten Beauty" (originally "O'Sullivan Rua to Mary Lavell," *Savoy,* July 1896); "The Secret Rose" (originally "O'Sullivan Rua to the Secret Rose," *Savoy,* September 1896); "He Reproves the Curlew" (originally "O'Sullivan Rua to the Curlews," *Savoy,* November 1896); and "The Ragged Wood" (in "The Twisting of the Rope," *Stories,* 1905).

26. Yeats, *Mythologies*, pp. 232–33.

27. See Frank Kermode's *The Romantic Image*, pp. 49–103.

28. Yeats, *Essays and Introductions*, pp. 304–5; see also "Symbolism in Painting," where Yeats states that symbolic art liberates its subjects "from the bonds of motives and their actions, causes and their effects" (ibid., p. 148).

29. Richard J. Finneran's collation of the printed texts of *John Sherman and Dhoya* is an exception.

30. W. B. Yeats, *The Secret Rose*, pp. 137–39.

31. I.e., to "O'Sullivan Rua," Yeats's earlier name for Hanrahan, in its first printing in the *Savoy*, September 1896.

32. *National Observer*, November 26, 1892, pp. 40–41.

33. Ibid., p. 41.

34. Bloom, *Yeats*, p. 351.

35. "Presences" (first printed June 1917), lines 7–8.

36. Yeats, *Memoirs*, p. 40.

37. Ibid., p. 46.

38. Ibid., pp. 132–34; Jeffares, whose *W. B. Yeats: Man and Poet* was published while both Maud and Iseult Gonne were still alive, refers to the latter as "adopted" (p. 183).

39. Virginia Moore, *The Unicorn*, p. 40; Hone, p. 155.

40. Yeats, *Memoirs*, pp. 123–25.

41. Ibid., p. 132.

42. Ibid., pp. 132, 134.

43. Both are summarized by Moore, *Unicorn*, pp. 73–80.

44. W. B. Yeats, *The Trembling of the Veil*, bk. III, sec. 1 (Yeats, *Autobiography*, p. 169).

45. Moore, *Unicorn*, p. 197; the journal is not that published in *Memoirs* but the still unpublished "white calfskin notebook" excerpted by Moore (pp. 197–203).

46. Ibid., p. 201.

47. Ibid., pp. 199–200. Emphasis in original.

48. Ibid., p. 201.

49. Ibid., pp. 200–201.

50. Ibid., pp. 202–3.

51. See above, p. 36; and Yeats, *Memoirs*, p. 125, where he says that "for nearly seven years" after 1897 there was no woman in his life.

52. Hone, p. 301; see also Richard Ellmann, *Yeats: The Man and the Masks*, p. 208n.

53. Moore, *Unicorn*, p. 229.

54. Ibid., p. 239.

55. See Jeffares, *Man and Poet*, p. 190.

56. Yeats, *Memoirs*, pp. 74n., 85.

57. Ibid., pp. 88–89.

58. I.e., in April 1897; if Yeats's "but a year" is accurate, he broke with Mrs. Shakespear some time in March.

59. "The Twisting of the Rope" was first published in the *National Observer* on December 24, 1892.

60. Yeats, *Memoirs,* pp. 125–26. "It was the most miserable time of my life" is deleted from the manuscript: see p. 125, n. 1.

61. Ibid., pp. 126–27

62. Ibid., p. 224; see also his letter to Florence Farr, March 1909: "My breakdown has left me much to do . . ." (*Letters,* p. 526).

63. Yeats, *Memoirs,* pp. 156–57. Yeats's sister Elizabeth preferred to spell her name "Lollie" (see Murphy, *Yeats Family,* p. 75), and I have followed her preference, her brother's ("Willie"), and her sister Susan Mary's ("Lily"), except in direct quotes; see below, chap. 4, n. 68.

64. Moore, *Unicorn,* p. 253; see also Jeffares, *Man and Poet,* p. 191.

65. W. B. Yeats, *A Vision,* pp. 8–9.

66. There is, however, the letter in which Yeats told J. H. Pollock that in the summer of 1933 he had once again had to give up "all the writing I could through some sort of nervous breakdown" (Murphy, *Yeats Family,* p. 83, n. 92).

67. Yeats, *Letters,* p. 634.

68. By 1908 the total lent had reached £500; see *Dramatis Personae,* sec. 9 (*Autobiography,* pp. 273–76); also Yeats, *Letters,* pp. 290, 292, 303, 330–31, 335, 363, 375–76, 392, 397.

69. Yeats, *Letters,* p. 288.

70. See letter to Lady Gregory, September 1902 (ibid., p. 379); the correspondence after the summer of that year takes on a markedly more intimate tone.

71. Yeats, *Memoirs,* pp. 160–61.

72. Ibid., pp. 229–30.

73. W. B. Yeats, *Reveries over Childhood and Youth,* sec. 33 (*Autobiography,* p. 71).

Two Sons and Mothers

1. Hone, p. 399.

2. Published November 5, 1926, and August 1926, respectively.

3. Passage from manuscript book quoted in A. Norman Jeffares, *A Commentary on the Collected Poems of W. B. Yeats,* p. 299.

4. Yeats, *Letters,* p. 719. A rapprochement between the two had begun as early as 1904, when Mrs. Shakespear sent Yeats a copy of her novel, *The Devotees* (ibid., pp. 436–37, 439). Their published correspondence does not become intimate again, however, until the fall of 1916 (p. 615).

5. Plato meant both the hetero- and homosexual "sexes." The "parable" oc-

curs in *Symposium* 189–92, where the origin of the desire for physical union is explained by a myth in which Zeus splits a primitive androgynous human form into two halves "as you cut an egg through with a hair."

6. W. B. Yeats, *Collected Poems,* pp. 455–56.

7. Thomas Taylor's translation (1917), pp. 22–25; quoted in Jeffares, *Commentary on the Poems,* pp. 301–2.

8. See Hesiod, *Works and Days,* 109–26; and Sigmund Freud, *Totem and Taboo.* Something of the circularity of Freud's cycle of revolt and repression is also suggested by the fact that Kronos has himself castrated his father (Ouranos) and that Zeus's attack on him is part of Gaia's plan to avenge his fall (*Theogony,* 154–210, 453–506). But see also n. 12 below.

9. See Sigmund Freud, "The Passing of the Oedipus Complex"; Otto Fenichel, *The Psychoanalytic Theory of Neurosis,* p. 91; Erik Erikson, *Childhood and Society,* pp. 247–74; and Heinz Kohut, *The Analysis of the Self,* p. 188.

10. See Fenichel, chap. 10.

11. The former is generally speaking the conclusion reached about Yeats by most of his biographers and critics: see chap. 5, pp. 194–97.

12. It is interesting to note that Yeats's "alteration" of his sources may have been an insight. Philip Slater argues plausibly and at length in *The Glory of Hera* that the nominally "oedipal" concerns of the art and mythology of classical Athens reflect underlying narcissistic anxieties.

13. This is the process Margaret S. Mahler calls "separation-individuation" and describes in detail in Mahler, Fred Pine, and Anni Bergman, *The Psychological Birth of the Human Infant;* its normal outcome is what Erik Erikson calls "basic trust" in *Childhood and Society* (pp. 247–51) and in *Identity: Youth and Crisis* (pp. 96–104). See also Fenichel, pp. 34–41; Phyllis Greenacre, "Considerations regarding the Parent-Infant Relationship," pp. 214–23; Donald W. Winnicott, "The Theory of the Parent-Infant Relationship," pp. 41, 48–50; Heinz Lichtenstein, "The Role of Narcissism in the Emergence and Maintenance of a Primary Identity," pp. 53–54; and Heinz Kohut, *The Restoration of the Self,* pp. 86–87.

14. See Fenichel, pp. 401–6, 415–17; and Kohut, *Analysis,* pp. 1–14. See also Donald W. Winnicott, "Ego Distortion in Terms of the True and False Self"; Erik Erikson, "The Problem of Ego Identity," and *Identity,* p. 97; Margaret S. Mahler, *On Human Symbiosis and the Vicissitudes of Individuation;* and Otto Kernberg, *Borderline Conditions and Pathological Narcissism.*

15. Thomas Parkinson, *W. B. Yeats: The Later Poetry,* pp. 104–5.

16. Ellmann, *The Man and the Masks,* pp. 251–52; Whitaker, pp. 274–75; and Bloom, *Yeats,* p. 369. The last has some reservations: see his p. 369.

17. See George Moore, *Vale,* pp. 160–61.

18. Hone, p. 9.

19. Yeats, "The Happiest of Poets," in *Essays and Introductions,* pp. 59–60.

20. J. B. Yeats, *Early Memories: Some Chapters of Autobiography,* p. 54.

21. W. B. Yeats, *Reveries over Childhood and Youth*, sec. 3 (*Autobiography*, p. 13).

22. Ibid., sec 1 (pp. 2–5).

23. JBY to Lily Yeats, February 1, 1922; quoted in Murphy, *Yeats Family*, p. 43.

24. J. B. Yeats, *Early Memories*, p. 14.

25. Letter to W. B. Yeats, July 30, 1915; quoted in Murphy, *Yeats Family*, p. 43.

26. See ibid., p. 42.

27. Lily Yeats's scrapbook, "Grandfather William Pollexfen"; quoted ibid., pp. 20–21.

28. J. B. Yeats, *Letters to His Son W. B. Yeats and Others*, p. 51.

29. Letter to Isaac Yeats, June 30, 1911; quoted in Murphy, *Yeats Family*, p. 83, n. 95. Emphasis in original.

30. Yeats, *Reveries*, sec. 1 (*Autobiography*, p. 5).

31. See Murphy, *Yeats Family*, p. 33.

32. Ibid., p. 35.

33. Ibid., pp. 34–35.

34. Ibid., p. 47.

35. Yeats, *Reveries*, sec. 5 (*Autobiography*, p. 19).

36. Ibid., secs. 5 (p. 19), 13 (p. 40).

37. Ibid., sec 5 (p. 19).

38. Ibid. (p. 21).

39. The impressions are those of Mrs. Ida Dewar-Durie and Oliver Elton; see Murphy, *Yeats Family*, p. 47; and J. B. Yeats, *Letters to His Son*, p. 5, respectively.

40. Yeats, *Reveries*, sec. 13 (*Autobiography*, p. 40).

41. Letter to W. B. Yeats, January 15, 1916; quoted in Murphy, *Yeats Family*, p. 87, n. 171.

42. Letter to W. B. Yeats, June 13, 1914; quoted ibid., p. 25.

43. Lily Yeats's scrapbook, "Grandmother Yeats"; quoted ibid., p. 22.

44. Letter to W. B. Yeats, April 25, 1915; quoted ibid., p. 87, n. 170.

45. Lily Yeats's scrapbook, "Mama's Health and Other Things"; quoted ibid., p. 53.

46. Letter to John Quinn; quoted in Benjamin L. Reid, *The Man from New York*, pp. 425–26.

47. Murphy, *Yeats Family*, p. 34.

48. Letter to Isaac Yeats, April 28, 1911; quoted ibid., p. 9.

49. Letter to Isaac Yeats, July 10, 1912; quoted ibid., p. 82, n. 90.

50. William Michael Murphy, "Father and Son: The Early Education of William Butler Yeats," p. 86.

51. November 1, 1872; quoted in Jeffares, *Man and Poet*, pp. 9–10.

52. See e.g., Kernberg, pp. 234–35.

53. See Winnicott, "The Theory of the Parent-Infant Relationship," p. 43.

54. See Kohut, *Restoration,* p. 87; on the importance of eye contact between mother and infant, see Mahler et al., pp. 45–46, 205; on the smiling response and the face "engram," ibid., pp. 45–46, 52.

55. See Sigmund Freud, *The Ego and the Id;* Fenichel, p. 40; Kohut, *Analysis,* pp. 25–27; Mahler et al., pp. 7, 11; and Kernberg, pp. 276–77.

56. See Bloom, *Yeats,* p. 373: "Nothing in the Self's wonderful declaration at the close of the *Dialogue* goes beyond re-affirmation of this ecstatic and reductive solipsism, since the source to which every event in action or in thought is followed will turn out to be the self. . . ." See pp. 68–69 herein.

57. See Kohut, *Analysis,* p. 135: the reactive mobilization of the grandiose self is "a rapid hypercathexis of an archaic . . . self image which is rigidly defended by hostility, coldness, arrogance, sarcasm, and silence."

58. Ibid., pp. 27–28.

59. Even Bloom, who has some interesting reservations about "Among School Children," finds the beatitude of "A Dialogue of Self and Soul" "attractive" and the poem as a whole "magnificent" (*Yeats,* p. 377; cf. p. 369).

60. W. B. Yeats, *Letters on Poetry from W. B. Yeats to Dorothy Wellesley,* p. 94. Emphasis added.

61. Whitaker, pp. 74–75; Bloom, *Yeats,* p. 280.

62. See Sigmund Freud, "On Narcissism: An Introduction." Kohut remarks that "the developmental step from autoeroticism to narcissism is a move toward increased synthesis of the personality due to a shift from the libidinal cathexis of individual body parts, or of isolated physical and mental functions, to a cathexis of an (albeit at first grandiose, exhibitionistic and unrealistic) cohesive self" (*Analysis,* p. 215). Consequently, he says, the threat against which the narcissistic personality's regressive hypercathexis of secondary narcissistic structures is mobilized is both "the dedifferentiating influx of unneutralized narcissistic libido (toward which the ego reacts with anxious excitement) and the intrusion of archaic images of a fragmented body-self" (p. 152). The symptom of the latter is "the regressively reinstated hypercathexis of isolated body parts and mental functions (elaborated as hypochondria)" (p. 120). See also his "Schema of Regressive Swings Which Occur during the Analysis of Narcissistic Personality Disorders," ibid., p. 97; Mahler's description of the "syncretic" character of the "normal autistic" phases in Mahler et al., p. 43; and Winnicott, "The Theory of the Parent-Infant Relationship," pp. 44, 47, on primary narcissism and disintegration anxiety.

63. The order of stanzas in the first version, dated October 1916 and published in the *Little Review* in June 1917, was 1, 2, 5, 3, 4 and ended with "Passion or conquest, wander where they will, / Attend upon them still" (23–24). The date of the revision is uncertain; the poem could have been rewritten at any time during the summer of 1917, although Yeats's letters indicate that he spent it writing *Dreaming of the Bones* (*Letters,* pp. 626, 628–29) and a series of lectures (pp.

627, 630, 631). According to Wade's *Bibliography*, the manuscript for *The Wild Swans at Coole* was complete on October 10, 1917; Yeats was married to Georgie Hyde-Lees on October 21.

64. See Thomas R. Henn, *W. B. Yeats and the Poetry of War*, pp. 301–6.

65. Cf. Greenacre's hypothesis about the prestructural origins of the aggressive "instinct" in "Considerations regarding the Parent-Infant Relationship," p. 212; and Kohut's discussion of "The Theory of Aggression in the Analysis of the Self," in *Restoration*, pp. 111–31.

66. "The Gyres" was originally the first poem in the volume of *New Poems* Yeats published in 1938. The volume included pieces now appearing in the *Last Poems* only through "Are You Content?"

67. See Bradford's examination of the poem's manuscripts, p. 5; see also the letter to Dorothy Wellesley dated June 22, 1938, in Yeats, *Letters*, p. 911.

68. Cf. Winnicott, "The Theory of the Parent-Infant Relationship," p. 47.

69. See Richard Ellmann's chronology in *The Identity of Yeats;* and Bradford, p. 164.

70. See Curtis Bradford, "On Yeats's Last Poems," in Stallworthy, pp. 96–97.

71. Yeats, *A Vision*, pp. 8–9.

72. Ibid., pp. 11–13.

73. Ibid., p. 19.

74. Ibid., pp. 24–25.

75. Ibid., p. 8.

76. In *Per Amica* (*Mythologies*, pp. 351–52), Yeats quotes More to the effect that "the general soul as apart from its vehicle is 'a substance but without sense or animadversion pervading the whole matter of the universe and exercising a plastic power therein, according to the sundry predispositions and occasions, in the parts it works upon, raising such phenomena in the world, by directing the parts of the matter and their motion, as cannot be resolved into mere mechanical powers.' I must assume that 'sense and animadversion,' perception and direction, are always faculties of the individual soul, and that, as Blake said, 'God only acts or is in existing beings or men.'"

77. Ibid., p. 352.

78. See Whitaker, who attacks Yeats the "system builder" (as opposed to Yeats the "dramatist") and cites Kierkegaard's condemnation of such "Hegelianisms" as an "intellectual delusion and a retreat from the ethical demands of life" (pp. 8–9); or Bloom, who finds in Yeats's systems all that is most "awkward" about him: "I refer not to the theosophy but to the inhumanity or the calculated anti-humanism of much in the poet in at least *A Vision* on to the *Last Poems*" (*Yeats*, pp. 210–11).

79. Yeats, *A Vision*, p. 263.

80. Ibid., p. 268. It is interesting to observe that Yeats's definitions of *"antithetical"* and *"primary"* suggest once again the complementary oral modes of narcissism. He says that the *"antithetical* dispensation" is, like the grandiose "I," absorbed in its own "immanent power," while the *"primary* dispensation" it is

about to destroy, like the ecstatic "we," "looks beyond itself towards a transcendent power" (p. 263). In life as in art Yeats could only imagine the integration and reintegration of the self in terms of the incorporative and incorporated imagery of narcissistic transcendence.

81. Ibid., p. 81.

82. Passages from the diaries are included in the *Autobiography* as *Estrangement* (see esp. secs. 22, 33) and *The Death of Synge* (see sec. 6).

83. See the "Anima Hominis" section in *Mythologies*, pp. 325–42.

84. Yeats, *A Vision*, pp. 83–84.

85. This is Kohut's distinction between the "horizontal" and "vertical" splits in psychic structure characteristic of narcissistic personality disorders. He is at pains to point out that the existence of the latter is what accounts for the "side-by-side, conscious existence of otherwise incompatible psychological attitudes *in depth*" (emphasis in original) often found in such personalities (*Analysis*, p. 177) and for the fact that the relationship between maternal ideals and the hypochondria and depression these personalities experience is indirect (via anxieties associated with unneutralized narcissistic demands) rather than direct (via anxieties associated with a castrating mother who has been internalized by the superego) (ibid., pp. 181–82). See also Winnicott, "Ego Distortion in Terms of the True and False Self," esp. p. 145; and Mahler et al., p. 202.

86. Yeats, *Mythologies*, p. 336.

87. Cf. Langbaum, *The Mysteries of Identity:* Yeats's "notion that our spontaneous thoughts are not really ours must inevitably change the idea of the self" (p. 173); see also his comments on Yeats's "exteriority of self," p. 161.

88. W. B. Yeats, *The Bounty of Sweden,* sec. 2 (*Autobiography*, p. 359).

89. Cf. Kohut's speculation about the "compulsive, involuntary quality" of Mr. M.'s creativity in *Restoration,* p. 176n.

Three Fathers and Sons

1. That mawkishness played its part is of course undeniable, as is attested by Yeats's numerous attempts to improve the poem by revision. The 1889 version of the passage quoted just below, e.g., was

> Oisin, tell me the famous story,
> Why thou outlivest, blind and hoary,
> The bad old days. Thou wert, men sing,
> Trapped of an amorous demon thing.

The fact that revision of such youthful infelicities has done little to make the poem as a whole more readable or more popular is itself suggestive. Indeed one could argue that *Oisin* was better received in its original form than it has been since: see above, pp. 127–28.

2. The phrase is T. W. Rolleston's (*Myths and Legends of the Celtic Race,* p. 152). By 1912 Yeats felt it necessary to preface *Oisin* with an explanatory note: see *Variorum Poems,* p. 793.

3. *Transactions of the Ossianic Society,* vol. 4 (1859); cited in Jeffares, *Commentary on the Poems,* p. 523. A more accessible translation can be found in D. H. Greene's *Anthology of Irish Literature,* following p. 105. *Oisín i dTír na nÓg* was actually written in the eighteenth century by Michael Comyn, and the "Ossianic" works as a whole appear to have been composed no earlier than the eleventh century. They should not, consequently, be confused either with the earlier "Fenian" literature or with James MacPherson's spurious "translations" of Ossian, *Fingal* (1762) and *Temora* (1763).

4. See Hone, pp. 145–46. Yeats met O'Leary at the meetings of the Contemporary Club in 1885. Hone says that although Yeats never took the IRB oath or attended its meetings, "he understood himself to be with the party on the major issues and wished to capture it for his imaginative movement."

5. See Kohut, *Analysis,* p. 66, where in evaluating the pathogenic elements of parental personalities in respect to the narcissistic personality disorders he observes that, while the mother's narcissism is decisive in the "early acquisition of narcissistic vulnerabilities," "the father's personality . . . may, in later phases, be of decisive influence with regard to the severity of the ensuing personality disturbance." Another psychoanalyst might suggest that the Oisin/Finn/Niamh/triangle represents a *negative* (homosexual) oedipus complex (see Fenichel, p. 88). I have not introduced the possibility partly to avoid confusion and partly because it is clear that the problem here is not that the mother and son are rivals for the father (i.e., that the *father* is being seduced) but, as I say, that the mother and father are rivals for the son. Cf. Kohut's discussion of a similar point in the analysis of Mr. M. in *Restoration, pp.* 6–15, 44.

6. Letter to Dorothy Wellesley, December 25, 1935, in *Letters,* p. 841. The series eventually included "Come Gather round Me, Parnellites," "The Three Bushes," "The Curse of Cromwell," "The Pilgrim," and "Colonel Martin": Wade, pp. 261–62. In describing his project to Lady Dorothy, Yeats noted that "the work of Irish poets, quite deliberately put into circulation with its music thirty or more years ago, is now all over the country. The Free State Army march to a tune called 'Down by the Salley Gardens' without knowing that the march was first published with words of mine, words that are now folklore." Yeats is presumably referring to *A Broad Sheet,* which published "Spinning Song" (from *Diarmuid and Grania,* not included in the *Collected Poems*) in January 1902 and "Cathleen, the Daughter of Houlihan" in April 1903. The *Bibliography* does not include a separate entry for "Down by the Salley Gardens."

7. I.e., a hound with one red ear pursuing a hornless deer and a knight following a lady with a golden apple (I.139–45; II.3–4; III.3–4). Both are in Yeats's source; the symbolism is explained in a note to the 1897 version of "He mourns for the change that has come upon him and his Beloved, and longs for the End of

the World" as "images of the desire of the man, and of the desire of the woman 'which is for the desire of the man'" (*Variorum Poems*, p. 153). The title of the poem, however, betrays once again the latent association between sexual excitement and Yeats's "apocalyptic" autoerotic anxieties—a common theme in the poems published in *The Wind among the Reeds:*

> I would that the Boar without bristles had come from the West
> And had rooted the sun and moon and stars out of the sky
> And lay in the darkness, grunting, and turning to his rest.
> [10–12]

8. See variants of *Oisin* II.247 (1889 and 1895), *Variorum Poems*, p. 46; and "The Circus Animals' Desertion," line 12.

9. See Greene, p. 122.

10. I.e., I.261–86; 300–342; 400–427.

11. More exactly, it is the rhetoric of the romantic revolutionary, which in the earliest version of *Oisin* meant Shelley and in the later Blake: cf. the 1889 and 1895 versions of I.269–73.

12. See II.25, 247.

13. See *Odyssey* 4.351–570.

14. Rolleston, p. 125.

15. See Kohut, *Analysis*, pp. 145–46, where he says that the oedipal grandiosity (e.g., Oisin's heroic temper while on the Isle of Many Fears) often manifested by narcissistic personalities is "the mobilization of the later stages of the grandiose self when its grandiosity and exhibitionism are amalgamated with firmly established object-directed strivings. Specific environmental situations during the child's oedipal stage foster this type of grandiosity, which is in these instances experienced within the framework of (and subordinated to) object-libidinal strivings. If the child has no realistic adult rival, for example, because of the death or absence of the parent of the same sex during the oedipal phase; or if the adult rival is depreciated by the oedipal love object; or if the adult love object stimulates the child's grandiosity and exhibitionism; or if the child is exposed to various combinations of the preceding constellations, then the phallic narcissism of the child and the grandeur which are appropriate to the early oedipal phase are not exposed to the confrontations with the child's realistic limitations that are phase-appropriately experienced at the end of the oedipal phase and the child remains fixated on his phallic grandiosity." See also Mahler et al., p. 215; and Kohut, *Restoration,* p. 229.

16. I.e., John Synge, who spent a good deal of time in Connemara and Aran learning Gaelic at Yeats's recommendation: see *The Trembling of the Veil*, bk. IV, sec. 19 (*Autobiography*, pp. 229–32).

17. I.e., the years represented in the *Collected Poems* by *In the Seven Woods* (1904), *The Green Helmet* (1910), and *Responsibilities* (1914),

18. "Craoibhin Aoibhin" was the pen name of Dr. Douglas Hyde, the poet,

historian, and folklorist who became the first president of Eire in 1938. Jeffares notes that Yeats thought him a "cajoler of crowds, and of individual men and women" (*Commentary on the Poems,* p. 111).

19. Yeats, *Memoirs,* p. 21; see Brenda Webster, *Yeats: A Psychoanalytic Study,* p. 23, where she observes that the sword is called a "Druid word sword" in a variant of line 174.

20. I.e., 148 lines; the rest of bk. III (lines 149–224) describes Oisin's return to Ireland.

21. *Representative Irish Tales,* 1891.

22. Cf. Ernst Kris, *Psychoanalytic Explorations in Art,* pp. 60–61; and Phyllis Greenacre, "The Childhood of the Artist," pp. 490–91.

23. W. B. Yeats, "Introduction to 'The Resurrection,'" in *Explorations,* pp. 392–93; first published in *Wheels and Butterflies* (1934).

24. Yeats, *Reveries,* sec. 4 (*Autobiography,* p. 14).

25. Yeats, *Letters,* p. 589.

26. Yeats, *Reveries,* sec. 4 (*Autobiography,* pp. 14–15).

27. Murphy, *Yeats Family,* p. 48.

28. Preface to J. B. Yeats, *Letters to His Son,* p. 6.

29. Yeats, *Reveries,* sec. 7 (*Autobiography,* pp. 26–27).

30. Ibid., sec. 12 (pp. 38–39).

31. Ibid., sec. 14 (pp. 40–42).

32. Ibid., sec. 15 (p. 42).

33. Ibid., sec. 16 (p. 43).

34. Ibid., sec. 22 (p. 52).

35. Ibid., sec. 25 (p. 59).

36. Quoted in Wade, p. 19.

37. See Ellmann, *The Man and the Masks,* pp. 46–47.

38. See Wade, p. 23.

39. Yeats, *The Trembling of the Veil,* bk. I, sec. 10 (*Autobiography,* pp. 89–90).

40. Ibid., sec. 13 (p. 98).

41. Ibid., sec. 17 (p. 111).

42. Yeats, *Letters,* p. 589.

43. Yeats, *Memoirs,* p. 19n.

44. Ibid., p. 19; the last two sentences are deleted in the manuscript.

45. Ibid., p. 33. I agree with Murphy (*Yeats Family,* p. 83, n. 92) in thinking that "does not" is "obviously omitted" from the manuscript.

46. Letters to Katharine Tynan, autumn 1887 and September 1888 (*Letters,* pp. 54, 87).

47. Letter to Katharine Tynan, April 20, 1888 (ibid., pp. 68–69).

48. Yeats, *Essays and Introductions,* p. 51.

49. Yeats, *Memoirs,* p. 33.

50. J. B. Yeats, *Letters to His Son,* p. 252. The letter is dated October 19, 1918; in it JBY promises to send Quinn the manuscript of his "Suppressed

Chapter," and it is followed by another (as yet unpublished) letter, ca. January 1919, that Murphy says "gives a detailed account of his emotional difficulties as an improvident husband and unsuccessful father (as he thought) in the 1880's and 1890's" (*Yeats Family*, p. 86, n. 166).

51. J. B. Yeats, *Letters to His Son*, p. 274; letter dated July 23, 1921.

52. Yeats, *Reveries*, sec. 23 (*Autobiography*, p. 55).

53. See Murphy, *Yeats Family*, p. 84, n. 107)

54. Ibid., p. 51.

55. Yeats, *Reveries*, sec. 5 (*Autobiography*, pp. 16–17).

56. J. B. Yeats, *Early Memories*, p. 62.

57. Murphy, "Father and Son," p. 83.

58. Jeffares, *Man and Poet*, p. 13.

59. Reid, pp. 88–89; letter to John Quinn dated January 3, 1909.

60. J. B. Yeats, *Early Memories*, p. 27–29.

61. J. B. Yeats, *Letters to His Son*, p. 273.

62. Ibid., p. 79. For an account of JBY's life in Dublin and New York after 1900, see Douglas Archibald, *John Butler Yeats*, pp. 49–59.

63. Ibid., p. 280.

64. In 1922 JBY informed John Quinn that it was still "in a very embryonic condition" (Archibald, p. 77).

65. J. B. Yeats, *Early Memories*, p. iv.

66. Ibid., p. 56.

67. Ibid., pp. 56–57.

68. Ibid., p. 10; see also J. B. Yeats, *Letters to His Son*, pp. 241–42 (to WBY, September 19, 1917), where he writes that he has "always maintained" that a man should keep a box of drugged cigars for anyone who "said such a sentence as, 'Excuse me, Sir, but what you are saying is quite inconsistent with what you said earlier in the evening, etc.'"

69. J. B. Yeats, *Early Memories*, pp. 12, 28. "The 'Life and Opinions of JBY,'" Douglas Archibald remarks, "forms a series of shifting, acute responses and valiant contradictions" (pp. 87–88).

70. J. B. Yeats, *Letters to His Son*, p. 262.

71. Yeats, *Reveries*, sec. 4 (*Autobiography*, p. 14).

72. J. B. Yeats, *Letters to His Son*, p. 50. Emphasis in original.

73. Ibid., p. 50, n. 1; see also Murphy, *Yeats Family*, pp. 36–37.

74. Murphy, "Father and Son," p. 94.

75. Yeats, *Reveries*, sec. 5 (*Autobiography*, p. 19).

76. Ibid., sec. 11 (p. 37).

77. Quoted in Jeffares, *Man and Poet*, p. 51.

78. J. B. Yeats, *Letters to His Son*, p. 117; dated March 24, 1909.

79. JBY's unpublished memoir, quoted in Murphy, "Father and Son," p. 90.

80. Ibid., pp. 91, 93.

81. Yeats, *Memoirs*, p. 33.

82. Murphy, *Yeats Family*, p. 52.

Four Fathers and Mothers

1. Yeats, *Letters*, pp. 353–54.

2. Yeats's only other narrative poem, "The Gift of Harun Al–Rashid" (1924), was not part of the plan he describes to Bridges but an elaborately disguised "Arabian" account of his wife's part in the writing of *A Vision:* see above, p. 84.

3. See Yeats, *Letters*, pp. 353–54; "Speaking to the Psaltery," in *Essays and Introductions*, pp. 13–27; and "Literature and the Living Voice," in *Explorations*, pp. 202–21. When the latter appeared in vol. 4 of the 1908 *Collected Works*, Yeats added a note: "This essay was written immediately after the opening of the Abbey Theatre, though it was not printed, through an accident, until the art of the Abbey had become an art of peasant comedy. It tells of things we have never had time to begin. We still dream of them."

4. Yeats, "The Irish Dramatic Movement," in *The Bounty of Sweden* (*Autobiography*, pp. 378–79).

5. See, e.g., Augusta Gregory, *Our Irish Theatre*; and S. B. Bushrui, *Yeats's Verse Plays: The Revisions, 1900–1910*.

6. The stories of the Red Branch heroes are told in the Gaelic epic *Táin Bó Cualgne* and retold in Lady Gregory's *Cuchulain of Muirthmne*.

7. *The Variorum Edition of the Plays of W. B. Yeats*, ed. R. K. Alspach, p. 526.

8. See Sophocles, *Oedipus the King*, lines 714–16; and Slater's reinterpretation of the Oedipus story, pp. 66, 135–36, 162, 165, 376, 382.

9. Texts and line numbers for all the versions of all the plays quoted in this chapter are those found in Alspach's *Variorum Plays*.

10. Ibid., p. 477.

11. Yeats's traditional sources disagreed as to whether the Young Man was Aoife's son or Emer's. The version Yeats uses in "The Death of Cuchulain" is attributed to Curtin's *Myths and Folklore in Ireland* in a note (see *Variorum Poems*, p. 799); the plays are probably based on the version in *The Yellow Book of Lecan* (see Jeffares, *Commentary on the Poems*, pp. 28–29; and note to *On Baile's Strand* in *Variorum Plays*, p. 526).

12. Yeats, *Reveries*, secs. 2, 9 (*Autobiography*, pp. 7–8, 29–30).

13. See Kohut, *Analysis*, p. 146: "...Behind the imagery concerning the relationship of the [narcissistic] boy's grandiose self with a depreciated father...lies regularly the deeper imago [related to the phase-appropriate need to idealize (see pp. 43, 105–6) "fixated" by traumatic disappointment] of the dangerous, powerful rival-parent, and, as stated before, the defensive oedipal narcissism is maintained to buttress the denial of castration anxiety."

14. The first version of the poem, "The Death of Cuchulain," ended thus: "For

four days warred he with the bitter tide, / And the waves flowed above him and he died."

15. Yeats's omission of the Young Man's name ("Connla") is interesting, since it was certainly available in his sources, as was the fact that in the traditional version of the Aoife/Cuchulain story Emer warns Cuchulain in advance who Connla is, upon which he decides to kill his son "for the honor of Ulster"; see Rolleston, p. 190.

16. Yeats, *Letters*, pp. 424–25.

17. The chorus was originally intended to be part of another play "about the capture of a blind unicorn": ibid., pp. 471–72.

18. See Mahler on the "fear of re-engulfment," in Mahler et al., p. 215.

19. Tradition supplies Cuchulain with two fathers: Lugh and the mortal Sualtim (see Rolleston, p. 190), an ambiguity referred to directly only in the 1904 version of the play and indirectly in *The Green Helmet* (line 125) and *At the Hawk's Well* (line 84), where the young Cuchulain refers to himself as "Sualtim's son." Yeats's omission of Sualtim in favor of Lugh in the 1906 *On Baile's Strand* is significant: the hero must have an idealized, absent father.

20. See Kohut, *Analysis*, p. 232: "Narcissistic personalities are in general not predominantly swayed by guilt feelings (they are not inclined to react unduly to the pressure exerted by their idealized superego). Their predominant tendency is to be overwhelmed by shame, i.e. they react to the breakthrough of the archaic aspects of the grandiose self, especially to its unneutralized exhibitionism." See also Winnicott, "The Theory of the Parent-Infant Relationship," p. 41; and Kernberg, p. 232.

21. See above, p. 140; citations here are from the later (1910) version.

22. See lines 30–46.

23. The fact that the Red Man calls himself "the Rector of this land" also suggests an association with John Yeats, the "ancestor who was rector" at Drumcliff named in the concluding lines of "Under Ben Bulben." John Yeats both gave his name to Yeats's father and was the father of the first William Butler Yeats (Yeats's paternal grandfather, "That red-headed rector in County Down, / A good man on a horse"), both of whose characters were cast in something more like the "heroic" mold of the "laughing lip" than later generations of Yeatses.

24. See *Variorum Plays*, p. 454. The play was based on the story called *The Feast of Bricriu* retold in Lady Gregory's *Cuchulain of Muirthmne* and is a variant of the Celtic sun-myth "game" described in *Sir Gawaine and the Green Knight* and Yuletide mummers plays.

25. Brenda Webster assumes throughout her discussion of *On Baile's Strand* (pp. 164–66) that Cuchulain's father is Manannan, the god of the sea. The error is an easy one to make and reflects, I think, Yeats's own considerable uncertainties about the attributes of the "absent" father.

26. See pp. 176–81. The end of *On Baile's Strand* is ambiguous in this re-

spect, as were the traditional sources upon which Yeats drew (see n. 11 above). He had, however, no obvious reason to resurrect his hero from the waves until after he wrote *The Only Jealousy of Emer* in 1919; "The Death of Cuchulain" did not become "Cuchulain's Fight with the Sea" until 1925, when the final lines of the poem were rewritten (in *Early Poems and Stories;* see *Variorum Poems,* p. 111; and n. 14 above).

27. Cf. Kernberg's description of "narcissistic personalities functioning on an overtly borderline level," p. 268.

28. This is Kris's distinction between psychosis and the regression in the service of the ego that occurs in artistic inspiration: see his pp. 60–63. Kohut differentiates between the narcissistic personality disorders and psychosis as follows: "As in the case of the narcissistic personality disturbances, the psychotic disorders should not only (and perhaps not even predominantly) be examined in the light of tracing their regression from (a) object love via (b) narcissism to (c) autoerotic fragmentation and (d) secondary (delusional) restitution of reality. Instead it is especially fruitful to examine the psychopathology of the psychoses—in harmony with the assumption that narcissism follows a different line of development—in the light of tracing their regression along a partly different path which leads through the following way stations: (a) the disintegration of higher forms of narcissism; (b) the regression to archaic narcissistic positions; (c) the breakdown of the archaic narcissistic positions (including the loss of the *narcissistically cathected* archaic objects), thus the fragmentation of self and archaic self-objects; and (d) the secondary (restitutive) resurrection of the archaic self and of the archaic narcissistic objects in a manifestly psychotic form.

"The last-mentioned stage is only fleetingly encountered during the analysis of narcissistic personality disturbances" (*Analysis,* p. 6). Cf. Kernberg's "three levels" of narcissistic pathology, p. 325.

29. Yeats, *Letters,* p. 524; dated January 17, 1909.

30. Yeats, "A People's Theatre," in *Explorations,* p. 250; see also n. 3 above.

31. Yeats, "Certain Noble Plays of Japan," in *Essays and Introductions,* p. 221.

32. W. B. Yeats, preface to *At the Hawk's Well* in *Harper's Bazaar,* March 1917; see *Variorum Plays,* p. 416.

33. Yeats, "Certain Noble Plays," in *Essays and Introductions,* pp. 225–26, and 230.

34. It is interesting to note that, according to Takeo Doi's psychological study of the Japanese national character in *The Anatomy of Dependence,* the country that produced the model for the dance plays is itself primarily narcissistic in its social and cultural preoccupations.

35. See above, p. 64; and chap. 2, n. 54.

36. See Winnicott, "Ego Distortions in Terms of the True and False Self," p. 147; and Kernberg, p. 234.

37. See stage directions in *Variorum Plays,* p. 529.

38. See the introduction to the play in *Wheels and Butterflies,* sec. I (1934)

(ibid., p. 567). The text of *The Only Jealousy of Emer* was itself significantly cut for the 1934 *Collected Plays* (ibid., pp. 557–61; and n. 42 below).

39. Freud, *The Interpretation of Dreams,* chap. 7, sec. E; and Fenichel, p. 47.

40. *Variorum Plays,* p. 531. Citations are from the 1934 version.

41. Introduction to *Wheels and Butterflies,* sec. VI (*Variorum Plays,* p. 571).

42. This is even clearer in the uncut (pre-1934) version, where their conflict is dramatized at much greater length: see *Variorum Plays,* pp. 559–61, lines 288ee–44.

43. See above, pp. 147–48. Yeats's sources for "The Death of Cuchulain" give the name of the concubine ("one sweet-throated like a bird") as Eithne Inguba (see Jeffares, *Commentary on the Poems,* p. 29).

44. See Mahler's discussion of "optimal distance" in Mahler et al., p. 230.

45. See above, pp. 116–17. In this observation and much of what follows I agree with and am indebted to Webster, p. 167, who, however, never specifically suggests that what she sees as a primarily oedipal conflict is either unresolved or ironic—a point which I think both ignores the oral content of the play's imagery and misrepresents its tone.

46. See lines 576–78, where Cuchulain calls his sword

> This mutterer, this old whistler, this sand-piper,
> This edge that's greyer than the tide, this mouse
> That's gnawing at the timbers of the world....

47. Notes to *The Resurrection,* pt. I, in *Wheels and Butterflies* (see *Variorum Plays,* p. 932).

48. See lines 23–28: "Don't tell it to anybody, Blind Man. There are some that follow me. Boann herself out of the river and Fand out of the deep sea. Witches they are, and they come by in the wind, and they cry, 'Give a kiss, Fool, give a kiss,' that's what they cry."

49. See above, p. 66.

50. Cf. Phyllis Greenacre, "Early Physical Determinants in the Development of the Sense of Identity," p. 116.

51. See n. 47 above; according to legend the fathers of all six of Cuchulain's opponents had been killed by him: see A. Norman Jeffares and A. S. Knowland, *A Commentary on the Collected Plays of W. B. Yeats,* p. 308.

52. The pillar stone is reminiscent of the one Aoife sets her son casting at: see above, p. 144. There are similar dances (perhaps first suggested to Yeats by Oscar Wilde's "lyric" play, *Salome*) in the early story called "The Binding of the Hair" (1896) and in the late plays *A Full Moon in March* and *The King of the Great Clock Tower.*

53. The ironic contrast between the two "shapes" is even more explicit in "Cuchulain Comforted" (1939):

> "Now we must sing and sing the best we can,
> But first you must be told our character:
> Convicted cowards all, by kindred slain

"Or driven from home and left to die in fear."
They sang, but had nor human tunes nor words,
Though all was done in common as before;

They had changed their throats and had the throats of birds.
[19–25]

Yeats's letter to Dorothy Wellesley about the prose draft for the poem makes it
clear that Cuchulain's "birdlike" soul is the remade "inner" self of "Sailing to
Byzantium": "Then they begin to sing...like linnets that had been stood on a
perch and taught by a singing master" (*Letters on Poetry from W. B. Yeats to
Dorothy Wellesley*, p. 193). Cf. Langbaum, p. 234.

54. In the traditional version Cuchulain dies of his six wounds, and his head is
removed by Lugaid: see Jeffares and Knowland, p. 306.

55. Peter Ure, "*The Death of Cuchulain*," in Stallworthy, pp. 256–57.

56. Cf. Kernberg's description of the "inner world" of pathologically narcissistic patients, which could stand for the world of the dance plays as a whole:
"Idealized representatives of the self, the 'shadows' of others, and...dreaded
enemies, are all that seem to exist [there].... At the very bottom of this
dichotomy lies a still deeper image...the image of a hungry, enraged, empty self,
full of impotent anger at being frustrated, and fearful of a world which seems as
hateful and revengeful as the patient himself" (p. 233).

57. See chap. 2, n. 37 above.

58. This aspect of his interest in the Pollexfens was not something JBY would
have admitted freely either to himself or to others, although it was a very real part
of his "fascination" with them. When his wife's brother George died in 1910
without leaving him a penny, JBY so far forgot himself as to remark in a letter to
his son that in death he saw his "dear friend" for what he was at last, "that
Colossus the Pharisee, the mouldy old, ancient Pharisee" (Murphy, *Yeats Family*,
p. 45).

59. Murphy, "Father and Son," p. 84.

60. Moore, *Unicorn*, p. 13.

61. Murphy, *Yeats Family*, p. 38.

62. Ibid., p. 50. His other reason for moving was his loss of income in the Land
War: see above, p. 131; and Jeffares, *Man and Poet*, p. 18.

63. Yeats, *Reveries*, sec. 13 (*Autobiography*, pp. 39–40).

64. Jeffares attributes JBY's failure to make a living at painting in Dublin to his
bad sense of business: "He had charged such low prices that his genius had not
been recognized...[and he] was equally engrossed in painting heads of chance
comers for nothing if their heads interested him" (*Man and Poet*, pp. 38–39).

65. Yeats, *Letters*, p. 36.

66. Hone, p. 56n.

67. Yeats, *Letters*, pp. 34, 35–36, 48. There is some disagreement about the
precise date of Susan Yeats's first stroke. Hone puts it "towards the end of the
summer" (p. 56), Jeffares "in the course of the summer" (*Man and Poet*, p. 39),

while Murphy says it occurred "that winter" (*Yeats Family*, p. 51). A date in late September or early October accounts for both this confusion and for the abrupt change in the tone of WBY's letters to Katharine Tynan from Sligo mentioned just below.

68. Yeats, *Letters*, pp. 51–52. Despite the fact that Yeats thought his sister spelled her name, as he told Katharine Tynan in 1887, "with a y and two l's," her preferred spelling was, Murphy says, "Lily" (ibid., p. 54; and Murphy, *Yeats Family*, p. 75).

69. Yeats, *Letters*, pp. 54, 87.

70. Murphy, *Yeats Family*, p. 51; Hone is probably incorrect in saying (p. 57) that the second stroke occurred after her return to London in the spring of 1888.

71. Yeats, *Letters*, pp. 67–69.

72. Introduction to J. B. Yeats, *Letters to His Son*, p. 5.

73. Murphy, *Yeats Family*, p. 52.

74. See Hone, pp. 56–57; Jeffares, *Man and Poet*, p. 39; and Ellmann, *The Man and the Masks*, p. 77.

75. Murphy, *Yeats Family*, p. 51.

76. See Webster, pp. 29–30, where she suggests that Yeats's collapses show his unconscious identification with his mother's symptoms.

77. Murphy, *Yeats Family*, p. 49; and Reid, p. 137.

78. J. B. Yeats, *Early Memories*, p. 12.

79. Ibid., pp. 34–35.

80. Ibid., p. 14.

81. Ibid., pp. 87–90.

82. Ibid., p. 17.

83. Yeats, *Reveries*, sec. 13 (*Autobiography*, p. 40).

84. See above, p. 66.

85. Reid, p. 426.

86. Murphy, *Yeats Family*, p. 54. Emphasis in original.

87. Archibald, pp. 39–40.

88. Murphy, *Yeats Family*, p. 10.

89. Ibid., p. 20.

90. Ibid., p. 11.

91. Hone, p. 9.

92. Yeats, *Reveries*, sec. 5 (*Autobiography*, p. 19).

93. See above, p. 61.

94. Murphy, *Yeats Family*, p. 49.

95. Yeats, *Reveries*, sec. 13 (*Autobiography*, p. 40).

96. Ibid., sec. 5 (p. 19).

97. Murphy, *Yeats Family*, p. 38; Hone, p. 39.

98. Murphy, *Yeats Family*, pp. 38; 84, n. 107.

99. Yeats, *Letters*, p. 67. Archibald says that Jack later "said flatly and several times that he painted because he was the son of a painter" (p. 99).

100. Yeats, *Reveries*, sec. 7 (*Autobiography*, pp. 26–27); see above, p. 125. Of

her children, it appears to have been her sons who afflicted Susan Yeats's weakened nerves most. Jack was sent away to live with his grandparents at the end of a period in which his mother's health had been growing steadily worse, and Willie too was a source of constant irritation. "When I used to spend those miserable weeks at Burnham Beeches," JBY recalled later in a letter to Lily, "I was no sooner in the house than I had to listen to [your mother's] dreadful complaints of everybody and everything and *especially of Willie*. It was always of Willie" (emphasis in original); undated letter quoted in Webster, p. 74, n. 38.

101. See Kohut, *Analysis,* p. 147; and his discussion of the case of Mr. X. in *Restoration,* pp. 200–201, esp. n. 14.

102. Murphy, *Yeats Family,* p. 55.

103. J. B. Yeats, *Letters to His Son,* p. 78.

104. Ibid., p. 97.

105. See Hone, pp. 234–44.

106. Reid, pp. 493–94.

107. Yeats, *Mythologies,* p. 325.

Five Conclusion

1. "Prelude to Poetry," is Jeffares's title for chap. 1 of *Man and Poet;* Ellmann calls his chapter on the early relationship of JBY and WBY in *The Man and the Masks* "The Prelude."

2. Ellmann, *The Man and the Masks,* pp. 24–25; see also Bloom, *Yeats,* p. 155: "The poet's early timidity, and his permanent, indeed programmatic credulity, were both indirect reactions to his father's vehemence and scepticism."

3. Ellmann, *The Man and the Masks,* pp. 21–22. The substance of my disagreement with this sort of interpretation should, I hope, need no repetition. It is worth noting—though it may have been the consequence of external rather than internal censorship—that Yeats's translation of *Oedipus Rex* omits lines 976–83, where Jocasta says, "Before this, in dreams too, as well as oracles, many a man has lain with his own mother."

4. K. G. W. Cross and R. T. Dunlop, *A Bibliography of Yeats Criticism, 1887–1965,* p. 254, lists only Seiden's work under "psychoanalysis."

5. *American Imago* 5 (1948): 259–300.

6. Ibid., pp. 264, 265–66, 263, 266–67, 267.

7. Webster, p. 1.

8. Esp. in chap. 2, pp. 38–85.

9. This, at any rate, seems to be what she is saying about Yeats's early work, e.g., on pp. 4–5. Unfortunately, it is difficult to know whether it is really a statement Webster would agree with, since one of her premises appears to be that Yeats constantly and therapeutically remade the psychological situation as he went along; for my objections, see pp. 203–4.

10. The one notable, but lamentably brief, exception of which I am aware is the late Ruth Sullivan's article "Backward to Byzantium."

11. Ellmann, *The Man and the Masks*, p. vii.

12. Murphy, *Yeats Family*, pp. 75–76.

13. Ibid., p. 8.

14. See Fenichel, chaps. 4, 17, 18; Freud, "On Narcissism" and *The Ego and the Id;* and Margaret S. Mahler, "On Child Psychosis and Schizophrenia."

15. See Kohut, *Analysis* and *Restoration;* for an opposing view, see Kernberg, esp. pp. 270–84. For a discussion of some of the metapsychological issues raised by the psychology of the self, see Heinz Lichtenstein, "The Role of Narcissism" and "Towards a Metapsychological Definition of the Concept of Self."

16. See esp. Slater, pp. 135–36.

17. Bloom, *Yeats*, p. vii.

18. Ibid., p. 5. Emphasis in original.

19. Ibid. It is interesting to compare my version of Yeats's story with Phyllis Greenacre's discussion of the artist's need for "collective alternates" and his overidealization of the father in "The Childhood of the Artist" and "The Family Romance of the Artist." We have different ways of accounting for the same sort of thing, and I wonder—assuming my interpretation is correct—whether Yeats's story is also, in some general way, the story of the creative personality. Many other creative men, and at least one creative woman, had weak, depreciated fathers too: e.g., Shelley, Dickens, Frost, Joyce, and Woolf.

20. See esp. chap. 1, "The Nature of the Problem," in *The Character of the Poet: Wordsworth in "The Prelude,"* pp. 3–28.

21. Ibid., p. 172.

22. See Kohut, *Analysis*, pp. 16–17, 22–23.

23. Cf. Kohut's discussion of the "compensatory" value of creativity in the (analyzed) cases of Mr. M. and Mrs. Y. (*Restoration*, pp. 21, 264–65). It is not clear whether he regards art as a cure for the narcissistic disorders or not: see his comments on Proust, ibid. p. 182.

24. Webster, p. 237.

25. Bloom, *Yeats*, p. v.

26. Webster, pp. 236–37.

27. Morton Irving Seiden, "Patterns of Belief: Myth in the Poetry of William Butler Yeats," pp. 285–86.

28. Kohut would add that the idealized "we" is less regressed than the grandiose "I": see *Restoration*, p. 179; and Mahler's distinction between the autistic and symbiotic phases in Mahler et al., pp. 41–51.

29. I.e., the breakdown following the end of his first "spiritual marriage" in 1898 (see above, pp. 37–38) and the breakdown of 1933 (see chap. 1, n. 66).

BIBLIOGRAPHY

Archibald, Douglas N. *John Butler Yeats*. Lewisburg, Pa.: Bucknell University Press, 1974.

Bloom, Harold. *The Anxiety of Influence*. New York: Oxford University Press, 1973.

———. *A Map of Misreading*. New York: Oxford University Press, 1975.

———. *Yeats*. New York: Oxford University Press, 1970.

Bradford, Curtis. *Yeats at Work*. Carbondale: Southern Illinois University Press, 1965.

Bushrui, S. B. *Yeats's Verse Plays: The Revisions, 1900–1910*. Oxford: Clarendon Press, 1965.

Cross, K. G. W., and Dunlop, R. T. *A Bibliography of Yeats Criticism, 1887–1965*. New York: Macmillan Co., 1971.

Doi, Takeo. *The Anatomy of Dependence*. Translated by John Bester. Tokyo: Kodansha International, Ltd., 1977.

Ellmann, Richard. *The Identity of Yeats*. New York: Oxford University Press, 1954.

———. *Yeats: The Man and the Masks*. New York: Macmillan Co., 1948.

229

Erikson, Erik. *Childhood and Society*. 2d ed., rev. New York: W. W. Norton & Co., 1963.

————. *Identity: Youth and Crisis*. New York: W. W. Norton & Co., 1968.

————. "The Problem of Ego Identity." In *Identity and the Life Cycle*. New York: International Universities Press, 1959.

Fenichel, Otto. *The Psychoanalytic Theory of Neurosis*. New York: W. W. Norton & Co., 1945.

Finneran, Richard J., ed. *John Sherman and Dhoya*. Detroit: Wayne State University Press, 1969.

Freud, Sigmund. *The Ego and the Id*. Translated by Joan Riviere. London: Hogarth Press, 1927.

————. "Formulations on the Two Principles of Mental Functioning." In *Case History of Schreber, Papers on Technique, and Other Works,* edited by James Strachey, pp. 213–26. Standard Edition, vol. 12. London: Hogarth Press, 1958.

————. *The Interpretation of Dreams*. In *The Interpretation of Dreams (II) and On Dreams,* edited by James Strachey, pp. 339–627. Standard Edition, vol. 5. London: Hogarth Press, 1958.

————. "On Narcissism: An Introduction." In *The Collected Papers of Sigmund Freud,* edited by Ernest Jones, 4:30–59. London: Hogarth Press, 1924.

————. "The Passing of the Oedipus Complex." In *The Collected Papers of Sigmund Freud,* edited by Ernest Jones, 2:269–76. London: Hogarth Press, 1924.

————. *Totem and Taboo*. Translated by James Strachey. London: Routledge & Kegan Paul, 1950.

Gogarty, Oliver St. John. *W. B. Yeats: A Memoir*. Dublin: Dolmen Press, 1963.

Greenacre, Phyllis. "The Childhood of the Artist." In *Emotional Growth,* pp. 479–504. New York: International Universities Press, 1971.

————. "Considerations regarding the Parent-Infant Relationship." In *Emotional Growth,* pp. 199–224. New York: International Universities Press, 1971.

———. "Early Physical Determinants in the Development of the Sense of Identity." In *Emotional Growth,* pp. 113–27. New York: International Universities Press, 1971.

———. "The Family Romance of the Artist." In *Emotional Growth,* pp. 505–32. New York: International Universities Press, 1971.

Greene, David H. *An Anthology of Irish Literature.* New York: Modern Library, 1954.

Gregory, Augusta. *Cuchulain of Muirthemne.* London: J. Murray, 1902.

———. *Gods and Fighting Men.* London: J. Murray, 1910.

———. *Our Irish Theatre: A Chapter of Autobiography.* New York: Oxford University Press, 1972.

Grossman, Allen R. *Poetic Knowledge in the Early Yeats: A Study of "The Wind among the Reeds."* Charlottesville: University Press of Virginia, 1969.

Gwynn, Stephen, ed. *Scattering Branches.* London: Macmillan Co., 1940.

Hall, J., and Steinmann, M., eds. *The Permanence of Yeats.* New York: Macmillan Co., 1950.

Henn, Thomas R. *W. B. Yeats and the Poetry of War.* Proceedings of the British Academy, vol. 51. London: Oxford University Press, 1965.

Hesiod. *The Works and Days; Theogony; The Shield of Herakles.* Translated by Richard Lattimore. Ann Arbor: University of Michigan Press, 1959.

Homer. *The Odyssey.* Translated by Richmond Lattimore. New York: Harper & Row, 1968.

Hone, Joseph. *W. B. Yeats, 1865–1939.* New York: Macmillan Co., 1943.

Jeffares, A. Norman. *A Commentary on the Collected Poems of W. B. Yeats.* Stanford: Stanford University Press 1968.

———. *W. B. Yeats: Man and Poet.* New Haven: Yale University Press, 1949.

Jeffares, A. Norman, and Knowland, A. S. *A Commentary on the Collected Plays of W. B. Yeats.* Stanford: Stanford University Press, 1975.

Kermode, Frank. *The Romantic Image.* New York: Chilmark Press, 1963.

Kernberg, Otto. *Borderline Conditions and Pathological Narcissism.* New York: Jason Aronson, Inc., 1975.

Kohut, Heinz. *The Analysis of the Self.* New York: International Universities Press, 1971.

———. *The Restoration of The Self.* New York: International Universities Press, 1977.

Kris, Ernst. *Psychoanalytic Explorations in Art.* New York: International Universities Press, 1952.

Langbaum, Robert. *The Mysteries of Identity: A Theme in Modern Literature.* New York: Oxford University Press, 1977.

Lichtenstein, Heinz. "The Role of Narcissism in the Emergence and Maintenance of a Primary Identity." *International Journal of Psycho-Analysis* 45 (1964): 49–56.

———. "Towards a Metapsychological Definition of the Concept of Self." *International Journal of Psycho-Analysis* 46 (1965):117–28.

Magee, William [John Eglinton]. *A Memoir of AE.* London: Macmillan Co., 1937.

Mahler, Margaret S. "On Child Psychosis and Schizophrenia: Autistic and Symbiotic Infantile Psychosis." In *The Psychoanalytic Study of the Child,* 7:286–305. New York: International Universities Press, 1952.

———. *On Human Symbiosis and the Vicissitudes of Individuation.* Vol. 1, *Infantile Psychosis.* New York: International Universities Press, 1968.

Mahler, Margaret S. ; Pine, Fred; and Bergman, Anni. *The Psychological Birth of the Human Infant: Symbiosis and Individuation.* New York: Basic Books, 1975.

Moore, George. *Vale.* London: W. Heinemann, 1914.

Moore, Virginia. *The Unicorn.* New York: Macmillan Co., 1954.

Murphy, William Michael. "Father and Son: The Early Education of William Butler Yeats." *Review of English Literature* 8 (October 1967): 75–96.

———. *The Yeats Family and the Pollexfens of Sligo.* Dublin: Dolmen Press, 1971.

Onorato, Richard J. *The Character of the Poet: Wordsworth in "The*

Prelude." Princeton: Princeton University Press, 1971.

Parkinson, Thomas. *W. B. Yeats: The Later Poetry.* Berkeley: University of California Press, 1964.

Plato. *"Phaedrus," "Ion," "Gorgias," and "Symposium," with Passages from the "Republic" and "Laws."* Translated by Lane Cooper. New York: Oxford University Press, 1948.

Reid, Benjamin L. *The Man from New York: John Quinn and His Friends.* New York: Oxford University Press, 1968.

Rolleston, T. W. *Myths and Legends of the Celtic Race.* 2d ed. London: Harrap & Co., 1911.

Rothenstein, Sir William. *Men and Memories.* Vol. 1. London: Faber & Faber, 1931.

Seiden, Morton Irving. "Patterns of Belief: Myth in the Poetry of W. B. Yeats." *American Imago* 5 (1948): 259–300.

Slater, Philip. *The Glory of Hera.* Boston: Beacon Press, 1971.

Sophocles. *Oedipus the King.* Translated by David Grene. In *Sophocles. I,* edited by David Grene and Richmond Lattimore, pp. 9–76. The Complete Greek Tragedies. Chicago: University of Chicago Press, 1968.

Stallworthy, Jon, ed. *Yeats: Last Poems.* London: Macmillan Co., 1968.

Sullivan, Ruth Elizabeth. "Backward to Byzantium." *Literature and Psychology* 17 (1967): 13–18.

Vendler, Helen Hennessey. *Yeats's "Vision" and the Later Plays.* Cambridge: Harvard University Press, 1963.

Wade, Allan. *A Bibliography of the Writings of W. B. Yeats.* 3d ed., rev. London: Rupert Hart-Davis, 1968.

Webster, Brenda. *Yeats: A Psychoanalytic Study.* Stanford: Stanford University Press, 1973.

Whitaker, Thomas R. *Swan and Shadow: Yeats's Dialogue with History.* Chapel Hill: University of North Carolina Press, 1964.

Winnicott, Donald W. "Ego Distortion in Terms of the True and False Self." In *Maturational Processes and the Facilitating Environment,* pp. 140–52. New York: International Universities Press, 1965.

———. "The Theory of the Parent-Infant Relationship." In *Maturational Processes and the Facilitating Environment,* pp. 37–55. New

York: International Universities Press, 1965.

Yeats, John Butler. *Early Memories: Some Chapters of Autobiography*. Dundrum: Cuala Press, 1923.

————. *Letters to His Son W. B. Yeats and Others, 1869–1922*. Edited by Joseph Hone. London: Faber & Faber, 1945.

Yeats, William Butler. *The Autobiography of William Butler Yeats*. New York: Collier Books, 1965.

————. *Collected Poems*. New York: Macmillan Co., 1960.

————. *Essays and Introductions*. London: Macmillan Co., 1969.

————. *Explorations*. London: Macmillan Co., 1962.

————. *The Letters of W. B. Yeats*. Edited by Allan Wade. London: Rupert Hart-Davis, 1954.

————. *Letters on Poetry from W. B. Yeats to Dorothy Wellesley*. Edited by Dorothy Wellesley. London: Oxford University Press, 1940.

————. *Memoirs: Autobiography—First Draft: Journal*. Edited by Denis Donoghue. London: Macmillan Co., 1972.

————. *Mythologies*. London: Macmillan Co., 1959.

————. *The Secret Rose*. London: Lawrence & Bullen, 1898.

————. *The Senate Speeches of W. B. Yeats*. Edited by Donald R. Pearce. Bloomington: University of Indiana Press, 1960.

————. *The Variorum Edition of the Plays of W. B. Yeats*. Edited by Russell K. Alspach. New York: Macmillan Co., 1966.

————. *The Variorum Edition of the Poems of W. B. Yeats*. Edited by Peter Allt and Russell K. Alspach. New York: Macmillan Co., 1966.

————. *A Vision*. New York: Collier Books, 1966.

INDEX